IRISH SETTLEMENTS IN EASTERN CANADA:
A Study of Cultural Transfer and Adaptation

University of Toronto
DEPARTMENT OF GEOGRAPHY
RESEARCH PUBLICATIONS

1. THE HYDROLOGIC CYCLE AND THE WISDOM OF GOD: A THEME IN GEOTELEOLOGY by Yi-Fu Tuan

2. RESIDENTIAL WATER DEMAND AND ECONOMIC DEVELOPMENT by T.R. Lee.

3. THE LOCATION OF SERVICE TOWNS: AN APPROACH TO THE ANALYSIS OF CENTRAL PLACE SYSTEMS by John U. Marshall

4. KANT'S CONCEPT OF GEOGRAPHY AND ITS RELATION TO RECENT GEOGRAPHICAL THOUGHT by J.A. May

5. THE SOVIET WOOD-PROCESSING INDUSTRY: A LINEAR PROGRAMMING ANALYSIS OF THE ROLE OF TRANSPORTATION COSTS IN LOCATION AND FLOW PATTERNS by Brenton M. Barr

6. THE HAZARDOUSNESS OF A PLACE: A REGIONAL ECOLOGY OF DAMAGING EVENTS by Kenneth Hewitt and Ian Burton

7. RESIDENTIAL WATER DEMAND: ALTERNATIVE CHOICES FOR MANAGE-MENT by Angelo P. Grima

8. THE ATMOSPHERIC ENVIRONMENT: A STUDY OF THERMAL COMFORT AND PERFORMANCE by Andris Auliciems

9. URBAN SYSTEMS DEVELOPMENT IN CENTRAL CANADA: SELECTED PAPERS edited by L.S. Bourne and R.D. MacKinnon

10. SPATIAL EVOLUTION OF MANUFACTURING: SOUTHERN ONTARIO 1851-1891 by James M. Gilmour

11. THE FORM OF CITIES IN CENTRAL CANADA: SELECTED PAPERS edited by L.S. Bourne, R.D. MacKinnon, and J.W. Simmons

12. IRISH SETTLEMENTS IN EASTERN CANADA: A STUDY OF CULTURAL TRANSFER AND ADAPTATION by John J. Mannion

Irish Settlements in Eastern Canada: a study of cultural transfer and adaptation

John J. Mannion

PUBLISHED FOR THE UNIVERSITY OF TORONTO
DEPARTMENT OF GEOGRAPHY
BY THE UNIVERSITY OF TORONTO PRESS

© University of Toronto Department of Geography 1974
Published by University of Toronto Press
Toronto and Buffalo
Printed in Canada

ISBN 0-8020-5303-3

Preface

During the first half of the nineteenth century an unprecedented number of peasants left their European homelands, crossed the Atlantic, and settled in North America. These people came from various parts of western Europe, but in all this massive flow the southern Irish were the largest ethnic or cultural group. Celtic and Catholic, they were largely a rural, pre-industrial people. Although the vast majority of the southern Irish opted for city life in North America, many settled in rural areas, particularly in eastern Canada or British North America as it was then called. While something of the community of Irish life may have been more readily reproduced in an urban setting than it was in the relative isolation of the North American farm lot, the immigrants continued their age-old occupation on the farm and could transfer and adapt there a wider range of the material folk culture and settlement morphology of their homeland.

This study attempts to assess the extent to which aspects of Irish material folk tradition and settlement morphology were retained, were modified, or were lost in a rural setting in the New World. Three small pockets of rural Irish settlement — in Peterborough, south-central Ontario; in Miramichi, northeast New Brunswick; and in the Avalon Peninsula of Newfoundland — are selected for analysis. The material folk culture and morphology of settlement in each of these pockets are described in detail and compared to homeland forms. The author's boyhood in rural Ireland, his work as an undergraduate in historical geography at University College, Dublin, his MA thesis there on the evolution of the cultural landscape in County Galway and his close acquaintance with the current research on Irish folk life, formed an indispensable background for this study.

Research in the three study areas depended on both archival and field investigation. Material of a quantitative nature, not obtainable in the field, was available in the archives. Census data giving the numbers of immigrants, their areas of origin, their destinations, their age-sex ratios, their marital status, their religions, their past occupations and dates of entry, and details of their agricultural practices during the early decades of occupancy in the New World form the documentary base of this book. Special government reports on pioneer agriculture and on pre-migration conditions in Ireland and the public and private papers of persons officially connected with Irish immigration and settlement in the study areas proved particularly useful sources of information. Local courthouse records supplied data on individual land grants, sales, wills, and litigation over ownership, as well as cadastral maps of initial and subsequent settlement. Local sources such as church archives yielded genealogical data to supplement those already acquired in the field; local newspapers, old diaries, and other private accounts, travellers' sketches, and even outdated local histories furnished much needed information.

The bulk of this work, however, is based on field inquiry. Any study which has as its focus the reconstruction of the cultural landscape requires extensive field traverse. Two types of information were collected in the field: the first based on personal interviews, the second on observation of the cultural landscape.

Interviews were conducted mainly among older male residents in the study areas. Questions were usually confined to the history of an informant's farm. The lack of mobility, especially among the Irish in the Newfoundland and New Brunswick settlements, often meant that the informant's grandfather or great-grandfather had first settled on the farm and that the informant himself had acquired it through his own father and had worked it for a lifetime. This stability greatly enhanced the informant's interest in, and knowledge of, the family farm, for he often possessed not only information personally gleaned during his late nineteenth-century boyhood but an oral tradition that often extended back to the initial occupancy stage. A distinction has been made between phenomena actually observed by informants, which are part of the *living or folk memory,* and information transmitted orally to informants by persons no longer alive, which constitutes the *oral or folk tradition.*

Approximately one hundred full interviews were conducted in the three areas of Irish settlement and at least as many more persons were called upon to verify some of the material collected from the principal informants. A full interview involved the completion of the basic questionnaire, recording all the items of settlement being studied for at least one farm. The more willing or more reliable informants were visited several times and questioned about contiguous or relatives' farms. In this way the number of farms described in field notes exceeded the number of informants. Wherever possible, an investigation of the farm was made after each interview to inspect and sometimes to photograph pertinent items of material culture and settlement. Many of the sketches in this book are based on these photographs.

There are some terms in this work which are widely used by geographers in Britain but have never gained currency on this side of the Atlantic. Gaelic terms are also frequently employed. All of these terms are explained on first usage and are collected in a glossary at the end of the book.

My deepest debt is to the cordial countrymen whose grandparents and great-grandparents form the subject of this study. These Irish-Canadians shared fully in my interest in their ancestors and antecedents and displayed great patience and understanding with my countless questions. Field rapport was easily gained and as an "old country" Irishman I was welcomed warmly. It is axiomatic that this study could not have been produced without them. Space does not permit a full list of informants but I deem it necessary to mention here at least two informants whose contributions were outstanding: Simon O'Connell of Peterborough and Aly O'Brien of St John's.

In its original form as a doctoral dissertation for the University of Toronto this work was supported for one year by an Ontario Fellowship and for two years by a generous grant from the Canada Council. Special thanks are due to the personnel of the National Archives, Ottawa, the Provincial Archives in Ontario and Newfoundland, the Public Library in Peterborough, the archives of the University of New Brunswick in Fredericton, the Gosling Library in St John's, and the Newfoundland Room of the Memorial University Library, St John's, and to the staff in the land registries and courthouses of each of the study areas.

Private manuscripts such as church records, diaries, and old wills were freely given on many occasions and the various contributors are gratefully acknowledged here. Thanks are due to Mr Michael Crane, Department of Geography, Memorial University, for cartographic guidance and to Mr Gilbert Learning who drew the maps. A special debt is owed to Dr Alan G. Macpherson, Department of Geography, Memorial University, who read this work in its original form and offered numerous suggestions. My principal academic debt is to Dr Cole Harris, Department of Geography, University of British Columbia, who first as thesis supervisor and later at the publication stage was a source of stimulation and encouragement.

The book has been published with the help of a grant from the Social Science Research Council of Canada, using funds provided by the Canada Council. I would also like to thank Mrs. Anne Alexander for preparing the index and Mrs. Lydia Burton for the onerous task of editing.

Finally, I would like to record my indebtedness to my wife, Maura, who devoted so much of her time working with me in the archives and in the field.

JOHN MANNION
Department of Geography,
Memorial University, St John's

Contents

PREFACE / v

FIGURES / xi

I
The Atlantic migrations and the transit of culture: Problems
and literature / 3

II
Irish immigration and settlement in the New World study areas / 15

III
The settlement pattern / 33

IV
Field systems / 55

V
Farm technology / 84

VI
Farm outbuildings / 118

VII
The dwelling house / 138

VIII
Transfer and adaptation: a summary / 165

Glossary / 175

Appendix / 181

Selected bibliography on European ethnic group settlement in rural
North America / 184

Index / 209

Figures

1 The Cape Shore 1836 / 22
2 St John's 1836 / 23
3 Miramichi 1851 / 25
4 Peterborough 1851 / 26
5 Freshwater, initial settlement 1815-30 / 37
6 Outer Cove, initial settlement 1815-30 / 38
7 St Brides, initial settlement 1800-30 / 39
8 Barnaby, initial settlement 1825-35 / 40
9 Downeyville, initial settlement 1825-38 / 41
10 Cuslett 1935, kin-group settlement / 45
11 Freshwater, land transfers / 47
12 Barnaby, land transfers / 49
13 Downeyville, land transfers / 50
14 Freshwater, O'Brien Farm ca. 1880 / 65
15 The Cape Shore, McGrath's, Patrick's Cove / 69
16 Barnaby, Power lot no. 9 ca. 1870 / 75
17 Downeyville, the Callaghan farm ca. 1880 / 77
18 Fences / 86
19 Mattocks and Spades / 91
20 Flails / 99
21 Vehicles / 105
22 Studded wall, linhay, and root cellar / 121
23 Barn and stables, root cellar, and hay barrack / 127
24 Farmstead layout / 135

25 Tilt, camp, shanty, and cabin; rafter joints / 145
26 Hearth and chimney / 150
27 Floor plan / 152
28 Kitchen furniture / 154
29 Gable chimney houses / 156
30 Cultural continuity and change 1800-1900 / 166

IRISH SETTLEMENTS IN EASTERN CANADA:
A Study of Cultural Transfer and Adaptation

I
The Atlantic migrations and the transit of culture: Problems and literature

When a cultural group migrates and settles in an alien environment the traits of material culture[1] that emerge in the new settlement may be acquired in several basic ways:

1 traits associated with the migrating group may be transferred either at the time of the migration or later from the homeland to the new settlement;
2 traits not found within the homeland at the time of movement, but associated with neighbouring cultural groups in the new settlement area or existing elsewhere, may be imitated or adopted;
3 traits may be independently invented by a member or members of the immigrant group; or
4 traits may be acquired in some combination of these processes.

Material culture traits characteristic of the immigrants' homeland can be physically transported by the emigrants, can be reproduced from memory in the new environment, or can be physically diffused to the new settlement through such agencies as trade. Whatever the mode of diffusion, transfer of items of material culture depends on the persistence in a new setting of the settlers' conception of the importance or rightness of these items. When, for one reason or another, this conception weakens, the immigrant can adjust his homeland traits, or adopt or invent new ones. Neither the immigrant's homeland culture nor that of the groups living around him in the new area of settlement is static.

1 Material culture is here defined as embracing all the physical manifestations of culture.

During the Atlantic migrations of the early nineteenth century, for example, the technology of the agricultural revolution was evolving on both sides of the ocean, each a different corner of an essentially western European civilization. However, the individual immigrant who utilized a given tool, whether a flail or a threshing machine, in his new setting did so because he had brought the conception of its importance from his homeland, because he had acquired a conception of its importance in his new setting, or because quite independently he had discovered its utility. In some cases he may have observed a culture trait common to both his homeland and the new area of settlement. The relative importance of the various influences in such cases is almost impossible to measure.

These influences − tradition, borrowing, and invention − bear on cultural change whether or not there is spatial displacement. However, displacement of a people from a familiar to an unfamiliar setting may have shifted the balance, decreasing the importance of tradition while increasing the extent of borrowing and invention. Conversely, it may be argued that the emigrant escaped strong pressures for change in his homeland − perhaps indeed these pressures contributed to his decision to depart − and in a new setting he was able to maintain a tradition that his countrymen in the homeland were discarding. General interpretations of New World settlement have adopted these and many intermediate positions.

This study seeks to approach the broad question of the modification of European customs in the New World through an analysis of aspects of the material folk culture and settlement morphology of three small pockets of Irish settlement in eastern Canada in the nineteenth century. Rural settlement patterns, field systems, farm tools and techniques, farm outbuildings, and rural house types represent the complex of traits studied. It may be assumed at the outset that some elements of Irish material culture and the layout of settlement were readily transferred across the Atlantic, that others were left behind and still others, although transferred, were modified almost immediately in the new environment. Within a single sample settlement some transferred traits might endure longer than others. The durability of any single trait may vary from one study area to another. This study, then, examines these similarities and differences, attempting in the process to establish a clear picture of the extent of Irish transfer in each of the study areas and to explain as far as possible the differences that emerged.

Cultural and historical geographers, among other scholars, have made numerous studies of the material culture of immigrant groups in North America. They have largely ignored, however, the European antecedent forms in their analyses of ethnic group settlement, and consequently the literature sheds little direct light on the question of cultural transfer.[2] Perhaps one of the reasons for this failure to study carefully conditions on both sides of the Atlantic is the macroscopic approach that has characterized almost all the geographical research on ethnic group settlement in the New World. In North America a county unit, or indeed a township, when peopled by even a single European ethnic group, would usually draw these settlers from a far broader territory in the homeland. Even in such sharply focused studies as these, a full description of the immigrants' background would necessitate a wide-ranging knowledge of the folk traditions of the country of origin. Most students of the ethnic group in rural North America, however, have chosen areas larger than townships or counties, in which there are several basic ethnic groups. In such cases no more than a skeletal treatment of antecedent forms or Old World conditions has ever been attempted.

Studies which consider a sizable population spread over a considerable territory also neglect field inquiry, if only because of the magnitude of the task. The failure to carry out extensive field work partly explains the slight attention historical geographers have paid to such items of material culture as farm tools and techniques, various farm outbuildings, and even field systems, despite the fact that these topics are carefully treated in the European geographical literature. For the most part geographers have sought to illustrate the distinctiveness of European ethnic settlements in North America with broadly based studies of the groups' reaction to different types of soil, the kinds of crops grown, the balance between pastoral and arable husbandry, territorial mobility, and so on; even if these features did vary from group to group in the New World there has been little effort to link these distinctive traits genetically to Old World conditions.

Nor has the geographic literature made ample use of the comparative method. Two or more cultural groups occupying the same or contiguous territories, or members of a single ethnic group settling two or more different areas can be compared and contrasted.[3] There is also need for an analytical procedure which

2 A list of pertinent works by geographers is included in the bibliography. Surprisingly few of these authors have undertaken detailed background research in Europe. Only Perret, Wright and Kaups have seriously considered relevant antecedent forms or pre-migration conditions in Europe. Conversely, European geographers, while often possessing intimate knowledge of the emigrants' background, rarely have as deep an understanding of conditions in the New World.

3 Most comparative research on ethnic groups either intermingled or settled in contiguous territories have been restricted to largely descriptive accounts of population distribution, eg., works by Bird, Lewis, Schultze, Tower, and Wolf. The analysis of ethnic group settlement using cross-cultural comparisons is demonstrated in the research of Kollmorgen, Kniffen, Wright, and especially Clark and Lemon. Only Jordan and Perret have made detailed comparisons of a single group settling in different areas.

allows for a quantitative comparison of the cultural adaptations made by groups occupying New World lands. Although elaborate statistical techniques may not be necessary or even appropriate to the data, it is always important to know as precisely as possible what percentage of the population was utilizing a given tool, or a field system, at a given time. Such an assessment is a basic step in the effort to understand more clearly why some traits crossed the Atlantic while others did not, and why some transferred traits endured longer than others in the New World.

In recent geographical literature there has been a good deal of explicit interest in the themes of spatial diffusion and environmental perception, themes which have almost always been implicit in geographical studies of historical migrations. Much of this recent work has relied on theoretical mathematical models, on studies of the psychology of perception, or on the intellectual history of a people. While it is axiomatic that any geographical study of cultural transfer and adaptation is concerned with the themes of spatial diffusion and environmental perception, the application of such methods to a study of the transfer of a wide range of cultural items across the Atlantic before the present century is extremely difficult. The great majority of peasant immigrants in the New World were illiterate, and the "representativeness" of the views of a small literary minority describing the New World environment can be seriously questioned. A psychological study of the perception of a people who have been dead for decades is probably impossible, while the use of abstract mathematical models when we do not have the data on which a reliable theory of cultural diffusion might be built is a misdirected interest in generalization.

American folklorists have largely restricted their study of cultural transfer to the non-material aspects of European folk culture;[4] even these studies are rare.[5] In recent years, however, students schooled in the German *Volkskunde* or

4 Over fifty years ago an eminent French-Canadian folklorist-anthropologist made an eloquent plea for the study of the folk traditions, both material and non-material, of the major ethnic groups in North America (Marius Barbeau "The Field of European Folklore in America," *Journal American Folklore* 32 (1919): 185-97). In 1953 a leading American folklorist complained that "both folklorists and ethnologists in America have failed to make adequate systematic studies of the material culture and customs of the dominant white groups, mostly of European origin" (Stith Thompson, "Advances in Folklore Studies," in A.L. Kroeber [ed.], *Anthropology Today: an Encyclopoedic Inventory* [Chicago: University of Chicago Press, 1955], pp. 587-96).
5 The question of the transfer and adaptation of the various genres of folklore by even recent European immigrants has not been an important concern in American folklore studies (see Elli Kaija Kongas, "Immigrant Folklore: Survival or Living Tradition," *Midwest Folklore* 10 [1960]: 117-23; Alan Dundes, "The American Concept of Folklore," *Journal Folklore Institute* 3 [1966]: 226-49; Richard M. Dorson, "The Shaping of Folklore Traditions in the United States," *Folklore* 78 [1967]: 161-83).

Swedish *Folkliv* concept have begun to investigate the transfer of material items of folk culture to North America.[6] One such student has written:

Into this vast space that is America there came a great variety of peoples who, bringing what was transportable of their folk, popular and higher cultures from Europe, settled here, and through acculturation with their neighbors produced new American regional cultures. It is these that we study, in the twentieth century, horizontally and vertically, using European folklife methodology.[7]

Inherent in the folklife approach is a consideration of cultural distributions and the establishment of culture areas. The temporal dimensions of culture are normally neglected for the spatial,[8] although some folklife students do analyze the changing character of culture areas. As in cultural geography the content of the cultural landscape forms the basic subject matter in American folklife research, with an emphasis on traditional architecture (see bibliography). Traditional country crafts and work tools – items geographers tend to ignore – are also important topics, but the study of settlement patterns, an integral part of the Swedish *Folkliv* tradition, has not yet been considered by American folklife students. All of the shortcomings in the geographical literature are repeated in the folklife research. Treatment of European antecedents has been shallow and microstudies rarely involve a consideration of more than a single trait, such as a house or a barn, in the context of a single culture or ethnic group. There have been no studies, as yet, of the transfer of trait complexes and only a superficial analysis of acculturation. Nor have there been studies of a quantitative nature,

6 Don Yoder, "The Folklife Studies Movement," *Pennsylvania Folklife* 13 (1963): 43-65; Norbert F. Riedl, "Folklore vs 'Volkskunde'," *Tennessee Folklore Society Bulletin* 21 (1965): 47-53; Riedl, "Folklore and the Study of Material Aspects of Folk Culture," *Journal American Folklore* 79 (1966): 557-63.
7 Don Yoder, "Folklife," in Tristan P. Coffin (ed.), *Our Living Traditions* (New York: Basic Books, 1968), pp. 47-57.
8 "In general," writes Henry Glassie, "folk material exhibits major variation over space and minor variation through time, while the products of popular or academic culture exhibit minor variation over space and major variation through time. The natural divisions of folk material are, then, spatial, where the natural divisions of popular materials are temporal; that is, a search for patterns in folk materials yields regions, where a search for patterns in popular material yields periods. . . . While ordering his data the student of folk culture should listen more closely to the cultural geographer than to the historian, for he must labor in the geographer's dimension and he shares a major goal with the geographer – the establishment of regions" (Henry Glassie, *Pattern in the Material Folk Culture of the Eastern United States*, University of Pennsylvania Monographs in Folklore and Folklife No. 1 [Philadelphia: University of Pennsylvania Press, 1969], pp. 33-34).

although the ethnic culture surveys and folk cultural atlases suggested for the states of Pennsylvania and Tennessee are introducing this dimension.[9]

Anthropologists have rarely studied European material culture traits in rural areas north of Mexico. To be sure, there is a growing anthropological literature on the acculturation of European immigrants, but almost all of this work has been directed towards problems of ethnic group adjustment in an urban environment.[10] There are few of these studies focused on pre-twentieth century immigrants and even fewer, if indeed any, dealing with the transfer of material culture across the North Atlantic. Because there has been little acculturation between native and European groups, anthropologists have apparently ignored the study of folk culture in the United States and Canada.[11] In Latin America, by contrast, there has been considerable anthropological interest in the transfer of European items of material and non-material culture. George M. Foster's work on the diffusion of Spanish cultural traits to the New World, for example, is the most important work to date on the problem of cultural transfer,[12] although the work is weakened considerably by the breadth of its approach and by the lack of archival research. The assumption that certain current items of the material culture of Latin America are identical to those initially transferred by Spanish immigrants over four centuries ago requires historical documentation. Although diachronic considerations are apparent in some anthropological

9 Norbert F. Riedl, "A Survey of Tennessee Folk Culture," unpublished questionnaire, Department of Anthropology, University of Tennessee (1967); Henry Glassie & MacEdward Leach, *A Guide for Collectors of Oral Traditions and Folk Cultural Material in Pennsylvania* (Philadelphia: University of Pennsylvania Press, 1968).

10 Melford Spiro, "The Acculturation of American Ethnic Groups," *American Anthropologist* 57 (1955): 1240-52; L. Mason, "The Characterization of American Culture in Studies of Acculturation," *American Anthropologist* 57 (1955): 1264-79. Up to 1955 Spiro found less than 30 publications by anthropologists on the problems of acculturation of American ethnic groups. Most of the research was completed in the 1940's. Such topics as leadership, language, marriage and the family, religion, folklore, youth and personality, formed the core of these studies. There is, of course, a more voluminous literature on the assimilation of native Indian groups by European settlers, with the emphasis almost exclusively on the unilateral borrowing of Euroamerican culture elements by native peoples. Spier is one of the few anthropologists who has worked on the transfer and adaptation of material culture traits by non-native peoples to North America (see Robert F.G. Spier, "Tool Acculturation Among 19th Century California Chinese," *Ethnohistory* 5 [1958]: 97-117).

11 George M. Foster, "What is Folk Culture?" *American Anthropologist* 55 (1953): 159-73. According to Foster, folk culture results from a continuing exchange of traits over several centuries between a creative elite or urban group and the mass of primitive peoples: these latter become the folk. In Latin America such symbiotic relationships have existed since the Spanish conquest, but in most of North America, where European expansion occurred much later, there was no comparative exchange of traits. As far as Foster is concerned, there is no folk culture in New World areas outside Latin America. For a discussion of the development of this perspective in American

research, the use of archival sources is rare in anthropology. Rowe has demonstrated the spurious conclusions sometimes reached because anthropologists fail to consider the possibility of short-term changes within a culture.[13] This neglect of the temporal dimensions of culture in anthropological methodology is the chief reason for the failure to consider European antecedents, even in the sharply focused studies of ethnic group assimilation in the North American city. Francis Ianni, in a recent plea for more studies of European cultures in North America, stressed the need for an historical approach in order to reconstruct more fully the pre-migration conditions in Europe and to see clearly the elements of culture transported by the immigrants to the New World.[14]

Probably the most voluminous work on immigration has come from the historians. In America at the beginning of the present century such research was focused mainly on the processes of assimilation and the contributions of different ethnic groups, or leading members of these groups, to the political and economic life of the nation. The concern was with immigrants' contribution to America. Much of this literature was coloured by hostility towards certain immigrant groups or pride in the author's own ethnic origins and identity. Few of these antagonistic or filiopietistic treatises are of use to the student of cultural transfer. The next generation of historians was freer of the malice and chauvinism of its predecessors and considerably raised the standard of immigrant

anthropology see Ake Hultkrantz, "Historical Approaches in American Ethnology," *Ethnologia Europaea* 1 (1967): 96-116.

12 George M. Foster, *Culture and Conquest: America's Spanish Heritage*, Viking Fund Publications in Anthropology No. 27 (Chicago: Quadrangle Books, 1960). The author's extensive inventory of pre-migration Spanish conditions illustrate a rich diversity of material culture traits, little of which crossed the Atlantic. The central question is: why did some traits reach the New World, while others, apparently equally useful, did not? Foster concludes that the sequence of presentation of traits by Spanish immigrants to the native New World peoples was all-important in the subsequent diffusion of these traits throughout Latin America. Those traits first transferred and presented spread widely and endures.

13 John H. Rowe, "Time Perspective in Ethnography," *Kroeber Anthropological Society Papers* 12 (1955): 55-61. The synchronic orientation of most anthropologists is concisely stated by Benedict: "The first essential, so it seems today, is to study the living culture, to know its habits of thought and the functions of its institutions, and such knowledge cannot come out of postmortem dissections and reconstructions" (Ruth Benedict, *Patterns of Culture* [Cambridge, Mass: Riverside Press, 1934], p. 230).

14 Francis Ianni, "Time and Place as Variables in Acculturation Research," *American Anthropologist* 60 (1958): 39-46. Glyn William's work on the Welsh in Argentina is a rare example of an ecologically oriented anthropologist who makes extensive use of archival sources to reconstruct the Old World background and initial patterns of adaptation in the new area of settlement. Glyn Williams, "Incidence and Nature of Acculturation within the Welsh Colony of Chubut: An Historical Perspective," *Kroeber Anthropological Society Papers* 39 (1968): 72-87 and *idem*, "Welsh Contributions to Explorations in Patagonia," *Geographical Journal* 135 (1969): 213-27.

historiography. Following a stimulating statement by Schlesinger on the immigrant's role in American history,[15] a group of scholars led by Stephenson, Hansen, Blegen, and Wittke began research on the Atlantic migrations.[16] As much sociological as political in emphasis, the new studies were more concerned with communities than with individual personalities. But for the student of cultural transfer the principal merit of this work was the emphasis on the immigrants' Old World antecedents and on immigrant adaptation to a new environment. Stress on the immigrant heritage was partly a reaction to the Turnerian emphasis on the frontier. Blegen wrote:

His frontier hypothesis was useful in focusing attention upon some of the mainsprings of our national life, but in its major concern, it failed signally to explain the diversity in the customs and attitudes and in the material and spiritual culture of the peoples living within the boundaries of the United States. As scholars have tried to understand the history of the American people in a wider framework, a new emphasis has gradually made itself felt which takes into account the varied backgrounds of the national elements and their part in the peopling and development of the United States.[17]

Blegen himself wrote not only of the movement of Europeans across the Atlantic, "but of the migration of ideas and institutions and techniques from the Old World, their modification in the New and their return to the Old World, in unfamiliar and sometimes explosive form."[18] It is important to note the

15 Arthur M. Schlesinger, "The Significance of Immigration in American History," *American Journal of Sociology* 27 (1921): 71-85. The immediate post-war years were characterized by nativist attacks on the immigrants' role in America. Schlesinger stressed the varied cultural antecedents and positive contribution of the immigrants.
16 The wide-ranging interests of this group in the great migrations were outlined by Marcus L. Hansen, "The History of American Immigration as a Field for Research," *American Historical Review* 22 (1927): 500-18. Three of the pioneers of modern immigration studies were of Scandinavian descent; Wittke was German. All were born in the Midwest, the sons of immigrants.
17 Theodore C. Blegen (ed.), *Land of Their Choice: The Immigrants Write Home* (Minneapolis: University Minnesota Press, 1955), p. ix. It is, however, a mistake to think that Turner was unaware of the significance of Old World cultures in America. His early writings stressed the importance of cultural heritage but he never explored the field.
18 Henry S. Commager (ed.), *Immigration and American History: Essays in Honour of Theodore C. Blegen* (Minneapolis: University of Minnesota Press, 1961), p. viii. Blegen, who drew the sharpest picture of immigrant groups in North America, devoted the entire first volume of his masterly two-volume account of Norwegian settlement in America (see bibliography) to background conditions in Norway. His contemporaries were equally sensitive to the importance of cultural antecedents or the culture the immigrants brought with them to the frontier, as were their disciples, notably Ander, Bjork, Handlin, Janson, Leyburn, Qualey, Rasmussen, and Shannon.

consideration given to the folk culture of the immigrants, especially in the literature on the Scandinavians. George Stephenson strongly emphasized the study of immigration as a human story of everyday life and for him the student of migrations

> will not concern himself with the people on whom fortune has smiled graciously, nor will he relate the exploits of the battlefield and portray the life of kings and nobles; he will study the documents that betray the spirit, hopes, and aspirations of the humble folk who tilled the soil, felled the forest, and tended the loom — in short, who followed the occupations that fall to the lot of the less favored majority in every land.[19]

Theodore C. Blegen emphasized the study of folklore and folk arts, sports and amusements, the immigrant farm and farm communities, material culture, the "migration of culture at the grass roots."[20]

Despite the wide historical literature on North American ethnic group settlement there have been few detailed cross-cultural comparisons and, with the exception of some discourses by agricultural, architectural, and regional historians, the ingredients of the cultural landscape have never been more than a secondary consideration. Only a few of these latter studies, such as Powell's, Pitkin's, and Greven's, are sharply focused studies of small groups and, Powell apart, none seriously consider the question of European antecedents.

Sociologists have been examining ethnic group settlement in North America for over two generations. Research has been focused almost exclusively on the problems of minority cultures and inter-ethnic relations and involves questions of assimilation, prejudice, discrimination, personality, family changes, and other social consequences of ethnic group membership. Most of this work deals with twentieth-century minority groups, many of them a product of recent

19 George M. Stephenson, "When America was the Land of Canaan," *Minnesota History* 10 (1929): 237-59.
20 See Theodore C. Blegen, *Grass Roots History* (New York: Kennikat Press, 1947). This interest in the ordinary folk is evident in the writings of Ander, Bjork, and Handlin, and especially in the work of agricultural historians such as Shyrock, Shannon, and Greven, and the architectural historians Shurtleff and Perrin. In South America the historian Bishko has stressed the need for a broader historical interpretation of the Iberian background of Spanish America. He emphasizes the need to investigate such subjects as traditional forms and techniques of crop farming and stock raising, the kinds and distributions of land-holdings and the patterns of village and urban settlement (Charles J. Bishko, "The Iberian Background of Latin American History: Recent Progress and Continuing Problems," *Hispanic American Historical Review* 36 [1956]: 50-80; *idem*, "The Peninsular Background of Latin American Cattle Ranching," *Hispanic American Historical Review*, 32 [1952]: 491-515). Regional and amateur historians, such as E.C. Guillet, usually emphasize cultural rather than purely political history.

migrations. As in the anthropological literature there is little discussion of longer term changes through time, and in the few exceptional cases, as in the research of Clark and Duncan, there is little discussion of material culture traits.

During the 1940s and early 50s a group of sociologists, working mainly at the University of Wisconsin, began to study ethnic group settlements in the rural areas of the Midwest. Townships with over 80 per cent of their inhabitants belonging to a single ethnic group were the units usually selected for analysis. The aim was to determine to what extent traits associated with a particular ethnic group persisted or were modified in the American environment.[21] Quantitative measures were made, and cross-cultural comparisons undertaken at a detailed level. Unlike the early sociological treatises of Park and Miller, Thomas and Znaniecki, or the later work of Schermerhorn (see bibliography), the Wisconsin group paid scant attention to the cultural traits the immigrants brought with them to America. The emphasis, instead, was on those traits that distinguished ethnic groups after a century in America. To be sure, many of these traits stemmed from the Old World heritage of the immigrants, but no effort was made to link them genetically to the homeland. This unwillingness to investigate to any great extent past patterns of cultural change is probably associated with the demise of sociological research on Midwestern ethnic groups: many of the traits that distinguish such groups were fast disappearing in the mid-twentieth century and could only be studied through historical reconstruction.

Although the agricultural technology of the different nationalities or "culture-types" was a prominent consideration for these rural sociologists, no attention was paid to the patterns of settlement or the origins and diffusion of items of material culture. "Our primary interest," wrote George Hill, "is to classify areas of social behaviour rather than material culture traits."[22] The notion that material items of culture are themselves indicators of social behaviour was not considered by sociologists; rather, such items were examined only as indicators of social conditions or of the level of technology.

21 For a statement on objectives and methodology, see George W. Hill, "The Use of the Culture-Area Concept in Social Research," *American Journal of Sociology* 47 (1941): 39-45.
22 Hill, "Culture-Area Concept," p. 39. The ignoring of material culture by both anthropologists and sociologists came partly as a reaction to Clark Wissler's early work on culture areas. Wissler concentrated mainly on items of material culture in delimiting culture areas. He believed material culture traits to be diagnostic of total cultures. The main objection to this concept was that non-material aspects of culture were not necessarily associated with material culture elements. This hardly seems reason enough to abandon the study of material culture.

The literature on the transfer and adaption of Old World traits of material culture to the New World has been under-researched and is too general in method and conclusion. The question of cultural transfer and adaptation, to be sure, is endlessly complex, as almost every variable associated with the Atlantic migrations may be of relevance. Partly because of this complexity students of cultural transfer all too often have fallen back on simplistic, deterministic interpretations. Yet it does not necessarily follow that, because of the complexity, controlled analysis is impossible. In such a study the first step is, perhaps, to try to minimize the effect of some of the variables. Some simplification might be achieved by selecting a single, culturally homogeneous, Old World group occupying two or more distinct areas in the New World; if these immigrants came from the same place, left at the same time under similar circumstances, shared common motivations, travelled in the same way and so on, differences emerging in occupance patterns between the new areas of settlement would be attributable, not to Old World conditions or to the Atlantic crossing but to differing conditions in the new settlement areas. Conversely, if cultural groups sailed under similar conditions and settled in an area of the New World where conditions were similar, differences in their patterns of adaptation would have to be explained largely in terms of their Old World cultural heritage. In each case the explanatory variables are confined primarily to conditions on one side of the Atlantic.

In this study a single, culturally homogeneous group, settling in three widely separated parts of eastern Canada, is chosen for analysis. Perhaps it is impossible to identify settlements of any size where the immigrants were totally homogeneous in the material aspects of their cultural heritage, but the immigrants to the three study areas represent as homogeneous a people at the time of emigration as it may be possible to find.[23] They came from the far south and southeast of Ireland, mainly from the counties of Cork, Tipperary, Kilkenny, Waterford, and Wexford. Although some aspects of the material folk culture in this source area varied regionally, these variations, which are noted in the

23 Some students of European migrations overseas have postulated a pattern of chain movement whereby one or two persons from a European village or parish settle abroad and then attract members of their family and neighbourhood to the new location; the transatlantic contacts subsequently broaden, immigration from the Old World neighbourhood to the new location gradually increases and sometimes reaches a thousand or more (see the works of Bailyn, Blegen, Galitizi, Yuzyk and Miller in the bibliography and especially C.A. Price, "Immigration and Group Settlement," in W.D. Borrie [ed.], *The Cultural Integration of Immigrants* [Paris: UNESCO, 1959], pp. 267-87). Extensive inquiry failed to uncover any such pattern of migration in the Irish parts of rural eastern Canada. It is indeed unlikely that there exist in eastern Canada three distinct rural settlements where the majority of immigrants came from a common county in Ireland.

following chapters, were trifling when compared to the great number of material traits that were shared.

The Irish settlements in Canada selected for study are:

1 The townships of Douro, Ennismore, and north Emily (parish of Downeyville) near Peterborough, south-central Ontario;
2 The settlements of Barnaby, Semiwagan, and Nowlanville in Nelson parish, Miramichi, northeast New Brunswick;
3 The settlements of Freshwater, Logy Bay, Outer and Middle Cove near St John's, and the Cape Shore on east Placentia Bay, all in the Avalon Peninsula of Newfoundland.

II
Irish immigration and settlement in the New World study areas

The migration from Ireland to the three study areas may be regarded as part of a single exodus of poor Catholic Irish across the Atlantic in the nineteenth century. The main motive for the departure of all of these emigrants was economic distress in the homeland. Since about 1770 the population of Ireland had been increasing dramatically. A reversion to commercial pastoral farming after the short-lived tillage boom during the Napoleonic wars meant that many small farmers could no longer support a large family or provide land for their sons. Landlords who had previously encouraged tenants to subdivide their holdings now more frequently discouraged or forbade it. Small tillage units were amalgamated into grazier farms. Many tenants were evicted and there was little industry in Ireland to absorb them. Over much of Munster, but especially in Cork where it was a particularly important adjunct to farming, the domestic linen industry declined.[1] Minor famines heightened the feeling of peasant unrest. In north Munster, source of the Peterborough and many Miramichi immigrants and one of

---

1 William F. Adams, *Ireland and Irish Emigration to the New World* (New Haven: Yale University Press, 1932), pp. 51, 56. See also S.H. Cousens, "The Regional Variation in Emigration from Ireland Between 1821 and 1841," *Institute British Geographers, Transactions and Papers* 37 (1965): 15-29. Emigration was heaviest from south Ulster and north Leinster, where the domestic linen industry was largely concentrated.

the most severely affected regions in Ireland, agrarian riots became endemic after 1815 and this was an important stimulus to migration.[2]

In the decades before the migrations the number of Gaelic-speaking monoglots in the southeast rapidly declined[3] and by 1850 Waterford and Cork were the only southeastern counties where half the population were Gaelic speakers.[4] As knowledge of English spread through the homeland, the peasantry became more and more exposed to emigration propaganda. Although local tradition asserts that Gaelic was spoken in all three New World study areas, there is no suggestion that the immigrants were ignorant of English. Armed with the language of the New World and having some prior knowledge of conditions there, the potential emigrant was in a position to assess the advantages and disadvantages of emigration.

Emigration was a highly individualistic solution to the economic and social ills that encumbered the Irish peasant. Although the extended family or kin group (Gaelic: *cineadh*) was still an important, if declining, element of Irish rural society, in the final analysis it was the single individual or nuclear (parent-child) family that made the decision to cross the Atlantic. Neither the dispersed farms that were mainly the product of landlord reorganization nor the indigenous joint holdings that all too often had been subdivided to miniscule proportions could support all the sons, but it rarely became necessary for the entire extended family to depart. Adams has shown that the great majority of Irish emigrants were between 15 and 25 years of age and that they were either single individuals or members of unrelated nuclear families.[5] The migration to the study areas was no exception. The diversity of surnames in all study areas (Appendix 1) and the diffuse nature of the location of emigrants' homes in the homeland suggest that almost all these families were unrelated. This is strongly supported by local folk tradition. The territorial extent of the Peterborough immigrants' homeland

2 Adams, *Irish Emigration*, pp. 11, 30. Clare, Limerick, and Tipperary formed the core of disaffected counties, but unrest overflowed into neighbouring Munster counties as well.

3 Seán De Fréine, *The Great Silence* (Dublin: Mercier Press, 1965), pp. 126-27. Arthur Young reported in 1776 and 1778 that Dublin and the baronies of Bargy and Forth in Wexford – the latter areas of Flemish and Welsh settlement since early Norman days – were the only places in the country where there were no traces of Gaelic. By 1800 only half the Catholic population of Ireland was ignorant of English.

4 For a distribution map see T. Jones Hughes, "Society and Settlement in Nineteenth Century Ireland," *Irish Geography* 5 (1965): 79-96. It is not known if many of these were bilingual.

5 Adams, *Irish Emigration*, pp. 108-9. There were instances, of course, when landlord clearances or natural disasters such as the potato famine swept an entire hamlet community across the Atlantic, but such cases were exceptional in the long history of Irish migrations, and did not affect the settlement of the three study areas.

was far more restricted than that of the Avalon or Miramichi Irish, yet even the Peterborough-Irish included no large groups of related people. The 307 nuclear Irish families in the Peterborough settlement came from no fewer than 90 parishes, mainly in the barony of Fermoy, North Cork.[6] Only in 9 of these parishes were there more than 10 families selected and in these latter cases the same surnames never occurred more than three times. There was even less repitition of surnames in Miramichi. Only 19 of the 153 nuclear Irish families recorded in the 1851 census had children born in Ireland[7] and genealogical evidence suggests that the majority of household heads had arrived in Miramichi as single adult males, and had married girls who came as child members of nuclear Irish families or the daughters of earlier Irish immigrants born in Miramichi. The Avalon migration appears to have been equally individualistic: probably more than half the nuclear families were formed by the marriage of Irish males to Newfoundland-Irish girls, some of whom were born in the study areas. As in Miramichi, duplication of surnames was rare and where surnames were repeated, kinship was rarely claimed.

The great majority of the immigrants came from a rural rather than an urban background.[8] In rural Ireland, the landlords apart, there were three main classes of people: the small farmers, the most numerous group, a few of whom were proprietors and the remainder tenants; landless labourers and cottiers with rarely more than an acre of land on a single year's lease;[9] and rural craftsmen such as blacksmiths, shoemakers, carpenters, and coopers. Of these groups the labourer-cottier class contributed least to the settlement of the study areas. Their annual income was often as low as £6 and rarely exceeded £10; they had little surplus to invest in a transatlantic passage. It was the small farmers, victims of the change to pastoral farming, and their sons, who could no longer acquire land, who left in great numbers after 1815. Even during the famine exodus in the mid-nineteenth century,

---

6 Canada, Peter Robinson Papers 1822-44 (MSS in Provincial Archives, Toronto), MS-12, "A List of Emigrants, 1825." Children comprised 65 per cent of the total migration and the average nuclear family exceeded 6 persons, a high figure when compared with the other migrations.

7 Canada, *Census of Canada, 1851* (MSS in National Archives, Ottawa), RG31, C-996, Nelson Parish, New Brunswick.

8 In 1841 over 75 per cent of the population in the southeast were dependent on agriculture and less than 20 per cent lived in towns or cities (T.W. Freeman, *Pre-Famine Ireland* [Manchester: Manchester University Press, 1957], pp. 25, 75, 77). A considerable portion of the latter was the result of rural-urban drift since migration to the study areas (see Cousens "Emigration from Ireland 1821-41," pp. 15-29).

9 The labourer-cottier class greatly increased during and after the migrations and by 1841 comprised 55 per cent of the adult male population of rural Ireland. This figure, however, included unmarried farmers' sons; the extent to which the labourer element was self-generated has not yet been determined.

17

when emigration from Ireland reached its apogee, the farmer element dominated the Atlantic migration.[10] Of the 307 heads of families who settled in Peterborough in 1825, 238 were farmers, 53 were artisans, and only 16 were labourers.

THE MIGRATION

The migration from Ireland to the study areas largely occurred between 1810-35, a brief time span in the long history of Irish emigration to North America. The first half of this short period saw the movement to the Avalon, the second half to Peterborough and Miramichi. The immigrants came from the same corner of Ireland, the southeast; within this source area most of the Avalon-Irish had been located in the east, the Miramichi and Peterborough immigrants in the west, but there was considerable overlap in the source areas of all three groups.

From at least the beginning of the eighteenth century Westcountrymen, who fished for cod each summer on the Grand Banks of Newfoundland, called at Waterford on their outbound journey to purchase provisions and enlist labourers for the season. Placentia was one of the major destinations for this seasonal Irish movement, yet no permanent Irish settlements were established on the Cape Shore until the beginning of the nineteenth century. By this time a Waterford merchant family, Sweetmans, controlled the Placentia fishing trade and annually transported hundreds of Irishmen, some of whom stayed on during the winter to cut timber for boat building.[11] Local folk tradition on the Cape Shore asserts that most of the Irishmen who first settled there fished for Sweetmans and worked as winter men before settling down. In 1794 four men who were shipwrecked on Cape St Mary's on the southern tip of the Shore, wandered along the coast for four days without seeing a single settlement.[12] The first indication of permanent settlement appears in 1802 when John Skerry, a fisherman with

10 Oliver MacDonagh, "Irish Emigration to the United States and British Colonies During the Famine," in R.D. Edwards and T.D. Williams (eds.), *The Great Famine* (Dublin: Browne & Nolan, 1956), pp. 331-2; Adams, *Irish Emigration*, pp. 34, 192-93, 221. See also J.H. Johnson, "The Two Irelands at the Beginning of the Nineteenth Century," in Nicholas Stephens and Robin E. Glasscock (eds.), *Irish Geographical Studies in Honour of E. Estyn Evans* (Belfast: Queen's University Press, 1970), pp. 224-43. Up to the famine there are several references to this farmer emigration in the reports of immigrant agents stationed at Quebec.

11 Newfoundland, Letter Book of Saunders and Sweetmans, Placentia (MSS in Arts and Culture Library, St John's). Pierce Sweetmans, Placentia, to Roger Sweetmans, Waterford, December 22, 1788: "Our winter crews are all gone into the woods where I hope they will be able to make good returns for the vast quantity of provisions they consume ...." Same to Same, May 29, 1789: "Our winter crews have done very great work. Fanning with eleven hands has got 600 very fine ship timbers."

12 Jean M. Murray (ed.), *The Newfoundland Journal of Aaron Thomas* (Toronto: Longmans, 1968), p. 125.

Sweetmans, petitioned for land in Ship Cove, ten miles south of Placentia.[13] Genealogical data suggest that a few immigrant Irish families settled on the Cape Shore before 1810, initiating a trickle of migration that endured until the late 1830s. In 1836 fifty-four families were recorded but close to half of these were second generation Cape Shore people.[14] Thirty-four nuclear families settled on the Cape Shore and established farms on their own. Reliable genealogical data have been collected for 20 of these families and reveal that only 8 were formed in the homeland while as many as 12 resulted from marriages of immigrant Irish adult males to Newfoundland-Irish girls, mostly from Placentia and the Cape Shore. Of the 34 families, 5 produced offspring between 1800-1810 on the Cape Shore, 7 others between 1810-1820, 11 between 1820-1830, and 7 between 1830-1840; this distribution of births suggest that the process of immigration and settlement extended over these decades.

Family tradition points to Wexford, Waterford, and Tipperary as the principal homeland counties of the immigrants to the Cape Shore. Documentary data on the precise homeland location of these immigrants are sparse. Surname evidence points clearly to the southeast, and since Waterford was the major port of exit there is little doubt that the homeland was largely confined to this corner of the country. Parish and family records reveal that 6 Cape Shore families or heads of families came from Wexford, 3 from Waterford, 3 from Tipperary, and one each from Kilkenny and Limerick.

The migration to the Cape Shore was but a small part of the wave of southern Irish immigration that reached the shores of the Avalon during the first two decades of the nineteenth century. St John's was the principal port of disembarkation and the Irish population of the city increased from 2,000 persons in 1794 to 14,000 four decades later.[15] Because of the distress caused by so numerous a body of immigrants in the city, the government probably for the first time in Newfoundland's history, openly encouraged agricultural settlement.[16] At the very time the Cape Shore settlements were taking root, indigent

13 Newfoundland, Surrogate Court Records, Placentia (MSS in Arts and Culture Library, St John's), December 16, 1802, p. 97. Petition of John Skerry "who has worked thirty-four years in the fishery, for a piece of land in Ship Cove, as he has recently brought his family out from Ireland. Petition granted, on condition that he doesn't sell or transfer any land which he may reclaim or cultivate." Through field interviews it was discovered that all present-day natives of Ship Cove are descendants of this man.

14 Newfoundland, Department of Colonial Secretary, *Census of Newfoundland, 1836* (in Memorial University Library, St John's), p. 10.

15 Newfoundland, Governor's Office, "An Account of Inhabitants Residing in the Harbour and District of St John's, 1794-95" (MSS in Memorial University Library, St John's), p. 40; *Census of Newfoundland, 1836*, p. 1.

16 Great Britain, Colonial Office Correspondence, Newfoundland (MSS in Provincial Archives, St John's), Series 194, vol. 23, Proclamation of Governor R.G. Keats, St John's, June 17, 1813.

Irish immigrants were establishing small farms around St John's. Freshwater valley, just west of the city, was occupied by Irish after 1815 while other immigrants moved four to six miles north of St John's to establish homes in Logy Bay, Outer and Middle Cove.

The first land grants were awarded in Freshwater in 1813, but apparently only one family actually occupied a lot at this date.[17] Petitions for grants normally came after a farm was established, and in Freshwater ten grants were awarded between 1827-30.[18] Family and parish records suggest that the bulk of the settlers took up land there in the decade after 1815. By 1840 the process of immigration was over and 37 nuclear families were working their tiny farms. During the same period over 50 nuclear families settled in the study area north of St John's.[19] Parish records, surname evidence, and family tradition indicate that the immigrants near St John's, like those on the Cape Shore, came from southeast Ireland and particularly from the counties of Waterford, Wexford, Kilkenny, and Tipperary.

After the Napoleonic wars, timber from the Maritimes had become an important British import and while Irish immigrants were still trickling into the Avalon, an increasing number, crossing the Atlantic in the holds of timber ships, made their way to the mainland. Along the banks of the Miramichi and its tributaries was one of the finest timber stands in the Maritimes. Timber ships docking at the ports of Chatham and Newcastle on the Miramichi after 1815 brought with them hundreds of poor Irish who often found initial employment loading lumber for the European voyage. Many of these immigrants eventually left for the United States, but others stayed and, after a period in the woods or on the wharves, sometimes turned to farming. By 1820 all the good lots fronting the main river had been pre-empted by immigrants who had arrived before the

17 Newfoundland, Department of Colonial Secretary, *Registry of Grants* (MSS in Department of Mines, Agriculture and Resources, Confederation Building, St John's), *Geographical Index to Crown Grants*, vol. A, Folio 122, October 1, 1813. Michael Dea (1775-1849) arrived in St John's in 1808 from Thurles, Tipperary, took out a grant in Freshwater in 1813, and died there in 1849; his son inherited the farm.

18 *Royal Gazette and Newfoundland Advertiser,* St John's, April 26, 1831 (in Arts & Culture Library, St John's). Between 1835-45, 30 grants were recorded in Freshwater, but a few lots were never occupied (Newfoundland, *Registry of Grants, Geographical Index to Crown Grants,* vol. 1, 1831-1930).

19 The earliest record of settlement is in Logy Bay where in 1818 Luke Ryan sought permission to build a fishing room and had already begun the building of a stage and flake. Between 1827-30 there were 9 petitions for land in Logy Bay, 30 from Outer Cove, 3 from Middle Cove; almost all of these settlers remained in the area (*Royal Gazette,* St John's, April 26, 1831).

Irish,[20] and so the Irish settled on lots fronting the secondary rivers. Between 1815 and 1835 tributaries of the Miramichi like Bay Du Vin, Bartibog, Barnaby, Bartholomew, Renous, Sevogle, and Cains were occupied by southern Irish.[21] Thirty-eight nuclear families settled on the banks of the Barnaby, 18 families moved to nearby Semiwagan, and 20 families to Nowlanville. These pockets of Irish settlement form the New Brunswick study area. While the bulk of these immigrants took up land in the decade after 1825, two families, or heads of family, had arrived before 1815, 16 arrived in the succeeding decade, 40 between 1825-35, and 17 thereafter.[22] These Miramichi Irish came mainly from Cork and Tipperary, with a few families from Offaly and Clare.

A few years prior to the main influx of Irish into Barnaby another group of Cork emigrants settled around Peterborough, in southern Ontario, or Upper Canada as the area was then called. A total of 307 families, numbering over 2,000 persons, were transported by the government to Peterborough in the summer of 1825. This assisted emigration was a test of a scheme devised to rid Ireland of its surplus population. The emigrants came mainly from the barony of Fermoy, North Cork, and were carried in nine vessels from the port of Cork to Quebec. The journey up the St Lawrence was made by boat. A thirty to forty mile trek overland brought them to their farm lots in the Peterborough backwoods. Here they formed discrete blocks of settlement, especially in the townships of Douro, Ennismore, and in North Emily, or the parish of Downeyville, where over 100 nuclear families settled;[23] this latter unit forms the core of the Peterborough study area. Several families settled in Downeyville after 1825, some of them victims of the Irish famine of the late 1840's.

THE NEW WORLD

While the relatively few Irish considered in this study came from generally similar Irish backgrounds, they settled in quite different areas. By and large,

20 New Brunswick, Department of Crown Lands, Land Petitions, Northumberland County (MSS in Newcastle Courthouse, New Brunswick), vol. 3, 1-257, 1783-90; vol. 4, 258-522, 1790-1809.
21 Land Petitions, vols. 5-9, 1810-35.
22 Census of Canada, 1851, Nelson. These aggregates disguise the concentrated bursts that brought 14 families in 1825 and 20 families in 1830.
23 Only 87 of the 142 grants awarded in Downeyville were settled in 1825, but 20 others were claimed shortly thereafter. By 1847, however, 25 lots were still not occupied (Great Britain, Parliament, Select Committee on Emigration from the United Kingdom. Minutes of Evidence [in National Archives, Ottawa], Paper 550, London 1827, pp. 421-25; Great Britain, Parliament, Papers Relative to Emigration to Canada [in National Archives, Ottawa], Enclosure 2, No. 4, London, 1847, pp. 12-13).

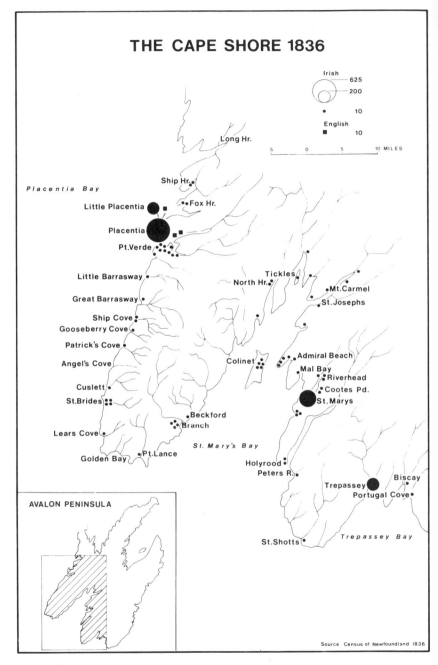

THE CAPE SHORE 1836

Irish
625
200
• 10
English
■ 10

5   0   5   10 MILES

Long Hr.

Placentia Bay

Ship Hr.

Fox Hr.

Little Placentia

Placentia

Pt.Verde

Little Barrasway

Great Barrasway

Ship Cove
Gooseberry Cove

Patrick's Cove

Angel's Cove

Cuslett

St.Brides

Lears Cove

Beckford
Branch

Pt.Lance

Golden Bay

St. Mary's Bay

Tickles
North Hr.

Mt.Carmel

St.Josephs

Colinet

Admiral Beach
Mal Bay
Riverhead
Cootes Pd.
St.Marys

Holyrood
Peters R.

Trepassey

Biscay

Portugal Cove

St.Shotts

Trepassey Bay

AVALON PENINSULA

Source Census of Newfoundland 1836

Figure 1

22

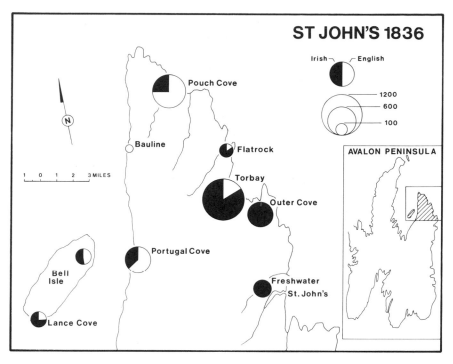

Figure 2

differences in the transferability and durability of Irish material culture depends not on distinctive Old World antecedents or on the conditions of migration, but on contrasting conditions in the study areas. For this reason it is important to describe as clearly as possible the basic differences between the study areas themselves.

Ethnic Isolation and Interaction

Generally, the Irish moved from a relatively homogeneous ethnic settlement to settlements that were ethnically diverse. But between the New World study areas there were striking differences in the degree of ethnic heterogeneity and interaction. At the local level, the Cape Shore immigrants were by far the most isolated ethnically. Along the fifty-mile stretch of shore from Pointe Verde to Branch there were no non-Irish settlers, and apart from some 30 English inhabitants in the more populous settlement of Placentia, the entire littoral from Long Harbour to Trepassey was exclusively southeastern Irish (Fig. 1). Indeed it is likely that many of these Cape Shore immigrants and their descendants lived out their lives without any contact with members of another ethnic group. By contrast, the Irish near St John's had English Protestant neighbours, most of

23

whom had settled prior to the Irish influx,[24] although the Irish themselves were settled in discrete blocks (Fig. 2). Because Freshwater and the Irish settlements north of St John's were only a few miles in extent, and because the English settlers were sandwiched between the city and these Irish areas, close — probably daily — contacts between the two groups were likely. The discrete block pattern of settlement was generally characteristic of Irish settlements near Peterborough and especially in the Miramichi district but in both these areas the Irish were in contact with several other groups of people. Within a few miles' radius of the Barnaby, for example, there lived Highland and Lowland Scots, immigrants from England, Loyalist and pre-Loyalist New Englanders, Acadians, and native Indians (Fig. 3). The Irish in Peterborough were even more closely surrounded by alien peoples. The movement of southern Irish into this area was part of a massive migration of land-hungry British settlers to Upper Canada after the Napoleonic wars. Ulster-Scots were the dominant element in the post-war influx and were particularly numerous in those townships adjoining the southern Irish settlements. The southern half of Emily township was almost exclusively Ulster Protestant, the northern half Irish Catholic (Fig. 4). Immigrants from Yorkshire had settled in Smith township in 1818-19, a few years before the Ulstermen arrived. Over the next two decades English and Scottish immigrants, descendants of American-born Loyalists and even some French Canadian lumbermen encircled and interpenetrated the Irish Catholic settlements, producing a greater cultural mixture than in any of the other study areas.

Agricultural Systems
In all study areas the immigrants settled on the land and, with the exception of the settlements north of St John's, the vast majority in each area were engaged in commercial agriculture. The first few years of settlement were characterized by a subsistence farm economy while the settlers struggled to clear enough land to produce a surplus. In the economy of the backwoods a farm lot was worth little more than the amount of labour invested in clearing it. Unlike the homeland, labour was scarce and expensive, land plentiful and cheap, so despite its abundance, land was cleared at a slow rate. The Peterborough-Irish cleared on the average less than two acres of land each year, but this was twice as much as the Miramichi-Irish and three times the rate of most of their countrymen in the

24 English fishermen had occupied the deeper inlets of Torbay, half a mile north of Middle Cove, and Quidi Vidi, three miles south of Logy Bay in the seventeenth century (Great Britain, Colonial Office Correspondence, Newfoundland [MSS in Provincial Archives, St John's], Series 1, vol. 35, "A List of Fishing Vessels and Colonists, 1675"). Because of the absence of harbours the study areas were not settled until the Irish came. Later some English and Irish Protestants and some Catholic Irish from elsewhere in the Avalon settled around the original Irish core.

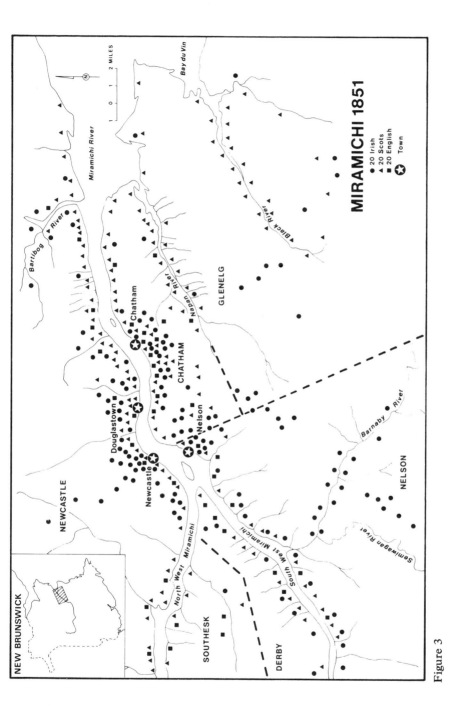

Figure 3

25

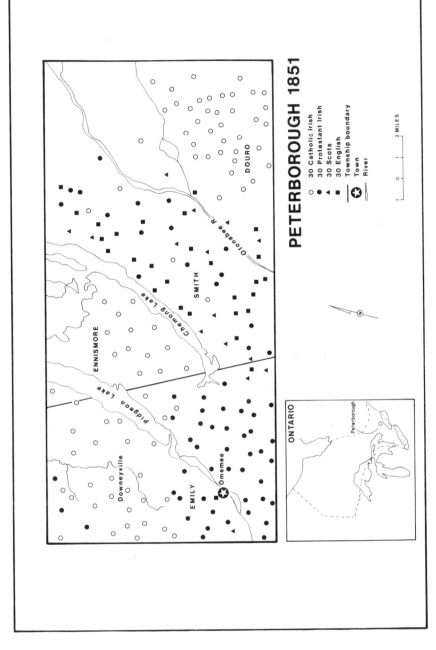

PETERBOROUGH 1851

- 30 Catholic Irish
- 30 Protestant Irish
- 30 Scots
- 30 English
- Township boundary
- Town
- River

0 1 2 MILES

DOURO

SMITH

ENNISMORE

Chemong Lake

Pidgeon Lake

Otonabee R.

Downeyville

EMILY

Omemee

ONTARIO

Peterborough

Figure 4

26

Avalon.[25] After twenty-five years of settlement the average clearing per family in Downeyville and Ennismore was 30 acres, 15 acres in Miramichi and along the Cape Shore, and 8 acres in the settlements north of St John's (Appendix 2). In the homeland, Waterford apart, 60 per cent of the farms were under 30 acres, and half of these were smaller than 10 acres. With the exception of the settlers north of St John's, it is almost certain that most of the immigrants had farmed fewer acres in southeast Ireland than in the New World in the mid-nineteenth century.

With a few exceptions the traditional crops of southern Ireland were grown in each of the New World study areas. Moreover, almost all the animals raised by the peasant farmer in the homeland were also raised by the immigrants. Between the homeland and the New World there were some sharp differences in the emphasis on certain crops or livestock and in the commercial orientation of agriculture, but there were even greater contrasts between the study areas themselves. Grain, especially wheat, dominated the economy of the Peterborough-Irish, although some of these immigrants early developed a more diversified economy, especially in Ennismore, where livestock products were a commercial adjunct to wheat. Grain was far less important commercially in Miramichi, where oats was the leading cereal, and was grown only sporadically in the Avalon. In Freshwater and on the Cape Shore, pastoral farming with an emphasis on the sale of dairy produce and beef was the dominant form of agriculture. Only in Miramichi did a mixed farm economy evolve, although the St John's settlers indulged in some market gardening, peddling potatoes, cabbages, and turnips in the town. Elsewhere these were subsistence crops.

Whereas the Peterborough-Irish were full-time farmers and were linked commercially to an international market, the farmers in the Avalon and Miramichi supplied local markets only. Up until the end of the 1820's the port of St John's had been supplied mainly from Waterford, Cork, and some West Country ports. Thereafter the farmers and farmer-fishermen settled near the city supplied this market. Traditionally, these goods were peddled and most farmers had an established core of customers in the city. There is no suggestion that there was a regularly scheduled market, but local tradition recalls that farmers often congregated on the city wharves to dispose of some products.[26] There was a small but significant local demand for fish, but the bulk of the catch was delivered to the city merchants for export.

25 In Ennismore, for example, the average clearing after a single year's occupancy was 3 acres per family. It increased to 3.4 acres in a year, to 4.2 after 3 years, but after 5 years it was still below 5 acres (Ontario, Assessment Rolls, Ennismore Township [MSS in Provincial Archives, Toronto], RG21, Section A, Newcastle District, 1827, 1828, 1830).
26 A cattle fair in King's Square, St John's is reported in *The Patriot*, St John's, Nov. 9, 1842 (in Arts and Culture Library, St John's). Milk cows predominated, but horses, hogs, and vegetables were also on sale. It is not known if this was a regular event.

The Irish in the St John's study areas were fully involved in this pattern of marketing. As early as 1837 a petition was entered that the roads north of the city be improved so that the inhabitants of Logy Bay, Outer and Middle Cove could take their farm produce and fish to the St John's market.[27] Two decades later 4,000 lbs of fresh butter, 1,140 lbs of fresh salmon, and £1,200 worth of cod liver oil were sold in St John's by Irish settlers in the study area north of the city.[28]

The farmers along the Cape Shore were too distant from St John's to peddle goods there; nevertheless trading links with the city were established early. According to local tradition, dry cattle — the most numerous type of livestock in the area in the mid-nineteenth century — were driven every fall to be sold in St John's. Despite the rugged nature of the terrain along the coast, a road from Placentia to St Brides was opened in 1844 and before 1850 was extended to Branch, in St Mary's Bay.[29] In supporting a petition for the improvement of the Cape Shore road, the inspector noted the agricultural emphasis in the area and suggested that the number of cattle driven from the Cape Shore to St John's would double if the road were improved. Three years later a St John's newspaper, reporting the arrival of cattle from the Cape Shore, referred to the "great advantages already afforded by the opening of a direct line of land communication between the capital and that valuable agricultural district."[30]

Boats from the city called in each cove at the end of the summer to collect butter. In the second half of the nineteenth century, codfish became the important commercial product on the Shore. As in other parts of Newfoundland, the cod were dried, salted and were stored in the stages in puncheons until the fall, when they were collected by the merchant's ship. There were no resident merchants on the Cape Shore: Sweetmans' business in Placentia had declined by 1850, so the Irish traded with merchants in St John's. Each fall the fishermen travelled to St John's and received provisions and other goods from the

27 Newfoundland, House of Assembly, *Journal* (in Memorial University Library, St John's), "Petition of Patrick Roche and Fifty-Five Others," July 19, 1837, p. 62. A later report on the Outer Cove road stated that the road commissioners "look forward with confidence to having this beautiful road in full operation by the month of September next, when the Planters residing in the settlements alluded to (Outer and Middle Cove) will be enabled to bring their fish and oil and other produce to the capital with a facility equal to the inhabitants of Portugal Cove" (Newfoundland, *Journal,* "Report of Board of Road Commissioners," Appendix, 1844, p. 47).

28 Newfoundland, Department of Colonial Secretary, *Census of Newfoundland and Labrador, 1857* (in Memorial University Library, St John's), p. 271. All of this was sold in the city.

29 Newfoundland, *Journal,* "General Account of Expenditure on Road from Great Placentia to Distress Cove," Appendix, 1845, p. 92.

30 *The Pilot,* St John's, March 13, 1852 (in Provincial Archives, St John's).

merchant in exchange for his fish. Apart from a little internal trading and some sales to Placentia, arable products, sheep and pigs were consumed on-farm.

From their very beginnings the Irish settlements in Miramichi were linked commercially to the trading centres of Chatham and Newcastle on the main river. During the first few years of occupancy, the Barnaby river was the main route of travel to these small towns. Beginning early in the 1830's new roads were built to connect the farm settlements to the Miramichi.[31] Lumber was the main Miramichi export when the Irish arrived.[32] Two large firms — Gilmour and Rankin of Newcastle on the north bank, and Cunards of Chatham on the south bank of the Miramichi — vied for control of this lucrative trade. Foodstuffs were imported in the early decades of the nineteenth century and the need for local agricultural development was stressed in the *Gleaner*.[33] As early as 1830 there were plans to erect a market house and public wharf in Chatham, where farmers could more readily dispose of their surplus.[34] The settlers sold cattle, sheep, hogs, poultry, butter, and some vegetables to the lumbermen and town dwellers, while hay and grain were purchased by the lumbermen to feed draft animals.

The Peterborough-Irish enjoyed far wider contacts in the world of commercial agriculture than did the immigrants in the other study areas. The town of Peterborough, situated at the northernmost navigable point of the Otonabee River, developed as the main collecting and forwarding centre for the wheat farmers of the surrounding area. Steamers were introduced in 1832 and Peterborough became the focus of seven roads, two of which led south to the lakeshore ports of Cobourg and Port Hope, where the merchants and farmers

31 New Brunswick, Department of Public Works, "Highways Recorded in the County of Northumberland" (MSS in Newcastle Courthouse), No. 20, 1831. "Proposed road from the village of Nelson to Barnaby River ...," *The Royal Gazette and New Brunswick Advertiser*, Fredericton, July 8, 1835 (in University of New Brunswick Library, Fredericton). "... £10 to open a road from the south side of Barnaby's River between lots numbers 8 and 9 to the Semiwagan Hardwood Ridge," *Gazette*, April 20, 1836. "... £20 for the road between Nelson Village and Barnaby's River; £15 to improve the road from Nowlan's farm, back of Nelson, to the upper settlement, Barnaby's River; ... £30 to explore and open a road from Dennis Kirk's on the northeast side of Barnaby's River to Joseph Hutcheson's place on that river," *Gazette*, May 17, 1837.
32 In 1825, for example 351 vessels left the ports of Chatham and Newcastle for Britain, carrying 155,040 tons of pine, 1,300 tons of hardwood, 3,161 cords of lathwood, 1,069,260 feet of deals, 1,752 spars, 615 price oars, 1,418 handspikes, 48,633 staves, 103,369 stave billets, 627 feet of birch plank, 288 poles, and 220 rickers (*The Mercury*, Newcastle, February 28, 1826 [in University of New Brunswick Library, Fredericton]).
33 *The Gleaner and Northumberland Schediasma*, Chatham, Oct. 13, 1829, Oct. 27, 1829 (in University of New Brunswick Library, Fredericton). A group of Scots settled along the river Nappan, a few miles east of Barnaby in 1825 and by 1829 were coming regularly to Chatham, peddling poultry, eggs, and butter to the inhabitants.
34 *The Gleaner*, Chatham, April 7, 1830. Through the sale of town lots the community in Chatham had acquired £75 for the construction of a market house.

unloaded their grain.[35] Wheat was a desirable commodity, capable of withstanding shipping costs across the Atlantic but with the rise of refrigeration in transatlantic shipping in the second half of the nineteenth century, meat replaced wheat as the leading export. Mixed farming replaced commercial grain in the Peterborough region after 1860 and finally changed to pastoral farming. Long before this the southern Irish had sold butter locally, and supplied local loggers with beef, bacon, mutton, vegetables, and fodder for the draft animals.

Not all of the Irish were full-time farmers. Twenty-six of 136 heads of household (all Irish-born) in Downeyville in 1851 were employed off the farm, mainly as artisans, but only 10 of these were landless.[36] Only 6 of the 60 or more families in Miramichi were not recorded as farmers in 1851, but it is certain that many of the Irish in this study area found seasonal employment in the local lumber industry, either logging in the woods, loading on the wharves, or working in the sawmills.[37] In the study area north of St John's, farming and fishing had been combined from the first years of settlement. Fifty-eight families and 62 fishing boats were recorded there in 1836.[38] In 1857 only 51 out of a total of 92 families were listed in the census as farmers, but the vast majority of the 51 were also engaged in the fishery.[39] According to tradition, few of the first generation of settlers on the Cape Shore were involved in a commercial fishery, at least until the mid-nineteenth century. In 1836 there were apparently only three fishing boats on the entire Cape Shore, all of them in Branch. Twenty years later all heads of household were listed as farmers but almost all adult males were engaged in commercial fishing.

The Physical Environment
The most conspicuous characteristic of the topography along the Cape Shore is a series of spectacular cliffs where the old eroded and sparsely wooded plateau meets the sea. Along this striking and windswept shore the 400′ plateau is dissected every few miles by narrow, stream-eroded valleys, many of which are the foci of settlement. Although subject to flooding, the alluvial soils of the "flats" were fairly fertile and are excellent for pasture. On the valley slopes the rocky till affords a poorer soil and the soil on the plateau is of low quality and was rarely cultivated. Near St John's the topography is rugged and the natural soil on the drift-laden slopes was shallow and stony with a low humus content.

35 Thomas W. Poole, *The Early Settlement of Peterborough County* (Peterborough: Peterborough Printing Company, 1867), reprinted, 1967, pp. 16-18. The Downeyville settlers used the Lindsay-Port Hope road for transporting grain.
36 *Census of Canada, 1851* (Emily Township), C-981/2.
37 *Census of Canada, 1851* (Nelson Parish).
38 *Census of Newfoundland, 1836*, p. 10.
39 *Census of Newfoundland, 1857*, pp. 352-55. Over 90 boats were recorded in this year. Folk memory recalls only 6 families in this study area who never fished.

Heavy rainfall and low rates of evaporation in both areas combine to produce highly leached, acidic conditions and the podzolic soils are generally too recent or immature to be fertile.

The Miramichi is a great, monotonous, forested lowland. Like the Avalon, soils are acidic and highly podzolized. Small pockets of alluvial soils are located along the Barnaby, but where the land slopes gently back from the river the natural soils were shallow and stony. Much of the Peterborough area is heavily drumlinized, affording a pleasantly undulatory topography further diversified by a myriad of small lakes, ponds, and streams. Drumlin soils were stony and the steep slopes made cultivation difficult. Drainage is often impeded and lowlying marshy swamps abound. Throughout the area there is a high lime content that enriches the predominantly clayey loam but the best soils were found on the broad clay plain of Downeyville, where the glacial drift cover is thinner.

The New World forest was a complete novelty to the Irish. Centuries of continuous occupation in Ireland had resulted in gradual removal of the native forest and by 1600 all but one-eighth of the land had been stripped of its trees.[40] In the homeland the peasants salvaged construction timbers and sometimes fuel from the fossilized remains of ancient oak forests buried deep in the bogs and it must have been especially galling for the emigrants from this timber-starved region to be forced to destroy so much timber in the New World in order to create a farm. Magnificent stands of balsam fir, maple, hemlock, and cedar existed in Peterborough and Miramichi but in the Avalon, by contrast, the Irish were confronted by stunted stands of spruce, fir, and larch. Poor soils and an unfavourable climate combined with the continual cutting of timber by fishermen for centuries before the Irish settled resulted in a sparse forest in this latter area.

The immigrants were ill-prepared for the long, cold winters of the New World. Irish winters are noted for their mildness, with mean January temperatures ranging from 41° to 44° in the southeast. Sheltered spots actually enjoy continuous growth in winter but everywhere in the homeland frost is rare. By contrast, the January mean in the Avalon dips to 24° and it is considerably lower in Peterborough and Miramichi. In all study areas the growing season is limited to less than 130 days. The summers vary from a long dry season in Peterborough with a July mean of 70° (compared to 60° in the homeland) to an Avalon summer that is cooler, wetter, and shorter than in the homeland. The southeast is the most favoured region, climatically, in Ireland; it is not only the driest and warmest but also the sunniest corner of the country. Whereas Ireland's mild moist regime favours the growth of oats, potatoes, and turnips and especially grasses, the southeastern Irish farmer can also grow wheat and barley.

40 Eileen McCracken, "The Woodlands of Ireland circa 1600," *Irish Historical Studies* 11 (1959): 271-90.

In the north and west these crops are ill adapted to the cold, cloudy, wet weather. Wheat cultivation reaches its climatic limits in the Avalon, but in Miramichi and especially Peterborough the climate is better adapted to wheat than is that of the homeland. The higher precipitation in the Avalon encourages the growth of root crops such as potatoes, cabbage, and turnips, and especially pastoral farming which is often rendered difficult in extended dry periods in the other study areas.

III
The settlement pattern

The traditional form of rural settlement in Ireland was one of dispersed dwellings or of clusters of usually fewer than thirty houses. According to the Gaelic rule of land inheritance – called "gavelkind" by the English – each son was entitled to an equal share of his father's property. A son who built a dwelling on inherited land normally placed it close to the parental house. Through this pattern of land succession and settlement, single farms often evolved into kin-group clusters, each distinguished by a common surname.[1] Deviations from this pattern occurred and sometimes more than one patrilineal extended family might occupy a cluster, but within such settlements farmsteads were still arranged according to blood ties. The arable land of a kin group was located close to the dwellings in an open field and was usually worked jointly by the group. Furthermore, Gaelic custom dictated that the lands of a kin group could not be alienated and if an individual died without direct heirs, the land became the property of the nearest kin. During periods of population expansion, as in

1 Jean Graham, "Rural Society in Connacht 1600-40," in Nicholas Stephens & Robin E. Glasscock (eds.), *Irish Geographical Studies in Honour of E. Estyn Evans* (Belfast: Queen's University Press, 1970), pp. 192-206; J.H. Johnson, "Partnership and Clachans in Mid-Nineteenth Century Londonderry," *Ulster Folklife* 9 (1963): 20-29; T. Jones Hughes, "Land Holding and Settlement in the Cooley Peninsula of Louth," *Irish Geography* 4 (1961): 149-73; D. McCourt, "Traditions of Rundale in and Around the Sperrin Mountains," *Ulster Journal Archaeology* 16 (1953): 69-84; *idem*, "The Rundale System in Donegal: Its Distribution and Decline," *Donegal Annual* 3 (1955): 47-60;

the decades prior to the Irish migrations, examples of single farms evolving into loose or compact cellular clusters were numerous, but once such settlements became overcrowded, sons usually waived or were denied rights of succession and sometimes established farms independently. Irish farm clusters were often dissolved or abandoned and the waxing and waning of these agglomerations was perhaps the most distinctive characteristic of Irish rural settlement since at least late medieval times. Dispersed and agglomerated settlements were not opposing types in Irish tradition, but alternative developments within a single dynamic settlement system.

The morphology of most Irish farm clusters was characterized by extreme disorder, with no discernible formal plan.[2] Unlike the continental European village, the *clachan* lacked any service establishments such as an inn, church, or stores. Sometimes dwellings were arranged in a close, compact manner but more frequently were disposed in a highly irregular fashion along or around the edge of the intensively cultivated openfield. Erixon, among others, has distinguished between the farmstead sites or building lots with their attendant garden plots and the adjacent open field or fields.[3] In re-allocating land in compact and enclosed blocks improving landlords sometimes replaced the untidy clusters with houses closely but regularly spaced on both sides of a road. A modified form of the true village of continental European tradition was also established in medieval times in the heavily manorialized parts of eastern and southeastern Ireland, mainly by Anglo-Norman settlers.[4] These agglomerations were often larger than the *clachans,* depended on a different field system, and often had

---

idcm, "Surviving Openfield in County Londonderry," *Ulster Folklife* 4 (1958): 19-28. A bilateral pattern of inheritance has been suggested by the anthropologist Fox for Tory Island, Donegal, but other anthropologists have reported a patrilineal emphasis in traditional Irish land succession practice. Conrad M. Arensberg and Solon T. Kimball, *Family and Community in Ireland* (Cambridge: Harvard University Press, 1940), pp. 76-93; J.R. Fox, "Kinship and Land Tenure on Tory Island," *Ulster Folklife* 12 (1966): 1-17; Eileen Kane, "Man and Kin in Donegal: A Study of Kinship Functions in a Rural Irish and Irish-American Community," *Ethnology* 7 (1968): 245-58; John C. Messenger, *Inis Beag: Isle of Ireland* (New York: Holt, Rinehart and Winston, 1969), pp. 72, 74.

2 In the dialect of Highland Scotland and Ulster these haphazard clusters are called *Clachans* and, although the word is unknown in modern Irish, it has been used to identify such settlements in the south of Ireland.

3 Sigurd Erixon, "The Age of Enclosures and its Older Traditions," *Folklife* 4 (1966): 56-63. There is still a clear distinction between the type of fences surrounding the farmstead and garden and the fences that enclosed the old openfield area. The garden, called *gort* in Gaelic, was enclosed much earlier and was worked privately by the individual family.

4 Pierre Flatrès, *Géographie rurale de quatre countrées celtiques: Irlande, Galles, Cornwall, Man* (Rennes: Plihon, 1957), pp. 266-67.

some kind of focal point – a church, manor house, or open space – within the village.

The medieval patterns of Irish rural settlement were being slowly effaced from at least the seventeenth century onwards. All over Ireland there was an increase in the individual ownership or operation of land, with the nuclear rather than the extended family holding the right of transmission. Although many factors influenced this drift towards agrarian individualism, the most potent force was the improving landlord. Reacting to the ideas of the agricultural revolution, Irish landlords were convinced that proper exploitation of the land could only be achieved if tenants resided on single, unified holdings, amid their fields. The traditional Irish openfield regime, with its mosaic of dispersed family plots, was inimical to the development of improved agriculture, and for a century prior to the migrations Irish landlords had been dissolving the agglomerated settlements, and amalgamating and redistributing the openfield plots in compact and enclosed units to their better tenantry. These newly created lots were sometimes long and thin in shape, called "ladder," "ribbon," or "strip" farms,[5] but whatever the shape, a single farmstead was relocated within each unified holding.

At the end of the seventeenth century most Irish farmland was still in open fields[6] but by 1770 the lowlands of southern and southeastern Ireland were largely enclosed.[7] The process of land redistribution and concomitant dispersal of farmsteads continued into the nineteenth century and was one of the major causes of emigration. By the time of the migrations to the study areas only pockets of openfields remained in the homeland,[8] but it should be remembered that enclosure was not always accompanied by the re-allocation of land or the dispersal of dwellings. The consolidation of holdings into single, enclosed tracts, the dispersion of habitations and especially the attempts to enclose the

5 This type of geometrical re-allocation of land represented a compromise between the landlord's desire for non-fragmented family holdings and the peasant's wish for an equitable distribution of different soils. On sloping terrain the quality of the soil deteriorated upslope, but the long narrow lots ascending the slopes normally enclosed the various soil types.

6 F.H.A. Aalen, "Enclosures in Eastern Ireland: A General Introduction," *Irish Geography* 5 (1965): 29-33. Only the baronies of Bargy and Forth, in south Wexford, and the lands around the towns were then enclosed.

7 J.H. Andrews, "Some Sources for the Study of Enclosure in Ireland between the 16th and 19th Centuries," *Irish Geography* 5 (1965): 36-37. Enclosure began in the eastern lowlands of the country and spread slowly to the more marginal west.

8 By 1841 less than 10 per cent of the population of the homeland practised joint farming. In the Union Districts of Mallow, Middleton, and Fermoy, homeland of the Peterborough-Irish, only 7, 1, and 2 per cent, respectively, of the tenantry held land in common. It is assumed that these figures refer to arable land only. Great Britain, Parliament, *Report of the Select Committee of the House of Lords on Colonization from Ireland* (in National Archives, Ottawa), London, 1847, VI, Appendix 22, pp. 173-79.

communally operated grazing grounds met with stiff opposition, often culminating in riots, from the Irish peasantry. In their view, ancient privileges and traditions were being repudiated by an alien aristocracy who sought to augment their estate income by improving the quality of farming. The improving landlord, George Hill, noted that "the pleasure the people feel in assembling and chatting together made them consider the removal of the houses from the clusters or hamlets in which they were generally built to the separate farms a great grievance."[9]

Wherever landlords did not interfere with native settlement traditions in the decades prior to the migrations the tendency was towards agglomeration rather than dispersion. It should also be noted that some landlords, in a reversal of policy, actually encouraged the subdivision of farms, especially during the tillage boom in the early nineteenth century.[10] Additional rents were collected from every new holding.

While, generally speaking, the move towards agrarian individualism had its landscape expression in the transformation of a traditional agglomerated settlement pattern into one of dispersed dwellings, enclosed fields, and compact independent farm units, this transformation of the cultural landscape did not disrupt greatly the traditional patterns of Irish peasant society. The reorganization of a cluster often involved the eviction of an indigent surplus tenantry and the creation of consolidated holdings within the townland for the remainder. In such a situation, an ingress of new families was rare. Despite resettlement, then, the move towards agrarian individualism was anything but complete: ties of kinship and friendship still existed and some aspects of communal organization could be maintained. The relative proximity of dwellings even under an *einzelhof* regime helped preserve the traditional social structure. Moreover, the isolated farmstead and compact farm sometimes reverted to an agglomerated form of settlement through renewed subdivision.

THE INITIAL SETTLEMENT PATTERN IN THE NEW WORLD

Along the valley of Freshwater the initial pattern of settlement was one of dispersed farmsteads (see Fig. 5).[11] Whether their farm lots were as small as 5 or as large as 50 acres, the Irish immigrants worked non-fragmented tracts with all

9 Lord George Hill, *Gweedore: Facts from Gweedore* (Dublin: Hatchard, 1845); 5th ed., 1887, p. 22.
10 For an example see T. Jones Hughes, "Landlordism in the Mullet of Mayo," *Irish Geography* 4 (1959): 16-34.
11 Farm boundaries are based on initial surveys and the location of dwellings determined through oral tradition and field observation (Newfoundland, Department of Colonial Secretary, *Registry of Grants* [MSS. in Department of Mines, Agriculture and Resources, Confederation Building, St John's], V-305, 0-13).

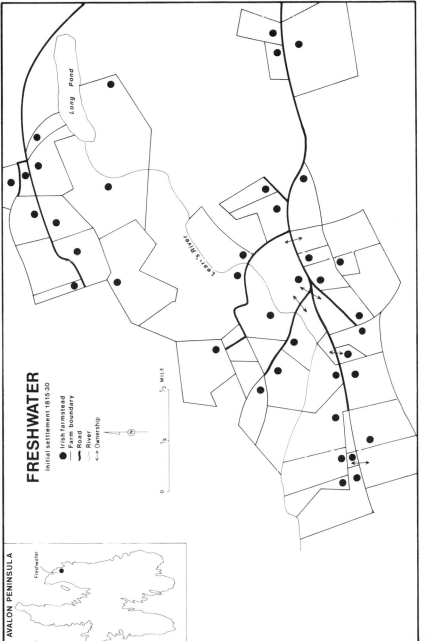

Figure 5

37

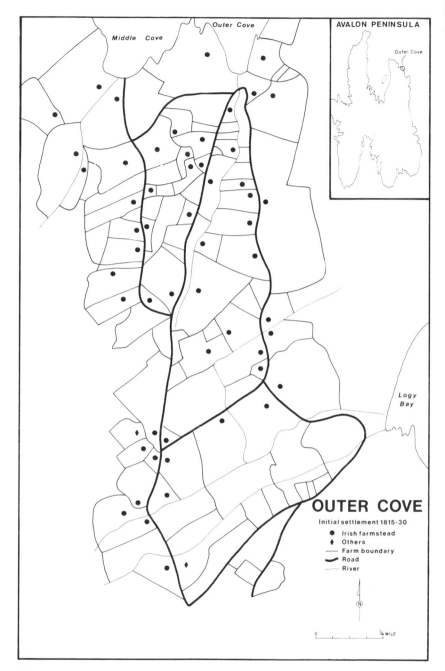

OUTER COVE

Initial settlement 1815·30

● Irish farmstead
♦ Others
— Farm boundary
▬ Road
— River

AVALON PENINSULA

Outer Cove

Middle Cove

Outer Cove

Logy
Bay

0   ¼ MILE

N

Figure 6

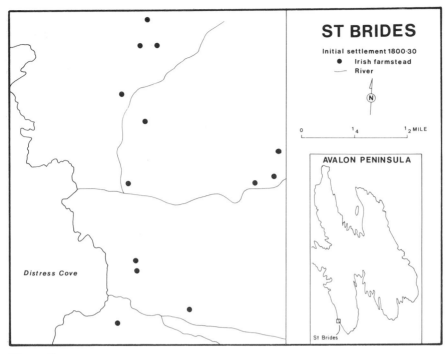

ST BRIDES

Initial settlement 1800-30
● Irish farmstead
— River

AVALON PENINSULA

Distress Cove

St Brides

Figure 7

farm buildings located within the farm boundaries. North of St John's, the Irish scattered their dwellings inland along the small streams leading to the coves and created haphazardly-shaped farm units similar to those of Freshwater (Fig. 6). Only in rare cases north of the city were non-contiguous portions of land occupied by a single immigrant family, and without exception, the farm buildings were placed within the boundaries of each compact unit. A similarly dispersed pattern characterized the initial occupation of the Cape Shore (Fig. 7). In all but two cases – Branch and St Brides – no more than two families initially occupied a cove. In St Brides the unified, compact farm unit was characteristic, but in the less populous coves a more fragmented pattern of landownership sometimes occurred. Immigrant families often cleared non-contiguous tracts or pockets of fertile soils in the flats and located their farmsteads in close proximity to each other, along the valley sides. Such farmsteads, however, were always located inside the boundaries of the farm.

Along the Barnaby river, and in its attendant settlements, the boundaries of most farms were drawn prior to settlement.[12] As elsewhere in Miramichi, the

12 Joseph Hunter completed his survey of Barnaby in 1830 and Semiwagan in 1833 (New Brunswick, Department of Crown Lands, *Crown Land Records*, Northumberland County [MSS in Confederation Building, Fredericton], vol. 9, 1833).

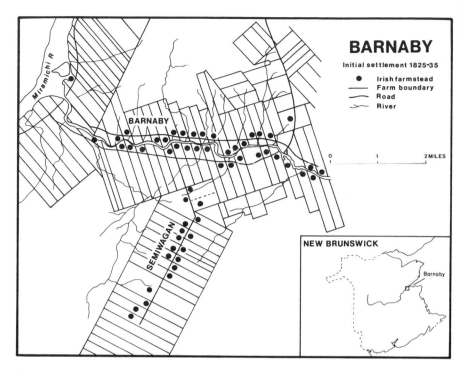

Figure 8

farm lots in the study area were long and thin in shape, with a narrow frontage along a river or road. The standard area of each lot was 100 acres. Farmsteads were located within the boundaries of each lot, close to the banks of the river, or beside the road (Fig. 8).[13] Because of the shape of these lots, farmsteads were initially more closely spaced than in the Avalon, although farm lots in the latter area were far smaller.

In Peterborough a superimposed cadastral plan determined the limits of every farm. The land was surveyed before the Irish arrived and allocated to individual families in 100-acre lots. These farm lots, with a few exceptions, were almost square in form, in contrast to the long, narrow lots in Miramichi. Each immigrant Irish family located their farmstead within the boundaries of the lot granted them, producing a more dispersed pattern of settlement than in the

13 The second round of buildings, dating from mid-century and before, is represented. These farmsteads are recorded in a map of the sample settlements drawn in 1876 (Roe and Colby, *Map of Northumberland County, New Brunswick* [in National Archives, Ottawa], R.220, Northumberland, 1876). The dispersed pattern of farmsteads in the middle of the last century is a continuation of the initial occupance form.

40

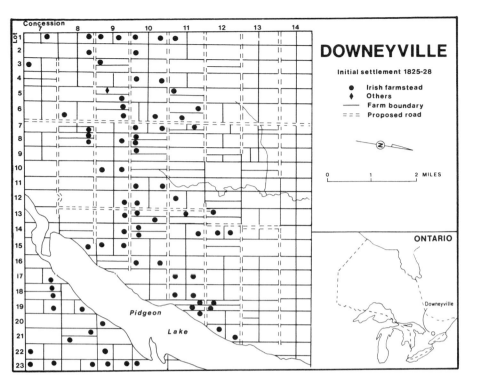

Figure 9

other study areas (Fig. 9).[14] As in Miramichi each family initially owned and worked a single tract of land.

Whereas in the homeland, farms were rented either by individual families or collectively by kin groups, land in the study areas was granted to single families who became outright owners on the completion of certain settlement duties and the payment of a small fee to the government. Both in Peterborough and Miramichi each settler had to clear 5 acres and build a dwelling house within his lot before full ownership was granted. In Peterborough, moreover, the concession line fronting the lot had to be cleared for a road. Most of the land in the St John's study areas was formally granted with settlement stipulations somewhat similar to those in Miramichi. Along the Cape Shore, with a few exceptions, and to some extent in the St John's study areas, the immigrants ignored or were ignorant of the legal procedures of acquiring ownership, and most of them squatted.

14 The farmsteads shown on Figure 9 represent the second round of buildings, dating from the mid-nineteenth century. Most of these are recorded in James A. Patterson, *Map of the County of Victoria* (in National Archives, Ottawa), Emily Township, Section C, VI, 420, 1877.

41

Although there were differences in the physical environment within and between study areas, dispersed settlement was characteristic of them all. By locating his farmstead close to the Barnaby, the Irish settler was near the physically favoured intervale soils but not every settler along the river had such soils on his lot. There were many springs strewn along the terraced slopes on both sides of the river, but in the non-riparian settlements of Semiwagan and Nowlanville each farmstead was similarly located at one extremity of the long lot. It is clear that the river, the avenue of transport in the first years of settlement, influenced farmstead location within each individual lot, but it is equally clear that the physical environment did not influence the basic decision to live on individual lots. Although dependent on the sea for part of their livelihood, the settlers north of St John's did not occupy all the available sites close to the beach but dispersed inland along the rivers, where they could establish tiny farms. Elsewhere in the study areas neither water, soil, nor slope influenced the decision to create an *einzelhof* pattern of settlement.

In Peterborough and Miramichi the apparent explanation for the dispersed pattern of settlement and non-fragmented nature of the farms lies in the influence of the superimposed cadastral survey. Every immigrant family in these two areas had to build a house within the boundaries of their lot, clear 5 acres for agriculture, and in Peterborough, help build a road along the concession line that fronted their lot. Until these settlement duties were completed, settlers did not acquire full title to the land they occupied. Such settlement stipulations were a powerful stimulus to the dispersion of farmsteads. Peter Robinson, who supervised the settling of the immigrant Irish in Peterborough in 1825, commented that "the location of the emigrants, by far the most troublesome and laborious part of the service, was completed before the winter commenced, and I had a small log house built for the head of each family on their respective lots. ..."[15] Yet in the Avalon, where there was no superimposed land survey, nor, indeed, any settlement duties to be performed, the Irish produced an *einzelhof* form of settlement.

Because the prevailing pattern of rural settlement in the homeland was dispersed at the time of the migrations, it is tempting to regard the pattern in the study areas as genetically linked to this homeland form. Certainly, it is likely that some if not the majority of emigrants who had worked compact farm units in the homeland were familiar with the economic advantages of such a system. But the dispersed pattern of settlement in Ireland just prior to the migrations was mainly a creation of the improving landlord, and in his absence, or sometimes through his encouragement, most peasants tended to subdivide and agglomerate. Because of the landlord's role in dispersing dwellings in the homeland, it is surprising that in the absence of landlordism in the New World

15 Canada, Peter Robinson Papers, (MSS in Provincial Archives, Toronto), 1822-44.

study areas (and especially in the Avalon where all elements of supervision were lacking) the immigrants did not establish farm clusters. Their failure to do so is best explained by an analysis of the social structure of the migrating groups.

In the traditional homeland clusters the exploitation of the land, as noted, was organized communally and based primarily on ties of kin. The Irish extended family is not a rigidly defined group, with constant boundaries, but may be taken generally to include all the descendants of a common great-grandparent.[16] Church law normally forbids marriage of second cousins (the descendants of a common great-grandparent) or any closer relatives. Recognition of kinship ties and respect for the obligations of kindred were more pronounced in the simpler society of the pre-industrial age and, it is safe to suggest, would extend beyond second cousinship in the Irish *clachan*. In order to reproduce the kin-based agglomerated settlements in the New World, the extended family had to be transferred across the ocean. However, the Irish migration was not a mass exodus of extended families, leaving behind deserted house clusters and open fields, but a steady trickle of dissatisfied sons and daughters from hamlets and isolated farmsteads scattered across the land. The ties of blood that had ordered the peasant's pattern of living on the land and had regulated their communal obligations were severed. No other centripetal force was substituted in their settlement of the New World. The total dominance of the single family farmstead in the study areas reflects the social structure of the migrating groups. They entered singly, family by family, and staked out their claims. The uprooted character of these immigrant families is strikingly illustrated along the Cape Shore, where a single family might occupy and hold an isolated cove for years. This individualism and isolation was in startling contrast to the kin-centred peasant society of Ireland. Even in those coves where more than one family settled, they rarely settled simultaneously. The first occupant would mark out his lot and clear some land. There was no reason why he should share his hard-won acres with the next incoming stranger; this latter immigrant was forced to settle outside the limits of the first occupant's farm. An initial pattern of dispersed farmsteads was thus assured. In Peterborough, where the immigrants did settle at the same time, there is no evidence of joint farming or of any tendency to cluster. Even a clustering of farmsteads at the four corners, where four contiguous lots met, was never attempted. Initially, there were some vacant lots, intermingled with occupied lots, which further dispersed the settlement pattern. When several contiguous lots were occupied the settlers often located their shanties towards the centre of the "square hundred," giving a maximum dispersal of farmsteads.

In many ways, the movement of nuclear families to dispersed farmsteads in the New World was but an extension of the Irish landlord's policy of dissolving

16 Arensberg and Kimball, *Family and Community in Ireland*, p. 90.

overburdened kin-group clusters and resettling the better tenants on consolidated holdings. It is likely that some of the tenants who failed to acquire land in these resettlement schemes joined the Atlantic migration.

The Avalon
The Irish custom of granting equal shares of the land to all male heirs was maintained in the settlements south of Placentia. An examination of land inheritance among 29 immigrant families reveals that out of a total of 98 sons in a position to inherit a portion of the ancestral farm, only 14 did not. During the second half of the nineteenth century partible inheritance almost trebled the number of farms without any commensurate increase in the area cleared.[17] It is not so much the rate of subdivision that concerns us here, as the manner in which the land was redistributed. Figure 10 illustrates the characteristic form of land inheritance and settlement evolution in a Cape Shore cove.[18] John Coffey, born of immigrant Irish parents in the settlement of Angel's Cove around 1845, moved to the neighbouring cove of Cuslett in the mid 60s, where he began clearing a farm north of the river, beside the old road. He married and had 7 sons and a daughter. The daughter married a farmer from a neighbouring cove – St Brides – and one son died while still very young. The remaining 6 sons acquired shares of the ancestral farm. There is no documentary record to indicate the size of these 6 shares, but the small parcels or "gardens" located along the road, close to the ancestral farmstead, represented the core of the old farm. Some of the parcels along the river, east of the original farmstead, were part of the old farm; others were cleared by the sons after the old farm was subdivided. The latter process partially accounts for the inequitable distribution of land among the sons in 1935.

Two similar, sharply defined kin-group clusters – the Mannings and the Reillys – are located south of Cuslett river, closer to the sea shore. Like the Coffeys, some of the younger sons (the third generation) had cleared lots well inland, along the river, after inheriting shares of the ancestral plots. Their

17 In 1857, 54 farmers worked 810 acres along the Cape Shore; in 1891, 153 farmers worked only 796 acres. It is possible that the 1857 acreage figures are too high but the pattern of increasing subdivision and much more leisurely rate of clearing during the second half of the nineteenth century is incontrovertible (Newfoundland, Department of Colonial Secretary, *Census of Newfoundland & Labrador, 1857*, p. 354; *Census of Newfoundland & Labrador, 1891*, Table II, Sect. B, pp. 364-65 [in Memorial University Library, St John's]).

18 Based on a cadastral map of Cuslett (Newfoundland, *Registry of Grants*, V-344, 1935). Subdivision of properties is shown only when heirs lived in separate houses. In all areas there are cases of unmarried brothers sharing part of the ancestral farm, but living together or with a married brother.

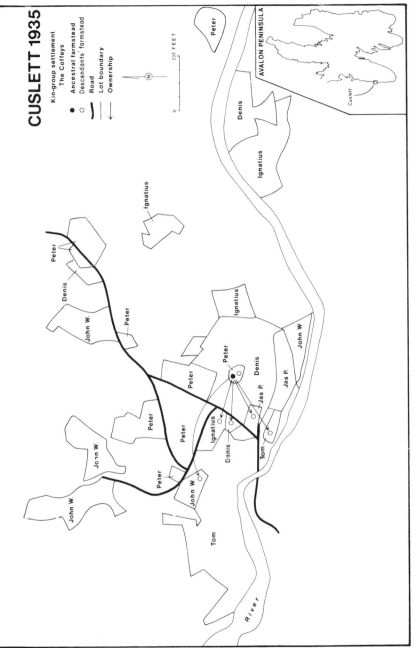

Figure 10

45

farmsteads remained clustered around the ancestral dwellings, with each son having a separately enclosed garden within which his farmstead was located. These several gardens represented the earliest cleared portion of the cove.

A similar pattern of farm transmission and settlement evolution is revealed among the sons of the immigrants, the second generation of settlers. In St Brides, for example, the practice of partible inheritance resulted in a pattern of closely clustered farmsteads, arranged according to blood ties. This tradition of land succession and settlement evolution has been rigidly maintained to the present day. Both in Branch and St Brides the distinctive kin-group clusters are commonly referred to as "squares." Since land inheritance was and is almost exclusively patrilineal, and residence patrilocal, each square is designated by the common surname of its occupants, e.g., "Dohey's Square" or "Young's Square"; the genitive is also always used. Of the 90 successors to land on the Cape Shore in the second generation, only 6 were women; two of these had no brothers, the others shared land with their brothers. In the second round of land transfers, 120 males and 3 females inherited portions of farms.

Only rarely was land sold. The kin-group clusters with their common surname have become more populous with each generation. In Branch, the ancestral house plots and gardens down by the sea shore had become so fragmented through successive subdividing between male heirs that some sons were forced to leave these nuclei early in the present century and clear new building sites up river.

The patterns of land succession in the area near St John's differed in some aspects from the patterns along the Cape Shore and these differences were clearly expressed in settlement morphology. In Freshwater, for example, only 3 of the 28 farms transmitted by the first generation to their descendants were subdivided (Fig. 11). In the second round of land transfers (from the second to the third generation) all but 2 of the 20 farms inherited remained undivided. Moreover, some farms in Freshwater were sold to non-relatives. Only 3 of the 31 farms recorded were sold by the first generation of occupants, but their descendants in the second generation sold 13 of the 35 units owned; none of these farms was subdivided. Where fragmentation of ancestral farms did occur, either in the first or second round of transfers, the farms were always split into compact units. The initial *einzelhof* pattern in Freshwater remained relatively unchanged.

North of St John's subdivision of the original farms was more widespread; 16 of the 49 ancestral units were divided among heirs by the first generation. In the second series of transfers, 26 of the 69 inherited farms were subdivided. In contrast to the Cape Shore, however, in only a few cases was a farm split between more than two descendants. As in Freshwater the farms were almost always divided into compact units so the initial pattern of dispersed farmsteads and single farm tracts was maintained. Farms did not pass as freely into the hands of non-relatives in these settlements north of the city as they did in

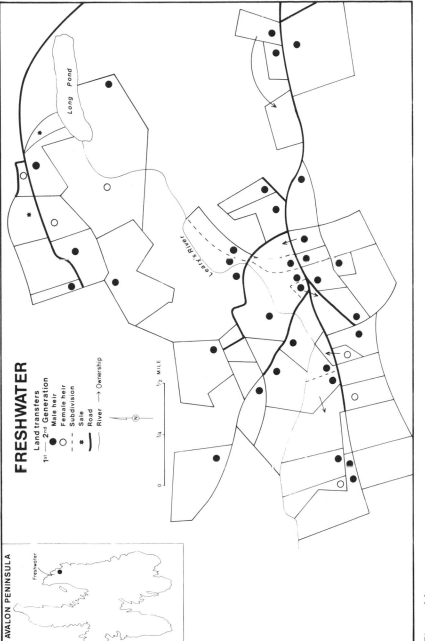

Figure 11

47

Freshwater, at least in the second series of transfers, but there was some selling of portions of farms.

The patrilineal pattern of land inheritance and patrilocal pattern of residence dominated in the St John's settlements as on the Cape Shore, but examples of female inheritance were more numerous in the former area. Of the 6 matrilocal residents among the second generation of Freshwater settlers, only one had a brother at the time of succession, but 5 of the 7 females inheriting in the next generation did have brothers, none of whom inherited land. North of St John's 7 of·the 15 females inheriting land in the second generation had brothers, but only 5 inherited a portion of the ancestral farm. As on the Cape Shore, marriage patterns were highly localized in the settlements north of the city, uniting the descendants of the original nuclear families in increasingly complicated kinship networks. In the second generation 41 of the 67 recorded heirs found marriage partners from within the three coves; of the 78 recorded marriages of heirs in the next generation, only 15 obtained partners from outside the study area. Society mirrored that of the Cape Shore in many ways, but lacked the distinctive kin-group clusters of the latter area. In Freshwater, by contrast, only 8 of the 18 marriages of heirs recorded for the first generation were local (i.e., both partners were born in Freshwater), and in the next generation 19 of the 26 partners came from outside, mainly from the city of St John's.

Miramichi

Although some farms were subdivided in Miramichi, the initial *einzelhof* pattern of settlement was preserved. Of the 68 first-generation farms recorded in Barnaby and Semiwagan, 54 were inherited and 14 sold; only 12 of the 54 inherited farms were subdivided (Fig. 12). In the second generation, 66 out of a recorded 161 males inherited land; 25 sons remained on as labourers or acquired land locally through purchase or marriage, and the remainder departed for work outside the study area, securing jobs either in the local lumbering industry or in the United States. Only 6 of the 98 females recorded inherited land in the first transfer; of the remainder, 41 remained in the settlement, and 51 departed. In the second round of farm succession in Barnaby and Semiwagan, 6 females and 44 males inherited land; there were no cases of subdivision in the first series of transfers; lots were split longitudinally, usually into equal shares. The original orientation of the cadastral survey was maintained. Inheriting sons received equal access to road, river, intervale, and rear woodlot, and probably an equal share of the cultivated segment of the ancestral farm. In some cases a farm lot, divided equally between two sons (there is only one example of a tripartite division, in Semiwagan) was worked as a single tract, but only when one or both of the sons did not marry. Farms were sometimes sold to relatives or neighbours but rarely to outsiders.

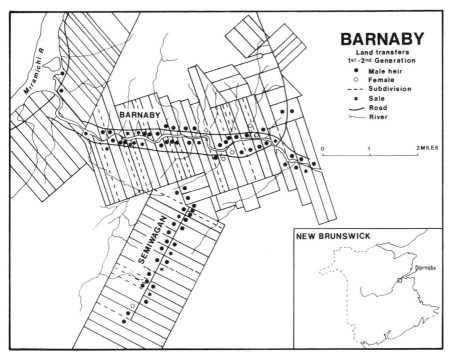

Figure 12

The multiplication of farmsteads along road and river further accentuated the line-village appearance of these settlements and, as in the Avalon, localized marriages produced strong bonds of kinship among the first and subsequent generations. Of the 65 marriages recorded for the second generation of Miramichi heirs, all but 11 were local unions. In the next generation, of the 42 marriages recorded, 29 heirs married locally, and 13 procured partners from outside the study area. Unlike the Irish settlements along the Cape Shore, there were few landscape manifestations of these kin-group networks.

Peterborough

Although the dwellings of the second generation of Peterborough-Irish usually were located closer to the roads, the overall pattern of settlement was still highly dispersed. Subdivision of farm lots was not as pronounced as in other study areas. Of the 104 lots owned by the first generation of settlers in Ennismore, 53 full lots were transmitted to descendants and 39 were sold. In 12 cases, a portion of the farm was inherited, another portion sold. 24 farms were subdivided; all of these were allotted to heirs in compact units, not in several discrete parcels. Rarely did more than 2 heirs inherit part of the ancestral farm. Almost all the

49

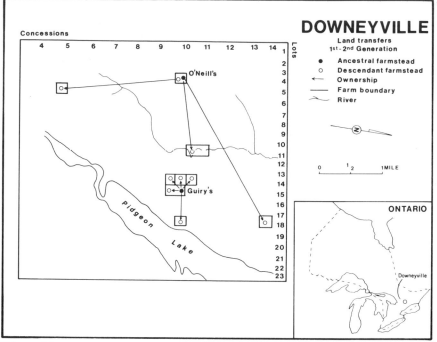

Figure 13

heirs were sons; daughters or collateral descendants rarely inherited land. Those sons who did not acquire the ancestral lot or a portion of it but wished to continue farming in the study area could procure unsettled lots, sometimes quite close to the ancestral farm. Figure 13 illustrates the settlement evolution of two families in Downeyville. In the case of the Guirys, the original settler purchased lots contiguous to his farm and settled his sons all about him; a similar pattern of settlement evolved in Semiwagan, Miramichi, where the Caseys and Sullivans expanded onto neighbouring lots. Because lots contiguous to the original farm were not available in the case of the O'Neills of Downeyville, the sons procured farms that were several miles from the ancestral unit.

Service Centres
Initially, religious and educational services, stores, taverns, and country crafts were housed in the ordinary dwellings of the immigrants, and thus were scattered across the settlements. In the Avalon the absence of a local service centre is a salient feature of its settlement geography to the present time. Only the church and school ever evolved into separate buildings from their origins in the farmhouse kitchen. Along the Cape Shore the more populous settlements of Branch and St Brides had both these institutions by the mid-nineteenth century

50

but in the settlements north of St John's there was no church until one was built in Outer Cove early in the present century. In Miramichi a small centre comprising a church, community hall, and store developed after 1880 at a crossroads point on the Barnaby. Distinctive rural service centers appeared much earlier in the Peterborough settlements. In function and morphology these settlement nuclei were similar in each of the Irish townships. Sites at the corner of intersecting roads were occupied by a store and one or more taverns, with a Catholic church, a hall, and a school located within 100 yards of the intersection. In Downeyville a blacksmith shop and a post office were added, but none of these Irish settlements had grist- or sawmills. The villages were centrally located within each tract of Irish settlement and were the foci of parish and community life.

Along the Cape Shore, the fragmentation of ancestral farm units by the second and subsequent generations was primarily a function of the growing emphasis on commercial fishing accompanied by an increasingly subsistent agriculture. As agriculture became more subsistent Cape Shore Irish families required less land, but could fish more efficiently by living close to the beach and to the other members of the fishing crew. Population expansion was not accompanied by a spread of settlement inland, but by the formation of a loose house cluster around the ancestral farmstead. This pattern of land succession and settlement is similar to that of the native Irish *clachan.* The only evidence of an orderly arrangement of houses is in Branch and, in one or two cases, in St Brides, where dwellings were disposed linearly or grouped compactly around an open space. It is difficult to say if the word "square" originally referred to the lay-out pattern of the kin-group clusters in these settlements. Certainly, not all of the clusters currently called "squares" have a regular, compact morphology. St Brides and Branch are the only settlements on the Cape Shore where several nuclear families originally settled, and several kin-group clusters have evolved; this may be an important factor in the introduction and use of the term. It is even more difficult to decide whether the compact morphology of the "square" is an inheritance from Ireland (a modification of the street-village, the Anglo-Norman cluster, or even the landlord town), is derived from some Newfoundland source, or had independently evolved *in situ.* In Ireland the word "square" is widely used to refer to an open space, in town or city, surrounded by buildings. The area is often a market or shopping centre, but may be purely residential. There is no record of the term being used in Ireland to describe any type of rural settlement, and it is likely that it first appeared with the improving landlords who planned so many of the towns. The word was used in St John's to indicate short streets and lanes. It is believed that a "square" was originally the plot and houses of an individual in St John's whose surname it carried. Sometimes, however, the "square" was named after a nearby institution.[19]

The contrast between the evolving settlement form in the St John's area and that of the Cape Shore is best explained by proximity to the city with its opportunity of alternative employment. In the former area surplus sons, instead of settling on part of the ancestral lot, found work in the city (usually as carters), or in the second half of the nineteenth century, emigrated to New England, especially to Boston. In Freshwater, where farming was a full-time occupation, local tradition strongly asserts that because of their small size it was not economically feasible to subdivide the original farm units. Uncleared land could be appropriated by the sons of the Freshwater immigrants, but its quality was low, and most of them opted for non-farm occupations. North of St John's where, as on the Cape Shore, fishing and farming were combined, the number of farms almost doubled between 1836 and 1891, but the average acreage cleared per farm also nearly doubled in this period.[20] In contrast to the Cape Shore, land clearing continued during the second half of the nineteenth century, and at a faster rate than previously. A nearby market provided a continuous stimulus to commercial agriculture in these coves and the compact farm appeared to be the most economic unit of production. Although the sea also offered a means of livelihood large house clusters never developed close to the seashore in any of these three coves.

Although access to the Barnaby was not important after the period of initial settlement, all of the cleared land there continued to be close to the river. The longitudinal division of some farm lots into extremely narrow strips satisfied both the Irish principle of allotting equal shares of different types or quality of land to male heirs, and the taste for agglomeration, without destroying the principle of the compact farm. This had been the landlord's rationale in creating, street villages in the homeland and there is a striking similarity between the

19 See William Kirwin, "Lines, Coves and Squares in Newfoundland Names," *American Speech* 40 (1965): 163-70. In the settlements near St John's the word "square" is used to designate a piece of land, e.g., "a fine 'square' of land" or "a 'square' of potatoes."

20 The actual figures are:

	No. of Families	Acres Cleared	Average Cleared
1836	58	174	3.0
1857	81	348	4.3
1869	95	380	4.0
1891	112	672	6.0

Newfoundland, Department of Colonial Secretary, *Census of Newfoundland, 1836,* p. 1; *Census of Newfoundland & Labrador, 1857,* Appendix 29, pp. 268-71; Newfoundland, Department of Colonial Secretary, *Abstract Census and Return of Population, etc., of Newfoundland 1869* (in Memorial University Library, St John's); *Census of Newfoundland & Labrador, 1891*, pp. 4-7.

Miramichi settlement pattern and the Irish street village. Whether the emerging pattern of settlement in Miramichi is closely related to the homeland form is difficult to say, but the pattern developed was well adapted to Irish social traditions. This was also true of the dispersed settlements in the Avalon, where the smallness of farms ensured that neighbours were not far away and close social contacts and the discharge of communal obligations were still relatively easy. The pattern of settlement evolved in Peterborough, however, was not well adapted to the gregarious Irish temperament. Lumbering was a commercial adjunct to agriculture for some Miramichi-Irish, lessening the demands made on the soil, but the Peterborough-Irish were full-time farmers and their principal objective was to operate a commercially viable farm. The emphasis on commercial agriculture is reflected in the relative unimportance of farm subdivision. One hundred acres was not an inordinate amount of land in a commercial wheat economy. The degree of farm commercialization is also reflected in the high percentage of farms, or portions of farms, sold to non-relatives. Moreover, mobility in the Peterborough settlements was far higher among the second generation of settlers than in any of the other study areas. Sons of families not satisfied with local conditions moved elsewhere. Under such shifting circumstances kin attachments were weakened and did not express themselves formally on the landscape. Even if surplus sons, like the Guirys, chose to settle close to the ancestral farmstead, they became individual operators, living on compact farm units, and were largely free of the communal restraints associated with agglomerated, kin-group farm settlement.

In rural Ireland, small service centres were rare. As in the Avalon and Miramichi, such services were dispersed through the settlement. This diffuse pattern was criticized by the landlords, who organized marketing centres for the peasantry during the eighteenth century.[21] The parish was relatively unimportant as a social unit in pre-migration Ireland and settlements which functioned as parochial centres were poorly developed.[22] This in part reflected the fugitive history of the Catholic church in Penal times. In all parts of Ireland the townland was the basic unit of agrarian organization. It was frequently co-extensive with the lands held by a co-operating kin group or groups, but this was becoming less common by the seventeenth century. Because individual homesteads lacked formal names, the townland was the major means of identifying areas locally and

21 The landlords regarded the Irish peasantry as being utterly without organization. "If Irish settlement is to be largely promoted in Canada, the land as well as the Church, the Clergyman, Drainage and Roads, the Mill, the Store, the Blacksmith's shop, the School, must be furnished by some Providence, some Organization, some Exertions; not those of the Bulk of the Settlers" (Great Britain, *Committee on Colonization from Ireland,* Appendix 25, p. 212).
22 T. Jones Hughes, "Town and Baile in Irish Placenames," in Stephens and Glasscock (eds.), *Irish Geographical Studies,* pp. 244-58.

is still the countryman's postal address. The townland normally included good and poor soils and the house cluster or clusters were strategically located in relation to the unit's resources. The settlements in the Avalon and Miramichi resembled the Irish townland in size, population, and pattern of settlement but were not, of course, genetically related to the homeland forms. Only in Peterborough was parish life — life around the church and community hall — developed to any extent. Service centres such as Downeyville were widely distributed over much of North America where dispersed farm settlements predominated.

IV
Field systems

Associated with the *clachan* form of settlement was a distinctive field system which comprised an infield and an outfield and detached summer grazing grounds. The infield was a more or less continually cultivated area lying close to the *clachan,* and often on its downhill side to facilitate the carrying of manure from the farmsteads. The infield area was normally located on the most fertile pockets of soil — fluvial and marine terraces and deltas were favourite sites — and received, moreover, almost all the manure produced and collected on the farm. Traditionally wheat, barley, oats, and sometimes rye were the staple crops of this restricted arable area, but for more than a century prior to the migrations potatoes and to a lesser extent flax, peas, beans, turnips, and cabbages were being incorporated into this ancient system of tillage. Around the intensively worked infield lay more extensive areas of rough pasture, parts of which were periodically enclosed and cultivated for a few years until the soils were exhausted, then abandoned for several years to reseed with weeds and wild grasses. These temporary and shifting arable plots comprised the outfield area which supplemented the produce of the infields.

Both infield and outfield were usually ploughed or dug into high-backed ridges of varying width, depth, and length and a family's plot comprised a number of ridges. Where the plough was the principal implement of cultivation, these plots were arranged frequently in long, narrow, rectangular, and contiguous strips but in areas where the spade or mattock was used the plots were often irregularly shaped. Whatever the shape, each family plot usually was

55

demarcated by uncultivated ribs of earth called *mearings, roddens, keelogues, stacán, crich,* or *bones,* and sometimes the infield or infield-outfield area was enclosed by a communal fence, dyke, or bank.[1]

Traditionally the land was held and worked jointly by the members of the *clachan,* often under the direction of a headman or *Rí* (King). Individual family plots were unenclosed and were intermingled with those of other families on the basis that every farmer received a share *(cuibhreann)* of soils of differing quality. Tenure of plots was rotated periodically among the families to reinforce this egalitarian division of the soil. This system of landholding was called "change-dale," "morrowingdale," or "rundale" in Ireland.[2] Both infield and outfield were traditionally the common property of the residents of the *clachan,* and the basis for joint tenure and exploitation of the soil was the extended family. According to the Gaelic law of inheritance, each son was entitled to an equal share of soils of different quality and like the *clachan,* the infield-outfield usually had its origins in a single farm. In the decades prior to the migrations, when the Irish population increased rapidly, successive subdividing of family plots produced a fantastically fragmented pattern of family holdings in the infield area.[3] Normally, all other resources were subdivided in a similar manner and even joint ownership of livestock was common. Joint or partnership farming was not restricted to the working of arable fields: the harvesting of sea shore, lake or stream, the cutting of turf, and the grazing of livestock in the rough pasture areas that abound in Ireland were organized communally. Labour was pooled for many years and such cooperation *(cooring)* was frequently based on blood ties.

The main characteristic of the traditional Irish agrarian system was the predominance of pastoral farming. The produce of the infields and outfields was primarily for home consumption but livestock, and especially cattle, were raised commercially. Under the old openfield regime it was necessary to hobble or tie the livestock from seedtime to harvest, or, alternatively, to drive them to the summer pastures. From May to November most of the farm animals were grazed in marginal areas often a considerable distance from the *clachan.* In such cases a system of transhumance evolved, where some of the *clachan* residents — usually the younger folk — spent the summer in the hills tending the flocks. Livestock were usually taken to the summer pastures on May 1st, an important date in the

1 D. McCourt, "Infield and Outfield in Ireland," *Economic History Review* 7 (1954-55): 369-76. These grassy balks often served as footpaths leading to the different arable plots.
2 As in the case of the farm cluster, there is no word in modern Irish to describe this land-holding system and controversy exists as to whether the system evolved locally or was introduced from outside. Both infield and outfield were recorded all over Atlantic Europe. See Ian M. Matley, "The Origin of Infield-Outfield Agriculture in Scotland: The Linguistic Evidence," *The Professional Geographer* 18 (1966): 275-79.
3 The property of a single family in a *clachan* was sometimes split into as many as 20 separate parcels and there are records of over 20 persons sharing half an acre (E. Estyn Evans, *Irish Folk Ways* [London: Routledge and Kegan Paul, 1957], p. 24).

Celtic calendar. During the summer the herders usually lived in crude huts in the hills, known as *boolies, clochauns,* or *machairs* and the practice of transhumance was called *booleying.* In the mountains unrestrained pasturing was uncommon. Each community grazed a designated territory, though several *clachan* groups might merge to form such a community. Grazing units were often regulated or allotted according to the number of ridges or area of land worked by the individual family in the infield.[4] As well as caring for the animals, the herders were also occupied cutting turf for winter fuel and making butter which was sometimes stored underground in specially built cellars. Around November 1st (Halloween), the herders returned to the homefields with their animals. By this time the crops were harvested, the animals were driven to the openfield area to graze the stubble and to tread and fertilize the soils in preparation for the following year's crops.

Despite the tenacity of Irish peasant tradition, openfield husbandry was becoming rare by the time of the migrations. With the precipitous rise in population and the introduction of new crops and techniques and new notions of agriculture, the old field system had gradually crumbled. Repeated subdivision had reduced family holdings and individual plots to almost ludicrous proportions. Time was wasted walking between plots and a good deal of cultivable land lay wasted in the grassy balks delineating each parcel. Squabbles over inheritance, boundaries, rights-of-way, and rents became interminable in the overcrowded clusters. New crops, especially improved grasses and turnips, changed the pattern of rotation. In an age of improved farming the landlords regarded the native field system as iniquitous and outmoded and did everything possible to obliterate it and replace it with a pattern of dispersed dwellings and enclosed fields. Through the eighteenth century the amalgamation or consolidatibn of the tiny openfield parcels into compact and independent farm units accompanied the dissolution of the *clachans.*

The new holdings were often arranged in long, narrow, segmented strips — the ladder or ribbon farms — fronting or straddling a new road with the dwellings disposed linearly along it. The regular rectangular fields of such farms greatly facilitated the task of ploughing. Many of the old wasteful balks were levelled and the mosaic of minuscule infield and outfield parcels were merged to form fields, each enclosed by a fence. Fields varied in shape and area according to the size, economy, and topography of the new holding but the unit favoured by the

---

4 Evans, *Irish Folk Ways,* p. 36. These units, called "collops" or "sums," were not reckoned by area but often equalled the amount of pasturage that would support a cow. Traditions of transhumance varied regionally in Ireland (see C. Ó'Danachair, "Traces of the Buaile in the Galtees," *Journal Royal Society Antiquaries Ireland* 75 [1945]: 248-52; J.M. Graham, "Transhumance in Ireland," *Advancement of Science* 10 [1953]: 74-79; *idem,* "Southwest Donegal in the Seventeenth Century," *Irish Geography* 6 [1970]: 136-53; B.J. MacAodha, " 'Souming' in the Sperrins," *Ulster Folklife* 2 [1956]: 19-21; F.H.A. Aalen, "Transhumance in the Wicklow Mountains," *Ulster Folklife* 10 [1964]: 65-72).

landlords was one whose length was one and a half times its breadth, with its long side running upslope, and a single holding usually had fewer than 20 fields.

Land re-allocation did not always entail the liquidation of old boundaries. In the Normanized areas of southeastern Ireland, for example, bundles of long, slightly curving strip fields are often openfield furlongs of medieval manorial three-field husbandry fossilized by enclosure. Nor was enclosure always accompanied by a geometrical redistribution of property. Some farms and fields were trapezoidal or highly irregular in shape, either preserving elements of the older patterns of land distribution or the products of eighteenth century piecemeal enclosure from marginal tracts. Indeed there are examples of enclosure with little redistribution or consolidation of openfield plots or dispersion of dwellings.

Despite the economic advantages of enclosure and resettlement, they were actively resisted by the peasants. Enclosure spelled eviction for the less well-to-do or more indigent tenantry. It widened the social and economic distinctions among the peasantry, creating a small-scale peasant capitalist class and a great number of cottiers or landless labourers. Enclosure, moreover, denied the peasants their ancient communal rights to other exploitable resources, especially the mountain pastures. Finally, with the proscription of subdivision, peasant heirs were denied their most cherished right — equal shares of the soil.

It is not surprising that in areas where landlords were absent or indifferent the old field system survived. Landlords often found that subdivision or subletting were impossible to suppress, since inheritance and tenure were regulated privately and informally in the *clachans*. Even after enclosure, peasants sometimes surreptitiously subdivided their compact farms. Since so much of the organization and labour on the land was communal, consensus on innovation was difficult to attain and the Irish peasantry rarely resettled of its own accord. During the Napoleonic Wars, the traditional pattern of uninterrupted grain cultivation in infields actually received a boost and some landlords openly encouraged subdivision and promoted the colonization of communal pastures and other marginal lands. This tillage boom was short-lived and the move to enclose thereafter became rampant, driving thousands of dispossessed Irish across the Atlantic. By the mid-nineteenth century, only in the Union District of Nenagh were as many as twenty per cent of the tenants holding land jointly, and in many of the districts the change to severalty (i.e., single tenancy) farms was virtually complete.[5]

The agrarian revolution brought great changes in the patterns of land management. With the intensification of land use and settlement in the

5 Great Britain, Parliament, *Report of the Select Committee of the House of Lords on Colonization from Ireland* (in National Archives, Ottawa), London, 1847, VI, Appendix 32, pp. 174-79.

homeland in the decades prior to the migrations, improved methods of maintaining the fertility of the soils were essential. The practice of liming and draining became widespread during this period and greatly facilitated the reclamation and settlement of marginal lands. Arthur Young refers repeatedly to the use of lime, limestone gravel, and marl on meadows and recently reclaimed land. In the 1770's they were used by improving landlords but in the following decades these techniques gradually were adopted by the peasantry. In the manor of Lismore, for example, the number of limekilns increased from 3 in 1773 to over 100 by 1841.[6] Sea sand, seaweed or wrack, and shells were used traditionally to fertilize grain and potato crops and farmers often travelled 20 or 30 miles to the coast to obtain them.[7] Ashes and the soot-infested thatch from the dwelling houses were also applied. Almost all the stable manure accumulated over the winter was used on the potato patches. Finally, one of the oldest methods of preparing rough or ley land for cultivation remained widespread in the homeland at the time of the migrations, despite the efforts of some landlords to suppress it. The tough sod was cut and turned with spade, mattock or plough, dried, then assembled into heaps and burned; and the ashes were sprinkled to fertilize the new ground. The technique was referred to as "baiting and burning," "paring and burning," or in the southwest, "graffawning and burning." While useful for reclaiming bog or rough meadowland in the absence of organic manure, the method destroyed shallow, sandy soils and landlords sometimes fined their tenants up to £10 per acre for adopting this practice.

Whenever the openfield regime survived, there were examples of continual cropping of infields. Arthur Young described a 70-acre joint or "rundale" farm in Wexford, where 90 crops of grain had been taken in succession without any fallow or grass intervening.[8] In neighbouring Kilkenny in the early nineteenth century some of the land had been cultivated annually for over 30 years and in Donegal tenants were unwilling to accept the introduction of a green crop because they could not afford to rest any of their arable land.[9] Pierre Flatrès found that in areas where elements of rundale persisted in western Ireland the uninterrupted cultivation of the open plots with grains and potatoes was

---

6 J.H. Andrews, "Changes in the Rural Landscape of the Late Eighteenth and Early Nineteenth Century Ireland: an Example from County Waterford," *Area: Institute British Geographers* 1 (1970): 55-56. Young reported that the peasants were composting lime and river mud or marl in Waterford in the 1770's.

7 A.T. Lucas, "Sea Sand and Shells as Manure," in Geraint Jenkins (ed.), *Studies in Folklife* (London: Routledge and Kegan Paul, 1969), pp. 184-203. The use of littoral deposits for fertilizer is believed to stretch back to pre-Celtic times and rights of access to the shore were carefully arranged and jealously guarded.

8 Arthur Young, *A Tour in Ireland 1776-1779* (Shannon: Irish University Press, 1970), vol. 1, pp. 88-89.

9 D. McCourt, "Infield and Outfield in Ireland," p. 370.

normal.[10] In the most arable baronies of the southeast in the decades before the migrations the dominant crop rotation was not one of unbroken tillage, however, but the cultivating of a tract for 5 to 10 years and then returning the exhausted soils to fallow for an equally long period. Such a system soured and leached the soils and to maintain the fertility of their estates, many landlords promoted improved pastoral farming, encouraging tenants to shorten the arable span and eliminate the fallow by introducing turnips, cabbages, vetches, clovers, and other rotation grasses. Irish peasant farming was traditionally pastoral, and the new green crops and system of long leys were adopted by many of the more well-to-do tenants even in the eighteenth century. Agricultural societies sprang up and landlords experimented with new breeds of livestock and different crop combinations, disseminating their knowledge to their tenents. Some landlords built roads and even towns to facilitate the marketing of agricultural produce from their estates. With the introduction early in the nineteenth century of steam transport on the Irish Sea the Irish farmers could dispose of their livestock more readily and the transformation of traditional Irish agriculture was assured. Ley farming could not be prosecuted properly under the restraints of a communal openfield system and the advent of a scientific and intensive pastoral system meant the demise of "rundale." The open arable plots were converted into enclosed grazing units, periodically ploughed and producing fodder crops and hay for winter feed. Other fields were used as summer pastures, replacing the traditional pattern of transhumance.

Despite the efforts of many landlords, the tradition of successive or intensive arable cropping continued in many parts of the southeast, and actually increased during the Napoleonic Wars. Weekly markets for grain and other arable produce were held and the number of flour mills, breweries, and malt houses greatly increased. Some landlords were quick to take advantage of the rising British market for grain and encouraged the old rundale agriculture. But with the decline of the grain market after 1815 many of the tillage landlords promoted pastoralism and a more advanced system of farming.

THE NEW WORLD FIELD SYSTEMS

The Avalon
One of the recommendations of an early nineteenth century Grand Jury with regard to land grants in Newfoundland was "that picketed fences at least five

10 P. Flatrès, *Géographie rurale de quatre countrées celtiques: Irlande, Galles, Cornwall, Man* (Rennes: Plihon, 1957), p. 480. Potatoes cleaned and enriched the arable soils for grain.

feet high should be put up to divide properties and that proprietors should share equally the cost of these fences."[11] Although there is one early reference to an Irish immigrant who erected a proprietory fence,[12] oral tradition asserts that normally only that part of the property cleared for crops was enclosed. Where family lots adjoined in the forest, or bordered on Crown Lands, boundaries were merely blazed. In Freshwater, for example, where many of the lots were surveyed and granted by the government, open paths or "lineways" acted as boundaries through the wooded sections of the property. Poles were nailed to trees at intervals along the boundary, and at the corners where they indicated the direction of the "lineways."

On many farms near St John's less than half of the property was ever cleared for agriculture. In the settlements north of the city, for example, only a quarter of the total area owned or held had been cleared by the middle of the nineteenth century.[13] The average family clearing in 1836 was 3 acres, in 1857 and 1869 4 acres, and 6 acres by 1891. During this period the numbers of families increased from 58 to 112. At the end of the last century few farms in Freshwater exceeded 15 acres.

By North American standards these acres were farmed intensively throughout the nineteenth century and considering the poor quality of the soils, yields were high. A Freshwater acre could produce either 3 tons of hay, 2 tons of fodder (green oats and straw), 300 bushels of potatoes or 400 bushels of turnips. In the settlements north of St John's the shallow soils were almost as productive and in both areas these high yields were as much the result of heavy manuring as of an enlightened rotation of crops.

Livestock manure was supplemented by other forms of fertilizer. As the immigrants cleared the land they collected sod and underbrush into heaps and burned them, using the ashes to fertilize the freshly cleared ground. The small

---

11 Great Britain, Colonial Office Correspondence, Newfoundland (MSS in Provincial Archives, St John's), Series 194, vol. 28, Grand Jury to Governor R.G. Keats, July 30, 1813.

12 C.O. 194/81, The King vs Luke Ryan, February 10, 1831. "That Luke Ryan did enclose, with posts and rails, three plots amounting to fifteen acres near Logie Bay. ..." He had prepared a petition for the land, but it had not been granted in 1831. No more than one-third of this area was ever cleared. Some of the ancestral farms north of St John's did have boundary fences all around the property but the wooded area on most properties there remained unenclosed.

13 Newfoundland, House of Assembly, *Journal* (in Memorial University Library, St John's), "List of Poor Employed by Governor in District of St John's," Appendix, 1848-49, pp. 329-31. Half of the 60 families listed had between one and 2 acres cleared and only 6 families had more than 4 acres cleared.

heaps of burning brush and sod were called "burn baitings."[14] A compost of fish offal (cod heads and guts), bog (decayed sphagnum), and clay was used to fertilize arable and especially meadowland. From the early phase of settlement the availability of bog around St John's was frequently alluded to in farm sale advertisements.[15] Every March Freshwater farmers transported bog from Keough's Valley, over a mile west of the settlement. Normally over 40 loads were hauled by slide to the "bog pit" out on the farm. One load of offal was mixed with 5 loads of bog and clay. Before spreading it on the meadows the Freshwater farmers turned the manure over several times in the pit. From 20 to 40 cartloads were spread on an acre. With the opening of a road after 1880 the farmers from Freshwater travelled 7 miles to Broad Cove on Conception Bay every June for cartloads of caplin which they purchased from the fishermen. Caplin were sometimes added to the compost but usually were dumped on low-lying, wet meadowland and older meadows. With the introduction of artificial fertilizer in the 1920's, the use of bog and fish declined.

In the settlements north of St John's the use of fish offal for fertilizer is attested to in early documents. In 1843 a projected road from the seashore to the inland farms of Logy Bay was expected to be "of much service to the farmers and other settlers in the neighbourhood. It will enable them to reach Logy Bay with horses, carts, etc., where a very considerable supply of fish offal and other useful manure can be had."[16] Great schools of caplin advanced to the beaches of Outer and Middle Cove late in June and these fish were spread on both arable and meadowland. Livestock manure was added sometimes to enrich the compost of offal and bog, but as in Freshwater it usually was applied separately to the root crops. Kelp was available on the rocky cliff base between Outer and Middle Cove and some settlers ventured out occasionally in boats to collect this valuable fertilizer for their meadows and potato ground.

Most fields in the St John's study areas were criss-crossed by a maze of hollow flag drains which in the damp climate of the Avalon greatly improved the

14 In 1829 Richard Comerford, servant of Luke Ryan, was clearing land in Logy Bay and "kindled twelve or fourteen fires in little heaps of peat for manuring the ground. ...." A gale blew the fires out of control and over 100 acres of Crown Land timber were destroyed (C.O. 194/81, The King vs Luke Ryan, February 10, 1831). There are several references to this burning technique around St John's in the nineteenth century and it is recalled by all older informants in the study areas.

15 See *The Patriot*, St John's, March 15, 1836 and October 11, 1845 (in Arts and Culture Library, St John's); *The Newfoundlander*, St John's, May 4, 1843 and May 18, 1843 (in Provincial Archives, St John's). For a Freshwater example see *The Morning Courier*, St John's, May 26, 1849 (in Arts and Culture Library, St John's). Some farms had private deposits of bog, but usually communal pits were used.

16 Newfoundland, *Journal*, "Report of Board of Road Commissioners," Appendix, 1844, p. 52. A year later the settlers in nearby Outer Cove petitioned for a road to cart manure to their farms (*ibid.*, "Petition of Richard Fox and Others," February 28, 1845, p. 65).

quality of the soil. Trenches almost two feet deep and a foot wide were dug and their sides lined with flat stones to support a horizontally placed flag which lay one foot below the surface and was covered over with clay.

Figure 14 describes the predominant pattern of crop rotation and land use on a typical Freshwater farm. John O'Brien had settled in Freshwater around 1820 and by 1849 had 14 acres of his 33-acre grant under cultivation.[17] The farm was divided into 7 fields, excluding the front garden. Six of these fields figured in the rotation. When cultivating a ley field, the O'Brien's normally began with an acre of turnips and cabbage. Nourished by the decaying grasses of the inverted sod, these crops grew best on ploughed ley. In the second year of cultivation they cross-ploughed the plot, breaking up the surviving sods, and planted this "red ground" with potatoes. Usually no more than an acre was sown and, provided the remaining area within the field was little more than an acre (as in the case of the "back meadow" in Figure 14), it was planted with oats. Potatoes were invariably followed by oats and hayseed (timothy grass and clover), with the intention of turning the arable back into ley. At least 4 crops of hay followed before the land was ploughed again and planted with turnips and cabbage. The kitchen garden, containing a variety of vegetables including carrots, parsnips, beets, and savoury, normally was separated from the root crops by an un-ploughed strip of earth or *bone*. The "front garden" was a fixed unit bearing such fruits as apples, raspberries, gooseberries, rhubarb, black and red currants, and a variety of flowers.

In the traditional pastoral economy of Freshwater the main objective of the rotation was the production of a good meadow. A horse or cow would consume over two tons of hay during the long winter and the O'Briens annually reserved at least 10 of their 14 acres for hay, in contrast to about one acre each for turnips and cabbage, for potatoes, and for oats. Potatoes, which were heavily manured, enriched the soil, so the crop was shifted each year to make way for hay. While the O'Briens retained one low-lying, marshy field as a permanent pasture, Freshwater farmers normally drove their livestock into the woods during the summer and, apart from a small area for the horse and cows, rarely reserved any portion of the cleared ground for summer grazing.

In the settlements north of St John's the pattern of crop rotation was much more complicated than in Freshwater. For many of these settlers the main objective of the rotation, as in Freshwater, was to maximize hay production. The majority shifted their arable plot around the farm as frequently as possible. Because of the small area of cleared land on many farms, however, the Irish could not afford to plough almost an acre of ley and shift their potato plot every year; meadows grew best in their second and third years and often an annual shifting of the potato plot would result in a premature encroachment on

17 *Morning Courier*, St John's, August 11, 1849. Little land was cleared after this date.

meadowland. Plots remained longer under cultivation than in Freshwater. The dominant rotational scheme at the end of the last century began with a crop of turnips and cabbage on the ley, followed by 4 to 5 crops of potatoes, then oats and hayseed, and finally 4 to 5 crops of hay. Turnips and cabbage, which occupied less than half the area under potatoes each year, were sometimes alternated with potatoes on the same plot for a few years, but usually the farmers ploughed a small area of ley each year for the former crops. Sometimes potatoes were planted on the ley. There are examples, however, of farmer-fishermen working an arable plot for 30 consecutive years or more before turning it back into ley. As in Freshwater, cleared land was rarely reserved for summer pasture.

In Freshwater field forms were haphazard and fields varied considerably in area. Their form and extent were in part determined by natural features: the distribution of steep slopes, stone outcrops, rivers, and marshland. Frequently Freshwater fields were divided by broad "wind-breaks" or shelterbelts, comprised of strips of uncleared woodland retained to preserve crops from over-exposure to cold winds and destructive gales. Field units were not necessarily conterminous with the fenced units within a farm, or with the unit area in the seven-year rotation. Sometimes 2 fields could be combined into a single unit for crop rotation and not have any partitioning fence as the "Top Meadow" and "Camp Meadow" in Figure 14, or conversely (and much more frequently), one large field might be divided into 3 units of rotation with temporary fences dividing the arable from the ley, as in the 4-acre "Meadow over the Pond" on the O'Brien farm. The size of the field bore little relation to the amount of arable in any given year.

Fields in Freshwater were best recognized by their names. These names sometimes described some physical characteristic in or near the field, its size or shape or location in relation to the farmstead, but more frequently it carried the Christian name of one of its owners — often the man who cleared it and first worked it — followed by the element "meadow." The high incidence of the term "meadow" in Freshwater field names reflects the dominant pattern of land use and crop rotation and it is significant that this term was predominant in field names not only in the St John's study area but also on the Cape Shore. The word "garden" is also used in Freshwater, not alone to designate the small vegetable and fruit producing unit near the homestead but arable plots as well.

In Logy Bay, Outer and Middle Cove, there were many farms where fields were not named. The area cleared was a small and often continuous parcel, rarely divided by either shelterbelt or even temporary fence; this single parcel needed no name. The absence of wind-breaks is perhaps best explained by the small size of the clearing, usually amply protected by the surrounding woods. Temporary fences were erected in Freshwater to protect root crops from cattle grazing the aftergrass in the fall; in the settlements north of St John's, the Irish

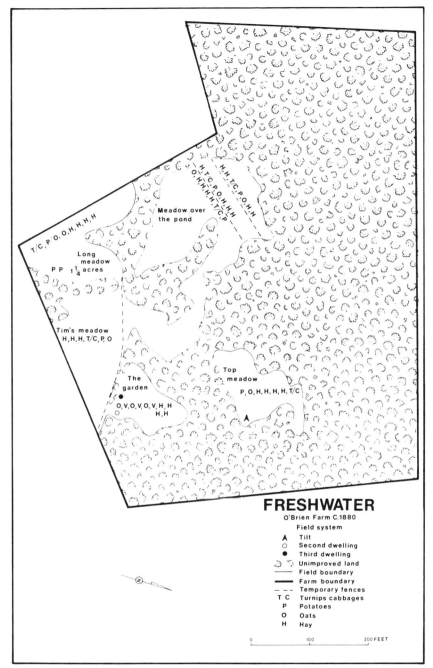

FRESHWATER

O'Brien Farm C.1880

Field system

人	Tilt
O	Second dwelling
●	Third dwelling
⌘ ⌐	Unimproved land
——	Field boundary
▬▬	Farm boundary
– – –	Temporary fences
T C	Turnips cabbages
P	Potatoes
O	Oats
H	Hay

0   100   200 FEET

Within the map:

H,H,T,C,P,O,H,H
O,H,H,H,T,C,P

T/C,P,O,O,H,H,H,H   Meadow over
                      the pond

Long
meadow
P P 1¼ acres

Tim's meadow
H,H,H,T/C,P,O

The   Top
garden   meadow
●   P,O,H,H,H,H,T/C
O,V,O,V,O,V,H,H
H,H

Figure 14

did not allow the cattle into the meadows until mid-November, when all the root crops had been harvested.

In 1836 the 34 families along the Cape Shore worked an average of 9 acres each. Apart from Branch and the Barrisways the number of acres cultivated coincided with the number of acres owned in each cove.[18] When woodland was claimed it was usually marked off rather than enclosed but all settlers traditionally fenced in their cleared land. According to the census of 1836 an average of 3½ tons of hay was produced, and an average of 240 bushels of potatoes and a single bushel of oats grown. Actually less than half the farmers grew oats and it is not certain if the returns refer to seed or yield. Over the next two decades the area of improved land increased to 15 acres per family, the average hay yield was 15 tons but oats and potato production remained relatively stable. Between 1836 and 1891 the number of families on the Cape Shore increased from 34 to 153. Subdivision of land resulted in an average farm size of 5 acres by 1891, and a commensurate decrease in average yields.

Land was worked as intensively on the Cape Shore as in the St John's settlements. The high livestock population meant there was a good supply of stable manure. It was composted with kelp during the winter and spread on the fields in spring. Kelp was also applied separately. During the fall it was collected from the beach and stacked by the shore to decompose. In the spring it was spread on both meadow and arable land. A compost of caplin, fish offal, and bog or clay was also prepared and widely used. When clearing land, settlers usually cut a 20 foot wide swath through the brush, heaping the refuse in a row along the centre. As in St John's this refuse was burned and the technique was locally referred to as "burnbrush."

The salient feature of the traditional crop rotation on the Cape Shore was the shifting of the small arable plot or plots around the ley every three years. Potatoes, turnips, and cabbage were sown for two years in succession and were followed by oats and timothy; potatoes often followed turnips, but the reverse never occurred. An extensive period of meadow followed, and was often further prolonged by the clearing and cultivating of new ground. Continual cultivating of fertile alluvial pockets over as many as 20 years also occurred, but most settlers maintained that "gardens" became weed-infested after the third year. Despite the frequent shifting of the arable, much of the farm remained in ley for long periods because the arable plot rarely exceeded an acre and was frequently less than half an acre. Meadowland was kept productive through intensive manuring and the application of timothy. As in Freshwater, a small field was reserved as pasture for the family horse during the summer.

18 Newfoundland, Department of Colonial Secretary, *Census of Newfoundland, 1836* (in Memorial University Library, St John's), p. 10. In Branch, 54 of the 144 acres owned were cultivated, compared with 97 of the 172 acres in the Barrisways.

Field forms on the Cape Shore were extremely haphazard. Figure 15A, B illustrates field patterns in a typical cove. The streams cutting through the flats were important field boundaries but, as in Freshwater, the distribution of slope and marsh also influenced both the size and shape of the meadows. Fences functioning as wind-breaks occasionally divided one meadow from another, but generally the only fences erected on a holding were between meadow and woodland or between separate operators. The arable plot was rarely fenced off from the meadowland. Farmers seldom had any part of their cleared ground in permanent pasture and, as in the settlements north of St John's, cattle were never admitted to graze the aftergrass until November, when all the arable crops were harvested.

Pastoral farming was the keystone of the Cape Shore economy and as early as 1836 the average farmer there kept 9 cattle, a horse, 2 sheep, and 3 pigs. Over the next two decades only 3 cattle and 4 sheep were added to the average livestock population but with the exception of the Peterborough Irish, the Cape Shore inhabitants owned more animals than any of the other settlers in the nineteenth century. By contrast there were few livestock north of St John's. Every second family owned a horse and cow in 1836; neither sheep nor pigs were raised. This paltry livestock population had barely increased by 1849, but in 1857 the average farm supported 3 cattle, a horse, and a pig. At the end of the last century most Freshwater farmers kept 10 or more milk cows, a few calves and 2 horses but rarely raised any sheep, pigs, or goats.

While arable produce was raised commercially in the settlements near St John's, dairying was the commercial staple of the farm economy. Milk from Freshwater was peddled in west and central St John's and was the principal source of income. During the peak grazing period in June and July the Freshwater farmer sold up to 50 gallons per day to his customers in the city. Male calves were usually sold as veal to the city butchers but female calves born on the farm were normally retained for milking and breeding. A similar dairying tradition obtained on some farms north of St John's, but dairy herds were not nearly so large as in Freshwater. Earlier in the century, the Outer and Middle Cove immigrants sold butter in the city but this industry had declined by 1900. By contrast the Cape Shore farmers, who were too far from the market to sell milk, continued with the selling of butter until well into the present century. Unlike the St John's settlers, the Cape Shore farmers rarely sold young calves, pigs, or sheep, or vegetables. Bullocks were the most important source of revenue until the rise of a commercial fishery in the second half of the nineteenth century.

In all Avalon study areas, the methods of livestock husbandry were essentially similar. During the summer the animals were driven out beyond the clearings to graze the surrounding unenclosed, uncultivated woodlands or "commons." The animals were branded, and a great variety of proprietory marks were needed. In every cove or settlement, neighbours and kin assembled in spring to decide on the different brand each family would adopt for the summer season. Duplication had to be avoided. Normally a family or extended family retained a particular mark for a lifetime and marks were transmitted over generations. Holes were branded on the horns or notches cut in the ears, all variously shaped and differently numbered. Sometimes initials were used.

Early each May, weather permitting, a group of families got together and drove their dry cattle, colts, sheep, and goats to grazing areas in the woods. Tending to these wandering herds was a shared task normally carried out by boys who combined berry picking, hunting, and trouting trips with the weekly chore of checking the stock. In Freshwater a herdsman was hired by the community for the task of tending to the herd. After all the crops were taken from the ground, around mid-November, the animals were returned to the home fields to graze the aftergrass on the meadows.

Neither cows nor horses were driven with the main herd to the woodland pastures. After the milking each evening cows were folded in a "pound" by the farmstead for the night and were driven out after the morning's milking to graze unfenced land around the settlement. The horse was in constant demand for summer work and was usually kept within the farm in a small pasture.

The initial pattern of compact family farms, with fields grouped contiguously or at least closely around each farmstead and worked exclusively by the nuclear family, sometimes changed after these ancestral units were transmitted to the second generation of settlers, the sons of the immigrants. Subdivision of original farms and fields between heirs produced a much more complicated pattern of land ownership and land working, based on co-operating kin groups.

The evolution of a joint farm and its associated openfield pattern in a typical Cape Shore cove is illustrated in Figures 15 A, B, C. Devil's Cove (later renamed Patrick's· Cove) was settled before 1810 by an immigrant Irishman, Bartley McGrath. No other nuclear family settled in this cove. By 1825 Bartley had 4 sons and 3 daughters. One of the sons died in infancy and the 3 daughters married men from nearby coves. Three sons – Paddy, Micil, and Bartley – remained in Patrick's Cove and both Paddy and Micil had married before their father died in the mid-nineteenth century.[19] During his lifetime old Bartley cleared about a dozen acres, all on the fertile alluvial flats, which he divided into three fields or meadows (Fig. 15 A). Bartley bequeathed these parcels to two of his sons, Paddy and Bartley, giving each son an equal share of each meadow. Young Bartley inherited his father's house, but individually cleared the Black Garden and The Hills Meadow, where he later built his dwelling house; he also

19 In 1857 three couples and 21 children were recorded; 3 of the children were born before 1840. There were 3 dwelling houses and 17 acres cleared. These records concur with oral tradition in Patrick's Cove (Newfoundland, Department of Colonial Secretary, *Census of Newfoundland & Labrador, 1857* [in Memorial University Library, St John's], Appendix 29, pp. 352-55).

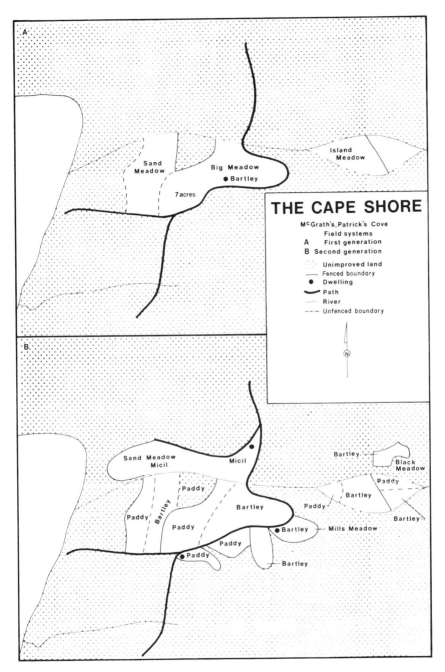

Figure 15A, B

cleared the Black Garden on the flats and another field close to his new dwelling, on a slope overlooking the flats (Fig. 15B). Paddy also cleared two fields on the southern slope and built his house in one of them. Micil, who apparently did not acquire any share of the ancestral clearing, moved across the river and individually cleared the flat Sand Meadow.

Between 1865 and 1890 the third generation of McGraths inherited or established farms. In the second round of subdivision on the flats, Bartley divided his share of the Big Meadow between his four sons, George and Antony, Pak and Ben, while Paddy split his share of the same meadow between his two youngest sons, Fran and Peter (Fig. 15C). Similarly each of these 6 sons acquired shares of the Island Meadow and the original Sand Meadow. The fields individually cleared by Bartley and Paddy were also subdivided. Pak and Ben shared the Black Garden and each of Bartley's 4 sons procured a share of his two meadows on the southern slope. Pak acquired his father's dwelling and George and Ben built houses nearby. After he married, Anthony moved to Cuslett and relinquished his shares to George. Like their father, George, Pak and Ben cleared extra parcels of land individually. Fran and Peter shared their father's two meadows on the slope, south of the road. Fran inherited his father's dwelling and Peter built his house on the same meadow and they jointly cleared a garden south of the road leading to the fishing stages. It appears that none of Paddy's 5 other sons — John, Jim, Richard, Patrick, or Denis — inherited land; like their uncle Micil these older brothers established separate farms well upslope but built their houses close to the father's dwelling. Both John and Denis cleared land on the north side of the river, but continued to live close to their nearest kin on the southern slope. North of the river Micil divided his Sand Meadow between his sons, Tom, Mick, and Peter. Mick inherited his father's house and Tom located his farmstead in a field he cleared individually. Peter, a bachelor, lived with Mick.

The fourth generation of McGraths continued the tradition of building their houses close to those of their parents. Thirteen of Paddy's grandchildren received shares of their parents' plots, greatly extending the cluster of habitations on the southern slope. By contrast, only 5 of Micil's and 3 of Bartley's grandchildren remained in the cove. Apart from George's daughter, Lucy, who married George, grandson of Paddy, there were no cases of endogamous marriages, female inheritance, or matrilocal residence in the history of Patrick's Cove. In 1891 there were 11 houses in the settlement, and after 150 years of occupance as many as 30 dwellings, all owned by McGraths, the direct descendants of the first settler.

The field systems evolved in Patrick's Cove expressed the close ties of kinship that characterized settlement in this and other Cape Shore coves. Until the present century the meadows on the flats remained unenclosed, despite their successive subdivision among male heirs. There were, of course, fences separating cleared ground from woodland. These alluvial meadows were the most endowed,

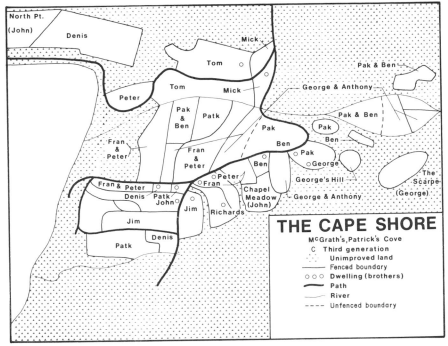

Figure 15C

physically, and were the primary cells of the joint farms. Although the open parcels were individually owned, they were worked communally, first by brothers and then by cousins. According to local tradition, Paddy and Bat farmed jointly the land they had inherited, sharing livestock, crops, stable, and cellar, but living in separate houses.[20] Paddy's sons, Peter and Fran, who acquired equal shares of their father's farm, were also joint operators; they planted their crops in a single plot each year and divided the produce. Hay was also jointly harvested and stored.

Fully fledged partnership farming was restricted, however, to pairs of brothers and was prosecuted only on land acquired through inheritance. Land cleared after the marriage of any one brother was never shared, with the exception of Fran and Peter's garden. Although plots on the flats remained unenclosed after subdivision, not all brothers chose to share crops and livestock; Micil's 3 sons on the north side had individual arable plots and separate stables, as had George on the south side of the river. Because plots remained unenclosed certain arrangements had to be made between brothers and cousins as to grazing of

20 It is possible that Micil was also involved in this joint farm: in 1857 there were 3 dwelling houses recorded, but only one barn (*Census of Newfoundland & Labrador, 1857,* p. 353).

openfields once the harvest was over. All crops had to be harvested by a set date to allow communal grazing of the meadows; it appears, however, that Micil's Sand Meadow was not included in this joint arrangement. Micil's sons grazed their livestock jointly in their father's Sand Meadow after they individually harvested their crops.

In Patrick's Cove land was acquired in two ways: (a) by inheritance, and (b) by staking one's own claim and individually clearing the land. First Micil and then 5 of Paddy's sons established separate or severalty farms. These two traditions — joint farming with its openfield arrangement, and individually enclosed separately worked holdings — existed side by side all along the Cape Shore during the nineteenth century. The social basis for these joint farms was the patrilineal extended family. It is interesting to note that in Ship Cove, where in the second generation two women (the only children of John Skerry) received equal shares of the farm and married two Irish immigrants, the farms were worked separately. Over the next two generations one of these families, the Tobins, continued to operate severalty farms despite subdivision, but the Brennans developed an openfield system almost exactly like that in Patrick's Cove.

The practice of partnership farming was closely connected with the operation of the fishery. When farms were subdivided between brothers on the Cape Shore stages, flakes, boats, and other fishing gear were transmitted in like manner and co-heirs frequently fished and farmed jointly. In the nineteenth century in both Avalon study areas fishing crews were predominantly dyadic (two males per boat) although in the settlements north of St John's some men fished single-handed ("cross-handed") or as triads. From at least the middle of the nineteenth century trap skiffs requiring crews of 5 to 9 men were operated in both study areas and such crews were normally recruited agnatically, especially on the Cape Shore, although affinal relatives and even non-kin were sometimes hired as share-men or labourers. Even when the crew was a partilineally extended family, sharing the same stage, flake and boat, fully fledged partnership farming rarely involved more than two of the crew members.

Miramichi

As in the Avalon, the Miramichi Irish enclosed only the cleared portion of their lots. Boundaries in the woods were usually blazed. Within each lot the first fields were laid out around the farmstead and close to the river or road. Clearing continued back along the longitudinal axis of the farm lot. Land was cleared at a rate of approximately an acre per farm each year. By the mid-nineteenth century the average clearing in Nelson parish was 15 acres and a decade later the Irish in the study area worked an average of 23 acres per farm. Farming was more mixed than in any of the other study areas. Seven of the 15 acres worked in 1851 were ploughed, producing an average 60 bushels of oats, 12 of wheat, 2 of barley, 2 of buckwheat, 140 of potatoes, 14 of turnips, and 2 bushels of peas and beans. The remainder was either under hay, in pasture, or in fallow. Ten years later the average farm produced 3½ acres of oats, 2 of wheat, 1½ of potatoes, ½ acre of other root crops, and 6½ acres of hay. Almost 10 acres of cleared land were either in pasture or fallow.

The average arable area per farm in Miramichi was far more extensive than in the Avalon and was far less intensively manured. The Miramichi Irish raised fewer livestock than the Cape Shore settlers in the nineteenth century, and unlike the latter group they usually did not supplement stable manure with any other form of fertilizer. To be sure, ashes from the burnt clearings were spread on the ground[21] and farmers composted wet clay or "bog," taken from the intervales, with stable manure,[22] but most Miramichi Irish relied solely on dung accumulated in the stables over the long winter to fertilize their root crops and meadows. It should be noted that the area under root crops in Miramichi, however, was little more than twice that of the average mid-nineteenth century Cape Shore farm and hardly exceeded the average in Freshwater but both these latter areas had more land under meadow.

The dominant schemes of crop rotation at the end of the last century began with an oat crop on the ley, followed by potatoes, turnips, and cabbage, then wheat, then oats and hayseed, four hay crops, and an indefinite period in pasture. Both grain and potatoes were also planted on freshly cleared ground. Hay, which occurred four times in the rotation, and oats, which occurred twice,[23] were the leading crops in Miramichi since the mid-nineteenth century. With the exception of some kitchen garden vegetables, all root and grain crops were grown commercially but were never exported.

Figure 16 shows field lay-out on a typical Barnaby farm around 1870, more than two decades before land clearing ended. The lot was occupied by 1830 and

21 Burning was widely practised during the nineteenth century. See evidence of Robert Young, Chatham (Great Britain, Parliament, *Appendix Colonel Cockburn's Instructions and Reports on Emigration* [in National Archives Ottawa], Paper 148, London, 1828, p. 86).
22 There is evidence that composting with "bog" was practised elsewhere in Miramichi early in the second half of the last century: "Compost heaps generally formed of swamp muck or bog, mixed with stable manure and occasionally with lime" (New Brunswick, Board of Agriculture, *Fifth Annual Report of Board of Agriculture* [in University of New Brunswick Library, Fredericton], "Report of Blackville and Derby Agricultural Society," Fredericton, 1865, p. 55; New Brunswick, *Seventh Annual Report of Board of Agriculture*, "Report of Northumberland Agricultural Society," Fredericton, 1867, p. 60). "A good deal of attention is paid to composting with peat, but many who have practised it have now given it up."
23 Oats was referred to by Richard Sutton, an immigrant Irish farmer in the study area, as "our never failing and most prolific cereal" (New Brunswick, *Fifth Annual Report*, 1865, p. 55).

there were 30 acres cleared three decades later; 8 of these acres were under hay, 5 under oats and 1½ under potatoes and other vegetables. Sometime in the 1860's the lot was divided between two male heirs, a division demonstrated by the continuous fence cutting longitudinally through the middle of the cleared ground. The older fields, on the river bank, were irregular in shape, being closely adapted to the distribution of workable intervale soils. South of the intervale, fields were more regularly laid out. Not all fields were as geometrically arranged, but the contrast between the riverbank fields and the others is fairly general. Temporary fences were rarely erected, so that there was a relationship between the amount of land under cultivation and the size of fields. Shelter was provided by surrounding forests in Miramichi and wind-breaks were few.

In 1851 there were in Nelson 6 cattle, 5 sheep, one horse and two pigs on the average farm; over the next decade, only a slight increase in the livestock population occurred. As in the Avalon, cattle were traditionally grazed in the "commons" during the summer. Abandoned fields, beaver meadows, marshland, and even the roadsides were used as summer pastures. The pattern of organization differed in some ways from that of the Avalon. Farmers did not allow cattle to stray very far from the homestead and dry cattle were usually kept on the farm overnight with milk cows. The elaborate branding of stock described for the Avalon was not practised. Within living memory neither horses, sheep nor young calves were grazed in "commons," and several acres of pasture land were reserved on the farm each summer for these animals. Once the hay was stored, livestock were grazed on the aftergrass. The Miramichi Irish grew less than half the amount of hay grown by the Irish on the Cape Shore, but hay was supplemented by straw and turnips for winter feed. Fat cattle were important commercially and there was a good local market for mutton, pork, butter and eggs.

Peterborough

As in the other study areas, the Peterborough immigrants fenced off only the cleared land and marked their boundaries through the woods. These immigrants cleared land at a much faster rate than in the other study areas. After one year's settlement the Ennismore Irish worked an average of 3 acres per family; the clearing increased to 5 acres by 1830 and 12 acres by 1839.[24] The average family clearing in both Ennismore and Downeyville was 30 acres in 1851, almost twice the size of the Miramichi farm.

In contrast to the Avalon, and to a certain extent Miramichi, the Peterborough-Irish practised an extensive type of land use. Apart from ashes produced while clearing land, and lime, stable manure was the only fertilizer. The dominant pattern of rotation in Upper Canada up to 1850 was a two-course

24 Ontario, Assessment Rolls, Ennismore Township (MSS in Provincial Archives, Toronto), RG21, Section A, Newcastle District, 1827, 1828, 1830, 1839-41.

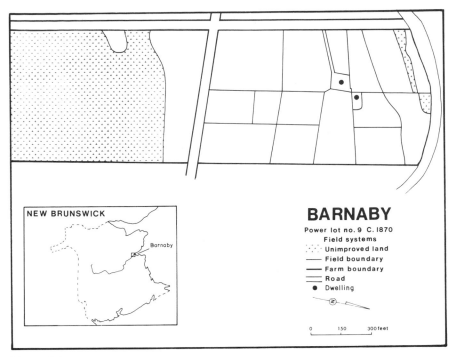

Figure 16

rotation where fallow followed wheat and wheat fallow: the land was put under wheat, rested for a year, then sown to wheat again. Wheat fields were not manured. This alternation of wheat with fallow was well adapted to a pioneer setting where there was a shortage of capital, labour was expensive, land cheap, and the market was for grain rather than for pastoral products.[25]

It is impossible to ascertain to what extent the Irish adopted either mixed farming or wheat/fallow/wheat during their first two decades of occupance. If the system of seeding down freshly cleared land to grass for several years were rigidly adhered to, enough land would have to be cleared each fall to carry all the crops sown. Between 1827 and 1830 only two acres were added to the first year's clearing in Ennismore; this would mean that on average only half an acre was available to each farmer for his annual crops. Undoubtedly, the average arable acreage exceeded half an acre so that immigrants must have introduced some form of rotation from the beginning. If this was a two-course wheat

25 Kenneth Kelly, "Wheat Farming in Simcoe County in the Mid-Nineteenth Century," *Canadian Geographer* 15 (1971): 95-112. In the Peterborough area some of the well-to-do English settlers practised a form of mixed farming, putting each new clearing into grass after one year in arable.

75

rotation then it certainly had disappeared on most immigrant Irish farms by the mid-nineteenth century. Recuperating crops such as peas and grasses were usually omitted in a wheat/fallow/wheat rotation and the area under wheat normally exceeded the combined area under feed crops. While in Ennismore the Irish had as much land under wheat as under feed crops in 1851, more than two-thirds of them grew an average of 4 acres of peas per farm. Peas were traditionally sown on ley land and this suggests that there was grassy fallow. Over two-thirds of the farmers grew an average of 6 tons of hay, and almost half the land in Ennismore was reported under pasture in 1851. It is likely, however, that some of the area returned as pasture was not seeded down to form a true grassy fallow. Cattle could be grazed in the woods, lessening the need for summer pasture within the cleared area. While some farmers may have been following a two-course rotation, by 1851 the majority had developed a wheat-feed or mixed farm economy. According to the census, over 25 per cent of the Ennismore farmers did not grow any wheat in 1851. Grain, however, did dominate most rotations. Potatoes and other roots crops were shifted around the farm, but occupied a small fraction of the arable and were unimportant in the overall crop rotation.

Fields in Peterborough were laid out in rectangular parcels similar to those in Miramichi, with their boundaries usually running parallel to the boundaries of the lot. Figure 17 shows a typical field layout on a standard farm lot in Downey-ville about 1870, after land clearing had ended. First settled in 1830, the lot was cleared at a much faster rate than was usual with the Irish in Peterborough. After a decade 35 acres were cleared[26] and by 1851 another 10 acres had been added. In 1861 there were 80 acres cleared, 60 of them under crops. The original farmstead was located at the northeast corner of the lot, on a well-drained patch of loam which extended diagonally across the lot in a southwesterly direction. By 1870 a road had been cut through the swamp on the southern end of the farm lot and the farmstead was relocated at a more convenient distance from this road. The oldest section of the farm, along the eastern boundary, was divided into 5 fields of equal size, and two small fields ("pigfield" and "little island") were created on the front of the farm after the farmstead was relocated. The remaining 50 acres of cleared land were divided up into various sized plots which were unenclosed but separated from the older cleared section by lanes or cartways. These open plots were worked as separate units in the rotation scheme and were called fields. At the rear of the lot, some 10 acres of woodland was grazed by cattle and was fenced off from the cropland. All fields were named, either according to size or function, physical characteristics, or location in relation to the farmstead.

26 Ontario, Assessment Rolls, Emily Township, 1840.

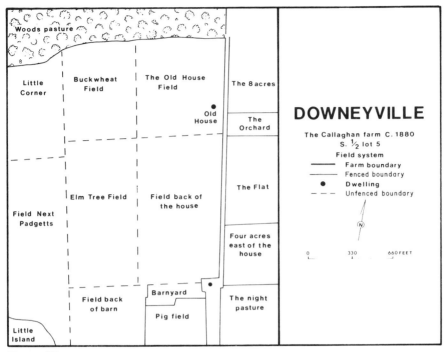

Figure 17

Temporary fences have not been used in living memory and wind-breaks were uncommon. While natural features, especially the distribution of different qualities of soil, influenced the size and shape of fields, their regular layout was a reflection of the strong arable tradition. Where soils were uniform and land was level the farmer in Peterborough often divided his lot into 9 enclosed fields, almost equal in size.

In 1851 the average Ennismore farmer kept 2-3 cows, 3 cattle, 3 oxen, 9 sheep, 7 pigs, and a horse. There was a small local demand for livestock, but most animals were consumed on the farm. Most animals were grazed in the open woodlands. The first township council meeting in Douro, for example, was devoted mainly to legislation concerning the grazing of common or ungranted lands. Cattle, horses, sheep, and pigs were permitted "to run at large" but all bulls, boars, rams, and stallions, as well as turkeys and geese were to be enclosed.[27] In order to protect crops from wandering livestock it was stipulated that fences were to be at least 4½ feet high and fence viewers were appointed to

27 Ontario, Douro Township Council Report, 1850 (MSS in Township Hall, Douro). In the following year the grazing of all pigs in the woodlands between April and December was forbidden.

enforce this legislation. The well-to-do English minority in Douro disapproved of woodland grazing and there was great alarm in the Langton home, for example, when the cows broke out and spent a day in the woods.[28] By the end of the nineteenth century only the roadsides and lake islands were used for communal summer pasturing, and by this time, with the advent of commercial cattle raising, most of the cleared land was in pasture or in meadow.

Traditions of landholding and farm technology transferred from the homeland or adopted from earlier settlers near the study areas, the social structure of the migrating groups, the new physical environment, and especially the new economy influenced the evolution of field systems. Every immigrant Irish family was determined to develop a commercially viable enterprise as quickly as possible. Like most North American pioneers these Irish settlers attempted to produce as much as possible from their land without destroying its fertility, but this objective had to be attained within particular physical, social, and economic conditions.

The task of clearing the forest did not influence the size or shape of fields. Although the land cleared each season was fenced off from the forest, these fences were temporary. There is no correlation between field size and the amount of land cleared in a season in any of the study areas.

Nor did topographical features or type of soil greatly influence field forms or size. To be sure, steep slopes or streams sometimes divided fields and drier or superior soils were often separated from wet clays or marsh. According to tradition the dry soils on the more elevated sections of the Peterborough farms could be cropped before low-lying areas, and were sometimes separately enclosed. But with extra drainage and manuring, wet soils were improved and united with the naturally dry soils into single fields. In the more heavily drumlinized parts of Douro township fields were often small and irregular, in contrast to uniformly regular units on the Downeyville clay plain. Field form on the intervale soils of Miramichi was often irregular but in both Peterborough and Miramichi the dominant field form was a rectangular block that paid little attention to topographic features. In the Avalon, where farms were small and there had never

28 H.H. Langton (ed.), *A Gentlewoman in Upper Canada: The Journals of Anne Langton* (Toronto: Clarke, Irwin & Company, Ltd., reprint, 1964), p. 92. Anne Langton refused to use the milk that evening. Samuel Strickland, who was President of the Douro Council, commented on the time wasted collecting cattle in the woods and advised settlers to reserve some pasture land.

been a geometrical land survey, field boundaries were far more sensitive to physical conditions.

Livestock had to be housed for a long period in winter and a considerable amount of hay was required to sustain them. The practice of long leys and rotation grasses in the Avalon and Miramichi, although adumbrated for almost a century on the larger peasant "stock" farms in the homeland, was mainly a reflection of the need for hay as winter feed. In the stables the livestock produced manure which was put on the meadows. Moreover, in the Avalon, grain was climatically marginal and this greatly influenced the development of a commercial pastoral economy and consequently many aspects of the field system. By contrast, the longer, drier summers and superior soils of Peterborough permitted wheat farming and this induced a more rapid rate of clearing and an extensive type of land use.

In both Peterborough and Miramichi cleared land was blocked off into regular parcels with fence lines running parallel to the straight boundaries of the farms. When a farm lot was subdivided, the new boundary was drawn parallel to the boundaries of the original lot. Squared fields (*blockflur*) and strip fields probably predominated in the homeland at the time of the migrations and it is certain that at least some of the immigrants worked such fields before emigrating. As in Peterborough and Miramichi the regular-shaped field units in Ireland were a creation or inspiration of a landlord or government survey, not a product of unsupervised peasant colonization. In the absence of a superimposed geometric survey, as in the Avalon and parts of the homeland, both the farm lots and the fields they contained were highly irregular in shape. Regular, rectangular field blocks were ideal for plough cultivation and the haphazard morphology of fields in the Avalon may reflect hand-tool cultivation. In Freshwater however, where the plough was the dominant implement of cultivation, most fields were irregularly shaped.

In the New World, in sharp contrast to the Old, cultivable land was plentiful and cheap but labour was scarce and expensive and was of paramount importance in determining the evolution of field systems. To be sure, some of the Irish peasant traditions of land use and management reappear in the New World, but most field traditions were altered or modified to adapt to local practices and the prevailing economy. Prior to the influx of Irish, the Peterborough farmers emphasized commercial cereal cropping, especially wheat, and the Irish immigrants adapted to this extensive form of land utilization. Whereas in the homeland, land pressure encouraged an intensive working of the arable area, the abundance of land in Peterborough permitted the immigrants to shift their crops, leave land fallow frequently and avoid elaborate rotations or intensive manuring and draining to conserve the quality of the soil. This practice, wasteful of land but not of labour, was adapted to the economics of the frontier; it not only saved on labour but speeded the rate of clearing.

79

Despite the availability of cultivable land, a more labour-intensive system of land management developed in Miramichi and especially in the Avalon. The intensive application of animal manure and kelp in the Avalon was similar to homeland practice. In the Avalon fish offal replaced lime, marl, and sea sand as fertilizer. Extended cultivation of fertile pockets also echoed old Irish infield practice but whereas in Irish tradition the cultivable land was often divided into an infield and an outfield area, no such division obtained in the New World. By contrast, both in Avalon and Miramichi, all cultivated land received manure. The rotation of crops and the draining of land in Freshwater and Miramichi were linked to the notions of improved husbandry gaining ground in western Europe and North America in the eighteenth century. Although discouraged by "improvers" the practice of "burn baitings" for land clearing persisted in the Avalon and was firmly based on Irish tradition. "Paring and burning" was regarded by Flatrès as a distinctively Celtic method of reclaiming rough land and ley for cultivation but was not recorded in Ireland until the thirteenth century. By the time of the migrations the technique was widespread amongst the peasantry. It was an intensive form of cultivation, greatly depleted soil fertility, and like infield agriculture was discouraged by improving landlords.[29] While the *grafán* was used for this task both in the homeland and in the study areas, "paring and burning" was important in the New World only as a reclamation technique and did not survive the period of clearing.

It is difficult to explain fully the labour-intensive farm management that evolved in the Avalon. Although extra land was available, farms remained small. Poor soils discouraged an extensive type of land use and an adverse climate ruled out commercial grain growing. Again, considerable labour that might have been invested in extra clearing was absorbed by the fishery, but even in Freshwater farms remained small. The pattern of rotation in this latter area allowed for 3 acres of arable, which was as much as a small family with a simple technology could handle and the practice of ploughing all ley every four years restricted the expansion of the farm. The extensive use of rough pasture in all areas also acted as a brake on farm enlargement. In Miramichi, the partial dependence on lumbering for a livelihood and the emergence of mixed farming slowed the pace of farm expansion. By contrast the extensive scale of land use in Peterborough greatly accelerated the pace of clearing.

Apart from the Cape Shore, few traces of the Irish openfield system appear in the New World. In the homeland such a system, wherever it survived up to the nineteenth century, was embedded in a layer of custom reinforced by ties of kinship in every hamlet. In Irish tradition the extended family was an important social unit in openfield husbandry. The replacement of this kin group by the

29 A.T. Lucas, "Paring and Burning in Ireland," in Stephens and Glasscock (eds.), *Irish Geographical Studies*, pp. 99-147.

nuclear family in the New World had the same effects on the field system in the study areas as it had on the initial patterns of settlement described in chapter iii. Individual families settled and arranged their fields contiguously around their isolated farmsteads. The failure to transfer the openfield system is closely related to the dismemberment of the native kin group, a concomitant of migration.

The evolution of a rudimentary openfield system in some coves along the Cape Shore was closely associated with the emergence of kin-group settlement clusters. Through successive subdivisions between male heirs the single farmstead developed into an agglomerated settlement and the compact ancestral farm into a joint farm with communally operated openfields. This pattern of land inheritance and land settlement is a reproduction of old Irish practice. The inherent flexibility of Irish rural settlement patterns has already been noted: just as farm clusters dissolved into a pattern of dispersed farmsteads and compact farms, a single farm sometimes developed into an agglomerated settlement with an openfield system. This was especially true in the period of population expansion in pre-migration times. The basic elements in the evolution of field systems in Patrick's Cove are analogous to the evolving pattern in a Donegal townland during the same period.[30] The townland was occupied by a nuclear family late in the eighteenth century, but through subdivision and internal expansion contained 29 holdings in 1845 and no fewer than 422 scattered plots. In both settlements all the inhabitants were either affinal or consanguineal relations and the openfield systems were based on co-operating kin groups. The patterns of inheritance in Patrick's Cove, the intermingling of open plots, the pooling of labour and sharing of crops, the joint ownership of livestock and the practice of allowing the cattle to graze in the "commons" during summer and on the openfields once harvest was over, have ample precedent in the homeland. Not all sons received shares, tenure of plots was fixed, not rotated, and the twofold division of the cultivable land into an infield and outfield did not occur in Patrick's Cove, but even in those pockets in the homeland where traditional agriculture prevailed, these traditions had often vanished by the time of the migrations. None of the terminology of the Irish openfield system appeared on the Cape Shore, but the Gaelic term *bowan*, used to indicate the unploughed strips of earth dividing infield parcels was used in Freshwater.

Apparently no single factor can explain the reproduction of elements of the Irish openfield system along the Cape Shore. Perhaps the absence of a cadastral survey was an important factor, yet open fields did not evolve in the St John's settlements, and here as elsewhere in the Avalon, there was never a regular survey. In Irish tradition, the creation of openfields was largely a result of the desire to share equally among sons soils of differing quality, and it may be that

30 E.E. Evans, "Some Survivals in the Irish Open Field System," *Geography* 24 (1939): 24-36.

the juxtaposition of good alluvial soils with less fertile soils on the slopes of the Cape Shore coves – a dichotomy not existing in the St John's settlements – influenced the evolution of openfields. Unlike the St John's settlements, houses along the Cape Shore had to be sited on the slopes, away from the fertile flats, and this militated against the developemnt of compact farms. Undoubtedly, co-operation at sea reinforced partnership on the Cape Shore, but did not have the same affect in the settlements north of St John's. It seems that the best explanation for the emergence of openfields along the Cape Shore, in contrast to the continuing compact farm units near St John's, is that there was considerably more subdivision in the former area during the second half of the nineteenth century. The rate of land clearing declined after 1860 along the Cape Shore, whereas the rate of clearing actually increased in tempo north of St John's. Moreover, young males in the St John's settlements could find work in the city or emigrate to the United States during this period; no such mobility existed in the more isolated Cape Shore coves. Again, some farms were sold in the St John's settlements, whereas sales would have been exceedingly difficult in a kin-based joint-farm operation. Farming was more commercially orientated in these settlements near the city, and the competition from the compact farms of their English Protestant neighbours may also have been influential. The striking cultural isolation of the Cape Shore settlers is certainly a contributory factor in the evolution of joint farming and openfields.

One of the major contrasts between the field systems of the homeland and the New World was that in the former area all exploitable resources were scrupulously subdivided but in the New World they were not. Rights to wrack or kelp on the seashore, to lime, sand, marl or bog, and even to grazing units in the summer pastures were as jealously guarded in Ireland as were the arable plots of the infield. Frequently, the division of such resources was based on the amount of land or number of ridges held by a family in the infield. Such meticulous allocation of resources reflected the extreme pressure of population on the land of Ireland before the migrations. In contrast, most of these resources were abundant in the New World, and were, moreover, readily accessible to the immigrants. While the Irish continued the practice of communal summer grazing in the study areas, none of the salient features of traditional transhumance were reproduced. In all study areas, the unimproved land beyond the farms, with its ample forage, stretched out almost interminably, and with such "commons" stinting or restricted grazing was unnecessary. Both in Peterborough and Miramichi pastoral products were relatively unimportant commercially in the pioneer period. Immigrants were more interested in clearing land for crops and could ill afford to send the young folk into the woods to tend to their few livestock. By contrast there was little arable land to be worked in the homeland and no extra land to be cleared. Surplus labour could be more profitably absorbed in the more intensive pastoral system of the summer *boolies*. On the Cape

Shore and in Freshwater, where commercial pastoralism was dominant, the demands on labour for clearing land and later for fishing on the Cape Shore, militated against the establishment of an intensive commercial pastoralism in the "commons." Only dry stock were driven and left in the woodlands, to wander at will. In Logy Bay there was a seasonal movement of families and livestock from inland farms to the coast each summer, but the commercial emphasis was on fishing, not pastoralism. Other resources that were communally exploited – kelp, bog, timber for fuel or construction, caplin – were equally and freely accessible to all. The abundance of such resources, in contrast to the homeland, was a major factor in the demise of the intricate rules and rights of access that typified openfield husbandry and society in the homeland.

V
Farm technology

The tools and techniques used in field and farmstead were important indicators of the immigrants' adaptation to a new physical and economic environment and reflected especially the contrasting conditions between the Old World and the New. A labour-intensive technology characterized the homeland, where land was limited and expensive, labour abundant and cheap, and where reserves of capital were low. Farm tasks were performed manually and everywhere in peasant Ireland this traditional technology endured long after the migrations. In the autarkic regime of the backwoods hand-tool methods were common, but as the farms of the immigrants attained commercial status in an economic environment where the premium was on labour, not on land, it can be posited that the retention of a simple technology would greatly inhibit the rate of commercialization. Technical traditions were often in conflict with the demands of a frontier economy and this chapter seeks to analyse the evolution of farm technology in the study areas against the background of Old and New World influences. Because of the extensive range of field implements and techniques examined relating to land clearing, cultivation, sowing, reaping, and farm transport, those of the study areas are first described and an investigation of possible Irish antecedents and New World influences follows.

LAND CLEARING AND FENCING

The formidable task of clearing the land continued in all study areas until the end of the nineteenth century. Much of the lore of land clearing survives. In the Avalon a light narrow axe was used to hack down the stunted forest and hatchets, picks and crowbars were used to clear away the underbrush and stones. By contrast, a heavy broad-axe was adopted by the immigrants to level the dense forests of Peterborough and Miramichi. Trees were cut close to the ground and the larger stumps left to decay. Small stumps were either prized from the ground with wooden levers, or were uprooted by oxen or horses. The introduction of stumping machines to the Peterborough farms in the second half of the nineteenth century greatly speeded the process of land clearing. In all study areas, soil covering the roots was removed with a mattock.

The business of clearing the land in the backwoods was best accomplished communally. Hired labour was costly and arduous tasks such as logging (i.e., gathering the already chopped logs into heaps for burning), or stumping, frequently were organized on a reciprocal, co-operative basis. "People in the woods have a craze for giving and going to bees," wrote Susanna Moodie, "and run to them with as much eagerness as a peasant runs to a racecourse or fair; plenty of strong drink and excitement making the chief attraction of the bee."[1] Logging bees are widely remembered in the Peterborough-Irish townships, but in Miramichi and the Avalon, land clearing appears to have been a more individual or family enterprise. Materials cleared from the land were used to build fences. Fence forms varied even within study areas. "Stake and longer" fences dominated the Avalon at the end of the last century. A post or stake was driven into the ground every 8 feet or so and 2 or 3 horizontally placed posts or "longers," each around 16 feet in length, were tied to the posts with withes or *gads*[2] (Fig. 18A). Alternatively the longers were tied to the upright posts by homemade tree-nails or "trunnels," or secured with strips of bark. Along the Cape Shore, and to a lesser extent near St John's, sticks and branches were woven between either the vertical posts or horizontal rails and were referred to as "wave," "bush," or "riddlin" fences. Another variant was the picket fence, formed of closely-spaced vertical sticks which were nailed or tied to the horizontally laid "longers."[3] This type usually enclosed the kitchen garden. Both in Miramichi and Peterborough the first fences were piles of wood and refuse from the clearings. The Irish also built fences with tree stumps, but in the Avalon, where

1 Susanna Moodie, *Roughing it in the Bush* (Toronto: McClelland & Stewart, 1964, reprint), p. 156. Thirty-two men, some of them recently arrived Irish, were invited to a logging bee at the Moodie farm near Peterborough. About 5 acres were cleared. Susanna Moodie called the bees "noisy, riotous, drunken meetings, often terminating in violent quarrels, sometimes even in bloodshed."
2 The post and rail fence dates back to the beginning of settlement in Logy Bay: Luke Ryan, an Irish immigrant, enclosed 15 acres with "posts and rails" in 1818 (Great Britain, Colonial Office Correspondence, Newfoundland [MSS in Provincial Archives, St John's], Series 194, vol. 81, 1831). Three "longer" fences were recorded in Logy Bay in the *Public Ledger*, St John's, December 2, 1828 (in Provincial Archives, St John's).
3 For an example near St John's see *The Patriot*, St John's, January 12, 1842 (in Arts and Culture Library, St John's).

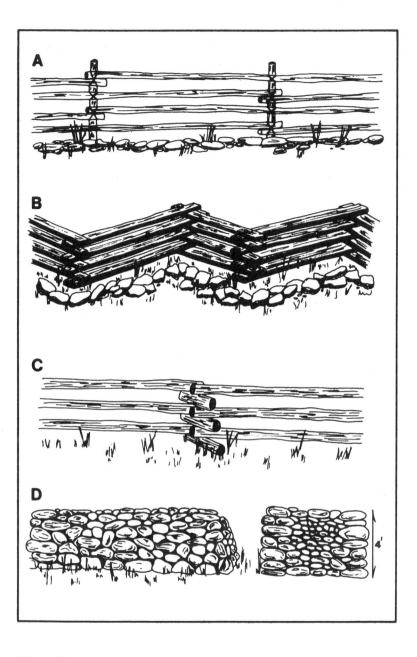

Figure 18
Fences: **A** — Avalon stake and longer. **B** — Peterborough snake. **C** — Miramichi log rail. **D** — New World stone.

stumps were small, this fence type was rare. "Snake" or "worm" fences appeared early in Peterborough[4] and many cedar examples still survive in the Irish townships, especially in marshy hollows and other areas of marginal agricultural activity (Fig. 18B).

In Miramichi the straight log fences still surviving on many farms (Fig. 18C) date from at least the mid-nineteenth century. Full spruce or cedar logs, rather than rails, were used. The logs, up to 15 feet in length, were placed butt to butt, each end resting on a transverse block of wood. Fences were 3 to 4 logs high and were sometimes reinforced at the joints by vertical posts bored into the bottom block on each side, and tied on top with an alder withe.

Stonewalls were erected in all three study areas, and were especially common on the rock-laden slopes of the St John's settlements and on the Cape Shore. Drywalling in Miramichi was restricted to the stony soils of Nowlanville and Semiwagan Ridge. Along the Barnaby river the clayey loam did not contain enough stone for such fences. In Peterborough, however, where stone was abundant in places, as attested by the numerous rock piles in the fields, stone walls were rare.

The walls varied little in form. Between 4 and 6 feet high, and 3 to 4 feet at the base, they usually tapered slightly to the top. The heavier and more regularly shaped stones were placed on the outside skin of the wall, which was neatly constructed, while the wide interior was filled with smaller stones (Fig. 18D). Frequently the wall was topped and reinforced with a layer of sod.

Another distinctive fence style, called a "ditch," was built on a few farms in Peterborough and along the Cape Shore. A narrow stone wall about 4 feet high was first erected, and an outer skin of sod, shovelled from a dyke dug on either side of the wall, was added. The structure was topped off with sods and sometimes crowned by a post-and-rail fence.

SEEDTIME

Vegetables

One of the first major tasks of the farming year was the preparation of the ground for arable crops. Depending on the weather, this task might begin early in April but was usually completed in May. Since at least 1850 the most popular cultivation implement in all areas, apart from the Cape Shore, and to some extent the settlements north of St John's, was the plough. With the exception of

4 Samuel Strickland, *Twenty-Seven Years in Canada West* (London: R. Bentley, 1853), p. 33. Trees of straight growth and grain were cut into 12-foot lengths and were split longitudinally by means of a beetle and wedges into rails approximately 4 inches in thickness; these were laid on top of one another in zigzag fashion up to a height of 5 feet. Oak, pine, cedar, white ash, and basswood (which split easily) were the timbers most utilized.

an iron or steel sock and coulter, this implement was wooden and usually was homemade. While local smiths sometimes made iron ploughs, they were frequently imported and were available in stores, but their cost in the early nineteenth century must have been prohibitive for many of the Irish.[5] By the end of the century, however, iron ploughs had replaced the old wooden implements on almost every farm.

Certain folk beliefs were associated with the task of ploughing in Freshwater. When starting the day's work the ploughman usually sprinkled some soil over the horses to bring good luck to his efforts and whenever possible he took care to turn his team with the sun. It was also considered lucky to begin the first furrow at the eastern end of a field, facing west. Bad luck might follow the ploughman who stepped over his plough, but he could avoid mishap by retracing his step.

In the settlements north of St John's many oldtimers remember the first introduction of ploughs to their fathers' farms. Snarled tree stumps, bushes or even fishing grapnels were sometimes used, but the spade or mattock were the principal cultivation implements on most farms in the nineteenth century. Along the Cape Shore ploughs were first introduced under a government assistance programme in the 1930's, but were widely rejected. Cultivation is still practised exclusively with hand-operated tools. Such simple technology probably predominated even in Peterborough during the pioneer phase. A plough could not be used when there were stumps in the ground, but freshly cleared land did not require ploughing during the first years in any case. The slow acquisition of oxen and horses in the Peterborough area and the small size of clearings during the first decade of settlement suggest that the Irish there used hand-tools.[6]

5 There is abundant documentary evidence on the availability and use of ploughs around St John's in store and farm auction advertisements and in wills (see especially *The Royal Gazette and Newfoundland Advertiser*, St John's, 1810-16 [in Provincial Archives, St John's]; the *Mercantile Journal*, St John's, 1816-24 [in Provincial Archives, St John's]; and Newfoundland, Supreme Court, *Registry of Wills*, [MSS in Courthouse, St John's], I, 1810-40). Ploughs cost £3-10-0 in Miramichi in 1826, the price of an Atlantic crossing (*The Mercury*, Newcastle, April 17, 1826 and June 13, 1826 [in University of New Brunswick Library, Fredericton]). A plough factory was established in Peterborough in 1840 and in 1856 an Irish immigrant paid $6 there for a plough (Thomas W. Poole, *The Early Settlement of Peterborough County* [Peterborough: Peterborough Printing Company, 1967 reprint], p. 100; Ontario, William Moher Diaries *1855-85* [Private MSS in Douro]).

6 In Ennismore, for example, only 7 of the 50 or so families owned oxen in 1830 and there were no horses. By 1839, 6 families kept horses but over half the farmers owned oxen and by 1851 there were few families without either oxen or horses and many kept both (Ontario, Assessment Rolls, Ennismore Township [MSS in Provincial Archives, Toronto], RG21, Section A, Newcastle District, 1830, 1839). In Douro "the land was worked by hacking it with a spade with a long eye made by the local blacksmith" (P.G. Towns, "Early Life in Douro," *Peterborough Daily Examiner*, Peterborough, May 15, 1925 [in Peterborough Public Library, Peterborough]).

The mattock (or in the Irish dialect of Avalon and Miramichi, the *gruff* or *grafán*) was widely used in place of the plough and is still the principle implement of cultivation on the Cape Shore. Similar in form to a heavy hoe, its long, broad, curved blade (Fig. 19A) was well adapted to cultivating arable soils. The *grafán* was usually purchased in a store. Memory of its use as a cultivation tool has disappeared in Peterborough but within living memory in Miramichi it was used in kitchen gardens and other areas where ploughing would be unmanageable. In Freshwater a man would often follow the plough with a *grafán*, turning over the sod and breaking up lumps of clay. In all areas the tool was used for cutting sods and clearing the land, and sometimes had a cutting blade on the opposite side of the digger (Fig. 19B).

A sharp-edged spade was often used for the creation of ridges on ley land. Spade blades could be fashioned by a blacksmith from an iron plate but were usually purchased in stores; the hardwood shaft was homemade. In the Avalon and in Miramichi blades were about 4 inches wide and 12-16 inches long. Sometimes in the former area blades narrowed slightly towards the middle and expanded towards a lightly concave mouth, giving a waist-like form, while in Miramichi the blade widened one-third of the way down and tapered towards the mouth (Fig. 19C, D, E). The majority of spades in both areas, however, had parallel sides and the blades were straight at the mouth. The blade was usually bent slightly forward about half way down, and this curve or lift gave the digger extra leverage when turning the sod and also lessened the need to bend over the task. On the upper portion of the blade the two sides or ears were bent backwards to form open sockets. Into one of these sockets – usually the one on the left – a straight and handleless shaft about 5 feet long was thrust and received by a nail driven laterally through socket and shaft. The other socket was fitted with an anvil-shaped wooden foot-piece or tread. Frequently a naturally curved tree-root or "knee" was selected for this purpose, and could be placed in the right or left socket to accommodate right or left-footed diggers. In the Avalon this spade type declined in use early in the present century and had virtually disappeared by this time in Miramichi.

In Peterborough there is memory only of a two-sided spade. Blades were shorter and broader than the one-sided variety, had less lift, and their sides were normally straight (Fig. 19F). The shaft was driven into a closed socket within the upper part of the blade and two metal strips extended from the socket along the front and back of the shaft, to which they were nailed or riveted. Two narrow strips of metal were forged on to the top edges of the blade to serve as treads. Folk memory recalls shafts similar to the one-sided spade but most shafts were shorter and had a T-shaped hand-grip at the end.

Both in the Avalon and Miramichi root crops were planted in ridges or "lazybeds," and in both areas the craft of ridge making was similar. On ley land a furrow or trench 1-1½ feet wide was first marked out with twine and pegs and this strip was then cut and dug with the spade, or the *grafán* in parts of the Cape Shore. The 3-inch sod was turned on to what was to become the "bed" or ridge on either side of the furrow. Furrows were carefully aligned to the shape of the land to aid drainage and the seed-bed was raised well above the water-table. Potato ridges were often less than two feet wide, especially on wet ground, but ridges sown to other roots were twice this width. The ridge itself was not dug. Manure was spread on the grassy sward and was covered by sod and clay from the furrow.

After the ridges were formed the spade was again used to bury the potato sets in the heart of the ridges. This was accomplished by sticking the long blade into the "bed," pushing the handle forward and placing the seed in the cavity formed at the back of the blade. The seeds were carried sometimes in a linen bag (*máilín* in the Avalon) which was strapped over the shoulder. This method of planting, called "spitting" or "setting" or "stabbing" was widespread in Miramichi but an alternative technique of leaving the sets on top of the bed and then covering them with soil from the furrow was dominant in the Avalon. The former method, although more painstaking, was also more efficient, for the seeds were placed just below the fertile layer of grass and manure, benefiting from a down-wash of nutrients as well as being sheltered from sun, wind, and rain.

After the seeds took root in the ridges the trenches were dug a second time, with spade or *grafán*, to a depth of around 8 inches and the soil shovelled or "earthed" onto the ridges. The deeper layers of soil, taken from the furrows, possessed extra nutrients to nourish the potato buds. In the following spring the beds were levelled with a bush harrow or *grafán* and new furrows were cut down the middle of the old ridge, so that ridge became furrow and furrow ridge. This alternation of ridge with furrow ensured that the uncut sod at the base of the previous year's ridge was dug. Deep digging and cutting with the sharp-edged spade not only hindered weed growth but also unearthed stones and roots.

Along the Cape Shore "lazy-beds" are still used for potatoes and other vege-tables, but in the settlements north of St John's the technique was gradually abandoned after the introduction of the plough. There is no memory of potato ridges in Freshwater or Peterborough and they were made by only a handful of settlers by the end of the last century in Miramichi. Drills, formed by the plough, have been used in these areas as far back as local memory extends. Drilling was introduced to most farms north of St John's only in the present century. Spade and "lazy-bed" culture lingered longest in the small kitchen gardens where the plough could not be used.

The common method of planting potatoes in the Irish settlements of Peter-borough was known as "hilling." After the settler ploughed and harrowed the ground he dragged a "marker," consisting of a log about 6 feet long with 3 or 4 wooden pins attached to it, over the soil, first lengthwise and then crossways. He dropped potato "sets" at each intersection of the grid and covered them by

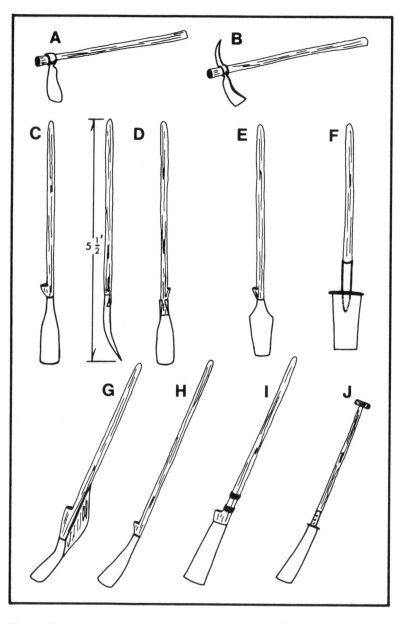

Figure 19

Mattocks: **A** — Avalon *grafán*. **B** — New World.

Spades: **C**, **D** — Avalon. **E** — Miramichi. **F** — Peterborough. Ireland: **G** — West midlands. **H** — South. **I** — West. **J** — North.

ploughing or hoeing up the soil. In the kitchen gardens each row was marked out with a line, and holes dug with a hoe. This method of planting has been described by contemporary observers in many parts of pioneer Ontario,[7] and was also used in Miramichi. Sometimes the potato "sets" were placed in every third furrow made by the plough, and manure placed on top.

Grain

In Miramichi and especially in Peterborough, the sowing of grain was usually the first and was certainly the major task of seedtime. From mid-May onwards the farmers along the Barnaby began planting and in Peterborough, weather permitting, grain occasionally was sown in April.[8] By contrast, in the Avalon, where grain was relatively unimportant, planting often did not occur until late in May after the potatoes were in.

The method of planting grain was similar in all three areas. The land was first harrowed to prepare it for the seed. Crude triangular-shaped harrows were used instead of ploughs in Peterborough to cultivate the soil between the stumps.[9] Harrows were available in stores in the Avalon and Miramichi when the Irish arrived, but most settlers made their own. Near St John's 5 spruce or larch poles, 5 feet each in length, were hewn and placed on the ground in a slightly fanned position, so that the front of the harrow was a foot or so narrower than the rear. Two holes were bored through the hewn timbers at the front and rear, but a heavy middle crossbar was mortised into the hewn timbers to reinforce and add weight to the structure. Twenty-five iron pins were then driven through the lower members only, 5 on each beam, at regular intervals. The swing or whiffletree was attached to one front corner of the harrow, so that the teeth or pins did not follow the same tracks or grooves as the implement was dragged over the ground. Until the present century on the Cape Shore a bush weighted with stones and logs was commonly used for harrowing and an iron handrake or *grafán* used to level the cultivation ridges for grain.

Grain seed was carried in a linen sack strapped around the shoulder, just as the potato setter carried his seed on the ridges. One hand held the mouth of the

7 William Hickey, *Hints on Emigration to Upper Canada* (Dublin: W. Curry, 1831), p. 71; Francis E. Evans, *The Emigrants Directory and Guide* (Dublin: W. Curry, 1833), p. 101; Joseph Pickering, *Inquiries of an Emigrant* (London: E. Wilson, 1832), p. 86; Catherine Parr Traill, *The Backwoods of Canada* (Toronto: McClelland & Stewart, 1968), p. 102.

8 In 1859 William Moher noted in his diary that he began sowing wheat on April 26. It was more usual, however, to begin early in May.

9 Traill, *Backwoods,* p. 70, called it "a queer sort of harrow that is made in the shape of a triangle for the better passing between the stumps; this is a rude machine compared with the nicely painted instruments of the sort I have been accustomed to in Britain." See also Moodie, *Roughing it in the Bush,* p. 207. Because of the scarcity of oxen the Irish in Ennismore buried the seed with hoes during the first years of settlement. Poole, *Peterborough,* p. 187.

sack open, the other was free to scatter the seed over the freshly harrowed ground. In Peterborough a wooden box tied around the sower's waist was used, leaving both hands free to broadcast the grain. The crop was harrowed over and rolled with a heavy log drawn by horses or oxen. If hayseed were sown with grain, it was broadcast separately, after the grain, and was harrowed in with the implement inverted so that the pins did not bury the seed too deeply. From 1870 onwards mechanical seeders were slowly introduced into Peterborough, displacing the older technique of sowing. It was only at the turn of the century that this machinery was introduced into Miramichi and the traditional technique is still employed in the Avalon.

The remainder of seedtime was taken up with the planting of various vegetables. Turnips usually followed grain and potatoes while cabbages and peas were the last plants sown. Farmers avoided planting vegetables when the moon was on the wane because they feared that such crops would fail. Cabbage seeds were sometimes sown in April in "hot beds"—a low pit covered by a glass roof resting on a light clapboarded frame. On the Cape Shore clay was sifted and placed indoors in a wooden box called a "plant bed." Warmed by the spring sunshine the seeds grew rapidly and were transplanted in June. By mid-June all crops were in, and a lull in agricultural activity followed, before the haymaking.

HARVEST

Hay
Because of the fickle nature of the weather, haymaking in the Avalon was the most strenuous and hurried task of the farming year. Traditionally, the settlers near St John's began mowing on "the day after the races in Quidi Vidi," in early August, and by Lady Day (August 15) most of the hay was usually "saved." Haymaking normally finished around Lady Day on the Cape Shore, late July in Miramichi, and around Orangemen's Day (July 12) in Peterborough. Wild grasses such as bents and fescues growing along streams and in marshes ("country hay") were harvested in September and were an important adjunct to the main crop. Such meadows were usually located in the "commons" but no stint was imposed on rights of usufruct.

Meadows were mown with scythes and grasshooks. Scything was a man's task and required both stamina and skill. Hay was cut close to the ground; a good mower cut half an acre in a day. Much of this work was performed co-operatively in "bees" or "frolics" and the competitive spirit in the hayfields ensured good progress. Sometimes women, using grasshooks, joined the men in the meadows, but in living memory the grasshook was used mainly in areas where the scythe could not be used or when a small portion of grass was required for the livestock. The grasshook was worked with one hand, using a short, slashing stroke, and progress was extremely slow.

Grass was cut out in swaths or "swarths" up to 4 feet wide, and on the following day the "swarths" were turned with hay forks. This task was often performed by women and children. Later in the day, weather permitting, the hay was shaken out evenly over the mown ground and formed into continuous piles or "winrows," stretching the length of the field. These rows were converted into small heaps – "smallcocks" in Miramichi and Avalon, "handshakins" or "coils" in Peterborough – from 3 to 5 feet in diameter at the base. In the Avalon these cocks were merged next day into larger "save-cocks" out in the meadow. The field cocks, up to 8 feet in diameter and 8 feet high, were secured with hay-ropes and left for several days before being hauled into the yard. Oldtimers insisted that hay would "soak" or "make" in a field cock and believed that if not well dried hay would burn in the large barnyard stack. A true test of its state of dryness was its degree of "crackle." Field cocks were sometimes made in Miramichi but in Peterborough hay was taken in from the "handshakins" directly to the barnyard.[10]

In all three areas some of the hay was stored outside in the barnyard. Great care was taken with the construction of this final hay-heap. A foundation of branches and straw and a surrounding boundary of stone were first laid. In the centre of this circle, sometimes close to 20 feet in diameter, stood a long pole which guided the stackmaker. This latter feature was not used in the Avalon. The stack was usually egg-shaped: from the base it broadened slightly towards the middle and tapered gradually to a peak on top. "If you want a good stack you must make it the shape of an egg," was the oldtimers' advice in Barnaby. Barnyard stacks were covered with wild grass and secured with hay-ropes weighted down with stones or logs. In the Avalon, fish nets were frequently used. In Peterborough and to a lesser extent in Miramichi a rectangular hay-heap or "reek" was sometimes built. Varying in size, its shape resembled the house and barn that stood close by. It was covered and secured with the same materials as the circular haystack.

Apart from rakes, the tools of the hay field – scythes, grasshooks, forks – were usually imported, but the helves or shafts of these tools – scythes excepted – were often replaced with local timber, such as juniper or, in the Avalon, mountain ash. In all areas the scythe shaft or "tree" was "hooped," curving around the mower's body so as not to impede his swing. Two short wooden hand-grips were fixed to ferrules about 2 feet apart and towards the centre of the shaft and could be adjusted to suit the mower. Another ferrule was fastened around the head of the helve and the 3- to 4-foot and slightly curving steel blade was attached to it. The angle of blade and helve was determined by holding the scythe out from the body, swinging the left foot forward and adjusting the

---

10 If the weather was hot and dry, the hay was carted in two days after cutting (Samuel Strickland, *Twenty-Seven Years in Canada West,* p. 35).

blade – there were 4 holes in the ferrule for this purpose – until the top of the blade touched the top of the left foot. If a scythe was not properly adjusted, it made cutting extremely difficult. The grasshook was a far simpler implement comprising a 2- to 3-foot smooth-edged curving steel blade spiked into a short wooden handle.

Two-pronged wooden forks, fashioned out of a single timber, were used in both Avalon and Miramichi, but the two-pronged or two-tine steel hayforks – "pikes" in the Avalon – were also used. A three-tine fork was more common in Peterborough and by the end of the last century had largely displaced the two-tine type in Miramichi. But in the Avalon and Miramichi hayrakes were homemade. About a dozen birch or juniper pins were driven through a two-foot long puncheon stave and a handle was attached to the stave at right angles to the pins; 2 or 3 *gads* were attached to one side of the stave and were passed concentrically through the wooden handle and jointed on the other side of the stave. A hayrake factory was established in Peterborough before 1840 and produced up to 20,000 rakes annually.[11] These rakes probably replaced homemade implements at an early date in the Peterborough area. Horse-drawn hayrakes and mowing machines had displaced hand tools in the Peterborough hayfields by 1880, in Miramichi by 1900, and in Freshwater by 1920. Hand tools still predominate in the other Avalon study areas.

Grain
Grain was cut in September. Initially the toothed sickle or the smooth-edged reaphook was used in all areas but as the area under grain increased the scythe replaced these older tools. Cutting with the sickle or reaphook was an extremely arduous task. Bending or kneeling, the reaper held the straw in one hand and drew the sickle towards him in a sawing action with the other, shearing the straw close to the ground. Each "cut" or "bunch" was placed across a prepared straw band and three to four cuts formed a sheaf. Reaping required considerable skill; in the settlements north of St John's it was asserted that "you must cut yourself three times before you are a reaper."

The sickle or reaphook enjoyed a longer life in the grain fields than did the grasshook in the meadows. The sweeping or slashing action of the scythe caused dead-ripe grain to shed, and often broke the straw. On stony arable ground the sharp delicate tip of the scythe was often blunted or broken and the straw could not be cut as low as with the sickle. Moreover, straw flattened by wind or rain could not be cut easily with a scythe. Despite these disadvantages, the scythe was by far the dominant grain cutting implement in all study areas by the end of the nineteenth century.

11 Poole, *Peterborough,* pp. 101-102.

After 1850 the cradle was introduced in Peterborough.[12] This comprised a 30-inch wooden rod set perpendicular to the sned at its head with 4 wooden fingers attached to this standard and running parallel to the blade. Straw was collected more efficiently with the cradle, and the blade was extended to expedite cutting. Instead of a wooden cradle a strip of cloth, called a "bow," was used in Miramichi, and the task of cutting was referred to as "bowing." By 1890 the horse-drawn combine harvester had reached Peterborough and was introduced to Miramichi by 1900, where it quickly replaced the old hand-operated implements. Neither the cradle nor the combine harvester ever reached the Avalon.

Throughout the nineteenth century grain was often harvested communally. Both men and women could operate the sickle, but only men worked the scythe and the task of binding ("bunching" in the Avalon, "bundling" in Miramichi) was performed mainly by women and children. Two or three families were often seen in a field together. The grain was first cut into "swarths" and the sheaves were erected into "stooks." Eight sheaves, 4 on either side, formed the character-istic Avalon or Miramichi stook, but the "long stook" of Peterborough had as many as 12 sheaves. Head sheaves were not normally used but sometimes the bar-ley "shocks" in Peterborough were covered with a single sheaf to protect the seed from the weather. In the Avalon, field stacks were made to give the grain time to season properly. Barnyard grain stacks were rare, but straw stacks were placed out in the barnyard after the threshing.

Flailing was the common method of threshing in all study areas but there was considerable diversity of flail forms and techniques of threshing. North of St John's this task was rarely undertaken until the first frost appeared. The farmer erected a board platform from 7-10 feet square out in the yard and drove wooden pegs around the perimeter to keep the boards secure. Beneath the wooden platform he spread a linen sheet or piece of schooner sail or canvas. Four to 8 sheaves were taken from the barn and placed, untied, in 2 rows along the platform, with the seeded heads overlapping in the middle. Two men would then stand at opposite sides of the platform and strike the grain alternately with their flails, slowly advancing and then retreating as they struck, so that each man covered the entire row of sheaves. The flail "striker" was swung in a wide arc over the head of the thresher and descended at an oblique angle, knocking the seed from the straw. After a few minutes striking, the straw was shaken out with a fork, and the threshers resumed with short, quick strokes descending directly on the straw and grain. When satisfied that the seed had been completely separated the flailers forked the straw back into the barn and the seed or chaff was stored in a puncheon or sack. On frosty days the wooden platform was often dispensed with, and the sheet was placed on the hard ground. In Logy Bay,

12 The first cradle in Douro appeared in 1857. Towns, "Early Life in Douro," 1925.

Outer and Middle Cove the sounds of the flail finally died with the decline of grain cultivation in the 1930s. In Freshwater although flails are still to be seen in tool sheds, none of the older people remember flailing. The only form of threshing recalled is "lashing" — beating the sheaf over a hard wooden object, such as a small wooden block or the rim of a barrel or puncheon. The grain was dislodged and fell into the barrel or onto a sheet on the floor. Unlike flailing, lashing did not crush the grain. It could be used for seed and the lashing technique was sometimes used instead of flailing when seeds were required for spring sowing. Within living memory Freshwater farmers generally cut their oats green, for fodder.

Along the Cape Shore the flail was unknown. A sheet was placed on the ground in St Brides and Cuslett and an upturned *kish* or woven basket placed on top. The thresher lashed the sheaf over the bottom of the basket and the dislodged seed fell through to the cloth below. In nearby Angel's Cove threshing was performed in the barn. A piece of sail cloth was placed on the ground and a block of wood on top. The thresher then placed the sheaf on top of the wood, its seeded section protruding over the edge. He held the sheaf with one hand and with the other beat the seed off with a short stick. In neighbouring Patrick's Cove a man knelt on the sheaf leaving both hands free to strike off the grain with sticks. Several informants in Branch stated that the seed was pulled off the straw by hand. In Lear's Cove 2 sticks, 5 feet long, were crossed and nailed near the butts to form a frame for the sheaves. The sheaves were placed in the "V" and secured by tightening the sticks with a rope drawn around both ends. This pincers was then suspended from the barn ceiling and the oats dislodged with a stick. As in the St John's settlements threshing disappeared in the present century when ripened oats were no longer harvested.

Within living memory stick threshing and lashing were performed only in emergencies in Miramichi. Flailing was the dominant threshing technique during most of the nineteenth century, and survived on some farms well into the present century. The Irish usually threshed their grain on the boarded floor between the barn "mows." Buckwheat was frequently threshed outdoors on a wooden platform similar to that used in St John's. Indoors and outdoors, the sheaves were laid out as in St John's but folk memory recalls only one thresher occupying the barn floor at a time. Outdoors, as many as four men threshed simultaneously. Sometimes the sheaves were thrown from the cart or from the "mow" on to the floor and the thresher would strike them in mid-air with his flail, striking them again after they landed on the boards.

Despite the introduction of an American mechanical thresher to Fredericton in 1827 "to serve as a pattern for New Brunswick mechanics,"[13] the "horsepower" or "beater" was not introduced to Barnaby until the last quarter of the

13 *The Mercury,* Newcastle, June 17, 1827.

nineteenth century. Until the present century, moreover, the mechanical thresher did not always arrive on time and the farmer sometimes threshed half his grain by flail. Flailing was an acknowledged skill among the Miramichi-Irish in the last century and some of the younger men in Barnaby migrated seasonally to Prince Edward Island to thresh in the barnyards there.

Horse-operated threshing machines were introduced earlier to Peterborough and few informants there have ever used the flail for threshing grain. Threshing machines were manufactured at Peterborough in the 1860s,[14] but they had been introduced to the area well before that date. One Irish immigrant who worked in Michigan brought back to Douro plans of a thresher which he had seen there, and had the model manufactured at the local foundry.[15] William Moher owned a "mill" in 1859 and threshed for 40 of his Irish neighbors in Douro that year.[16]

Despite the predominance of the mechanical thresher the flail was used on most farms in living memory. Some farmers might have to wait until Christmas before getting their grain threshed mechanically and used the flail to supply grain in the interim. Flailing was done on the threshing floor of the barn as in Miramichi. At the end of the last century the Peterborough-Irish used the flail extensively for threshing peas, and for this reason many flails are still to be seen in the area. The flail comprised two slender sticks fastened together by a flexible joint or link. It was homemade and never appeared in the lists of implements offered for sale in stores. There was considerable diversity of form even within individual study areas. North of St John's the handle was about an inch in diameter and 3 to 5 feet long. It was often made out of a soft wood such as spruce. The "thresher" or "striker" was usually heavier and shorter and was fashioned out of birch, ironwood, or some other hardwood. Sometimes both timbers were of the same wood and were similar in size, no distinction being made between helve and striker.

Flail types can be classified by the techniques of joining the two timbers. Figure 20A illustrates the dominant jointing technique north of St John's. The farmer cut two strips of leather about 14 inches long and an inch wide, either from one of the high "Logan" boots fashionable in the last century, or pieces of horse or pig skin, and doubled one strip over the end of each stick, leaving a small space or "eye" between the head of each flail stick and the leather loop. The loops were interlocked and a distance of 6 inches separated the sticks at the joint. The leather was secured to the timber in two ways: (a) a number of nails or tacks were driven through leather and timber and bent on the other side; (b) hemp was woven around the leather and timber, and secured by a half hitch

14 Poole, *Peterborough,* pp. 101-102.
15 Towns, "Early Life in Douro," 1925.
16 William Moher Diaries. He began threshing on August 30th and continued until Christmas.

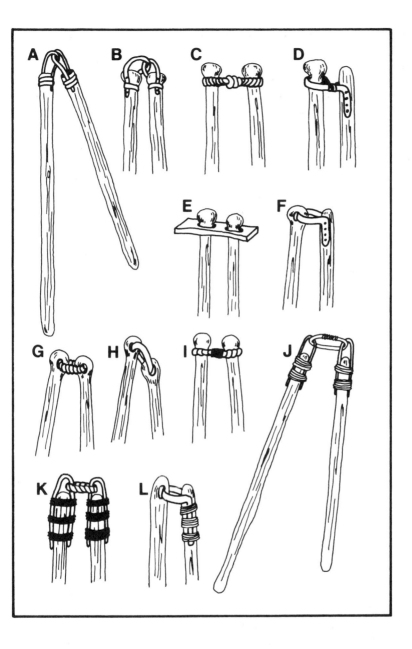

Figure 20
Flails: A, B — St John's. C, D — Miramichi. E, F, G — Peterborough. Ireland: H, L — north. I — southwest. J, K — southeast.

every few rotations. The latter technique was considered superior, because nails often caused the wooden members to crack when striking. Sometimes nails and hemp were combined to strengthen the jointing. A variation of this jointing style involved cutting two grooves about two inches apart, close to the head of each helve and tying the leather strip into these grooves (Fig. 20B). The leather cap could then rotate on the head of the stick without slipping off, and the handle did not twist in the thresher's hands as the flail was swung about. In one example in Outer Cove the farmer attached an iron swivel to the wooden helve instead of a grooved jointing.

In Miramichi a strip of "greenhide," one-quarter inch thick and varying in length, was passed around two grooves, one in the handle, the other in the striker, about two inches from the end of both sticks (Fig. 20C). The knob at each end of the sticks ensured that the leather did not slip off when striking, yet both timbers could rotate in their loops, easing the strain on the hands of the thresher. Various knotting techniques were adopted but the leather tie always remained a single continuous piece and the basic principle of a double loop lying in grooves remained unaltered. A free rotation of the striker in its loop is unnecessary, however, and in some cases the leather was attached to the striker with nails, as in the Avalon (Fig. 20D). Usually the flail handle was 5 feet long, and the striker about 3 feet. Yellow birch and rock maple made good strikers, while ash and beech were commonly used as handles.

Rock elm, white ash, maple, birch, and oak were all used for Peterborough flails, but no distinction was made between the wood used in handle and striker. The grooved joint of Miramichi flails reappeared in Peterborough, only the leather strip was wider and shorter and it was slit close to both ends and drawn over the knob into the grooves (Fig. 20E). To keep the leather in place, the slits were sewn on each side of the grooves.

A second type of jointing, less common among the southern Irish of Peterborough, was the "hole" style, of which four subtypes occurred. A hole was bored through the striker, near the top, and threaded with a leather strip which was (a) secured to the handle with either nails, tacks, staples, or hemp (Fig. 20F); (b) passed through a hole in the handle and was similarly secured (Fig. 20G); (c) bound to a wooden swivel fitted over the flail handle, or (d) tied around a groove cut two inches below the head of the handle. No rotation of the striker about the handle was possible in any of these subtypes. The joint or "souple" twisted and straightened as the flail was swung and the grip on the handle had to be relaxed to allow it to revolve in the thresher's hands. These flails usually required a new piece of leather each season.

In all study areas the Irish winnowed their grain by either dumping it on a sheet outdoors and tossing into the air with a shovel or a bucket, or by holding the bucket aloft and allowing the grain to fall out gradually. In both cases, the breeze blew the chaff away while the grain fell onto the ground sheet.

Sometimes a shallow basket made out of hide, with an ash rim, was perforated like a sieve and the grain and chaff were tossed into the air; only the grain would fall back through the sieve onto the sheet. In both Peterborough and Miramichi winnowing was usually performed in the threshing floor of the barn, benefiting from a strong breeze through the open double doors.

The disappearance of this form of winnowing was closely connected with the decline of flailing in all three areas. In Peterborough fanning mills became common at the same time as the mechanical thresher (in the second half of the last century), although a fanning mill was used in Downeyville in the 1840s.[17] Towards the end of the nineteenth century, winnowing with a bucket or shovel was adopted only in emergencies in either Peterborough and Miramichi, but in the Avalon it remained the only technique used.

Vegetables

Potatoes were dug in October. Up until the end of the nineteenth century the spade was used by most settlers in Miramichi and the Avalon but was gradually replaced by a four-pronged fork or shovel. In Peterborough only the fork is remembered and some farmers were using the plough to dig potatoes before the end of the century. While the plough was also introduced to Miramichi at this time, and was used in Freshwater to unearth the potatoes early in this century, it was not used in the settlements north of St John's for digging potatoes until very recently. Potatoes, when dug, were either transported to the barnyard and stored in a root cellar or pitted outside in long, shallow troughs. In the latter case a heavy covering of potato stalks, straw or hay, and clay was needed to protect them from winter weather. Turnips and cabbages, the last crops to be harvested, were pulled by hand and were stored outdoors in pits or kept in a root cellar.

METHODS OF HAULING

According to local tradition the immigrants themselves did a great deal of carrying over the rough terrain of the clearings in pioneer times. Hand-barrows comprising two poles and a centrally placed wooden platform were used within living memory for haulage both in the Avalon and Miramichi. Two men were required to carry a single barrow. Hay and other crops were transported down steep slopes or across wet land with these implements. In the Avalon hay cocks were also "swept in" on the ground to the yard by means of a long rope tied around the base of a stack. The rope was secured to one side of the horse's harness and the horse then driven around the field cock with the rope left "streelin" on the ground. After the rope tightened around the base of the cock the loose end was attached to the harness and the cock dragged over the ground.

17 Ontario, Will of George O'Connell, 1848 (Private MSS in Emily Township).

The hamper was one of the first implements of transport adopted in the Avalon. A forked branch or crutch was fitted across the horse's back, with straw padding underneath. On to this primitive straddle two *kishes* or baskets were hooked, one to each side of the horse. Along the Cape Shore, animal manure, fish offal, kelp, potatoes, and other farm crops were transported in these baskets. The manure *kishes* sometimes had a hinged bottom or "trip" which allowed the load to be dropped directly to the ground. North of St John's canvas bags were used and in the early days, according to local folk tradition, grain, fish, potatoes, and even building stones were transported to St John's in this manner.

Instead of placing the *kish* on the horse's back, it was more frequently fitted onto a wheelless sled or "streel-car" specially designed for rough terrain. Until the 1870s, and in some of the more inaccessible Cape Shore outports such as Point Lance and Golden Bay well into the present century, this was the dominant means of transporting hay and other produce. Two strong parallel poles or shafts were set about 3 feet apart and connected at one end by 3 or 4 cross-timbers or "cleats" to form the platform on which the *kish* was placed. At this end both poles curved slightly upwards to facilitate sliding or "streelin" over the ground (Fig. 21A). The poles acted as shafts and runners and the curved ends or "knees" were reinforced with hardwood blocks. When used for carrying hay a light timber frame was built around the platform or, alternatively, the *kish* was retained and was secured on the platform by 4 stout uprights. Outside the Cape Shore there is no record of this implement.

The *kish* was invariably homemade. Depending on the size or shape required, 40 to 80 withes were stuck into the ground 2 to 3 inches apart, forming a square, or a circle. Working from the ground up, more flexible rods were then "riddled" or woven horizontally into this frame. Once the sides had been built the standards were bent over and tied in the centre to form a framework for the bottom of the *kish*. After the bottom section was woven the *kish* was turned over and a rim or hoop, comprising several long rods tightly intertwined, was mounted over the standards previously rooted in the ground. This was considered the most difficult part of the operation. The heavy rim kept the *kish* secure and the vertical standards usually projected above the rim like short, sharp spikes.

An even more primitive wheelless vehicle was used by the Peterborough-Irish during the pioneer stage. A small tree with a branch or crutched top was cut; the long butt was used as a shaft, yoked between two oxen, and one or two timbers were nailed to the forked members to form a crude platform.[18] A box was placed on the platform and was supported behind by two uprights mortised into the forked timbers (Fig. 21B).

18 Towns, "Early Life in Douro," 1925.

In all study areas the flat slide was used. In the Avalon the settler cut a spruce pole around 12 feet in length and curving slightly at one end, and "ripped" or split to form the two runners for the slide or catamaran. Two stanchions, 12 inches high, were mortised into each runner about 8 feet apart and each stanchion was supported by two triangular blocks of timber called "knees." The runners were set about 3 feet apart and linked by two parallel cross-timbers or bars resting on the stanchions, on to which planks were sometimes placed parallel to the runners to complete the platform. Each runner was shod from nose to tail with a strip of metal. The Peterborough "jumper" and Miramichi "jump-sled" or "drag-sled" were similar to the Avalon slide (Fig. 21C). Instead of stanchions an extra pole was placed on top of each runner to the "jumper" and "jump-sled" to give the crossbars that formed the platform ample clearance over rough ground. In all three areas the slides were drawn by a horse. Two holes were bored close to the tip of the noses of the runners and a pole, iron bar or chain inserted, on to which the swing was attached. The slide or sled was an extremely versatile vehicle and is still used for transporting farm produce, wood, and manure in the Avalon and Miramichi.[19]

Local tradition asserts that many families did not work wheeled vehicles on the Cape Shore until the 1870s, when two-wheeled carts became widespread, but carts were used in the other study areas in the first decades of settlement. Initially wheels were homemade. Two hardwood hubs some 8 inches long and the same diameter were bored and fitted with metal or steel cups to take the iron or steel spikes of the axle-tree. On the Cape Shore triangular pieces of spruce, fir, or "dale" (hardwood from shipwrecks) curved on their short sides were mortised ("joggled") into the hub ("nabel") and an iron or hardwood ("green-heart") rim secured the blocks. When heated the iron band expanded and easily encircled the blocks. Sometimes the blocks were overlapped to a thickness of 6 inches. Block wheels are not recalled near St John's but blocks 50 inches in diameter and 8 inches wide were cut in Peterborough and Miramichi and fitted with a maple hub and iron band to form a solid wheel. Even on the Cape Shore block wheels had virtually vanished by the end of the century in favour of locally made spoke wheels. Six slightly curving pieces of timber – felloes – were trimmed and 12 spokes were mortised into hub and felloes, two spokes per felloe, and secured with an iron rim. Elsewhere spoke wheels were normally manufactured by a wheelwright.

In all areas the body of the cart was traditionally homemade. Two 15 to 18-foot poles were trimmed and placed on top of the 4-foot axle-tree, one at each end, to form the shafts. Four to 6 cross-timbers were mortised into the

19 Slides and catamarans were mentioned in farm auctions near St John's early in the nineteenth century (*Royal Gazette,* St John's, 1810-25). Ox and horse sleds were used in the 1820's in Miramichi (*The Mercury,* Newcastle, July 29, 1828).

shafts, each about a foot apart. Two boards were placed on top of the cross-bar, parallel to the shafts. The shafts projected inwards around the shoulders of the horse. Near St John's this vehicle was called a "long cart," a "long car" or "dray-car" on the Cape Shore, a "truck" in Miramichi, and a "wagon" in Peterborough. In the two latter areas this cart has 4 wheels (Fig. 21D), but was two-wheeled in Miramichi up to the end of the last century. It was used in all areas to haul hay, grain, or wood. Another type of cart had a much shorter platform enclosed by a front and tailboard, and was two-wheeled (Fig. 21E). The shafts of this box-cart were sometimes cut close to the axle-tree so that the body could be tipped without raising the front shafts. In all areas this small cart was used for hauling vegetables and manure on the farm.

Coming from an almost treeless terrain in the homeland the Irish immigrants had little knowledge of the techniques and tools of woodland clearing. With the exception of the *grafán* and the technique of burning the refuse of freshly cleared land before cultivation, there were no homeland precedents for the land-clearing implements or methods adopted by the Irish in the New World. In northeastern North America trees were usually either ringed and left to rot or blow over, or cut down with an axe, leaving only the stumps in the ground; in some cases, however, small trees were pulled up directly by the roots. The fact that the Irish immigrants' method of using an axe or hatchet and leaving the stumps in the ground was indistinguishable from that of other, earlier settlers clearly points to cultural borrowing. Imitation was made easier in Peterborough through government patronage. The Irish were given axes and other land-clearing tools and told how to use them. Adjustment to a new physical environment was sometimes slowly and painfully made. In Ennismore, for example, the immigrants tried without success to burn the trees as soon as they had cut them down.[20]

Some of the Irish in Miramichi worked for a spell in the lumber camps or as labourers on established farms before they cleared their own lots. Knowledge of local land-clearing techniques could be quickly learned and transmitted to those other Irish who settled directly on the land. Robert Young of Miramichi, who hired Irish labourers to clear his farm, stated that he had known immigrants "who had never previously touched an axe became first-rate choppers in three months."[21]

20 Poole, *Peterborough,* p. 187.
21 Great Britain, Parliament, *Appendix Colonel Cockburn's Instructions and Reports on Emigration* (in National Archives, Ottawa), Paper 148, London, 1828, p. 35. Samuel Strickland held a different view of his Irish neighbours in Peterborough, maintaining that they could neither log, chop, nor fence (*Twenty-Seven Years in Canada West,* p. 101).

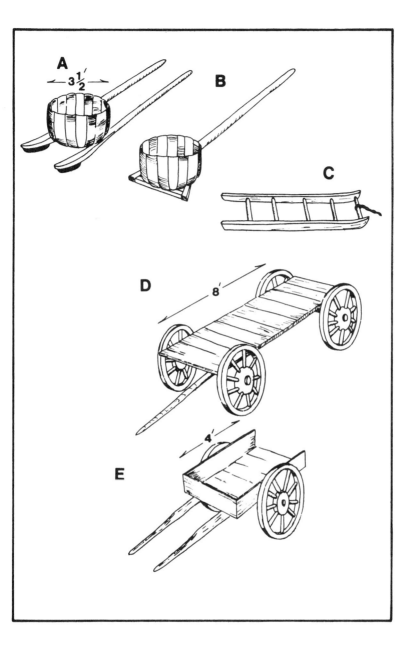

Figure 21
Vehicles: A — Streel-car and *kish*, Cape Shore. B — Peterborough sled. C — New
World sled. D — Four-wheel wagon, Peterborough. E — New World box-cart.

105

Whereas in Peterborough and Miramichi the Irish settled fairly close to farmers familiar with the techniques of clearing, the immigrants in the Avalon, and especially along the Cape Shore, had little access to this frontier heritage. It is perhaps partly because of this cultural isolation that the heavy broad axe, symbol of the pioneer farmer or backwoodsman in northeastern North America, was never used in the Avalon. It can also be argued that the smaller axe or hatchet was better adapted to the task of cutting the stunted trees of the Avalon. Such a tool would have been inadequate in the forests of Peterborough or Miramichi.

Although the communal spirit of the logging or other "bees" suited the gregarious or sociable character of the Irish, and local co-operation was a major characteristic of Irish peasant life, it cannot be regarded as simply an Irish transfer. Labour-pooling was an economic necessity in the backwoods, where labour was costly, and the "bee" or "frolic" flourished on the frontier before the coming of the Irish. The existence of a more reciprocal co-operative tradition in Peterborough is perhaps partly an expression of the highly dispersed and socially diffuse pattern of settlement there. The conviviality of a clearing "bee" was a welcome relief from the monotonous routine and lonely existence on the isolated backwoods farm. But the pressure to clear land rapidly also stimulated co-operation. In Ireland, where the pooling of labour was called *cooring,* the work-group or *meitheal* was normally recruited or based on ties of kinship; by contrast, the Peterborough "bees" were composed of basically non-kin and non-formalized neighbourhood groups. Indeed, in the absence of kin ties on the frontier, mutual aid was a useful means of gaining social rapport among new neighbours. Where fishing and farming were combined in the Avalon, joint activity amongst neighbouring kin was normal, but such co-operation was different to the Peterborough "bee" which was a spontaneous gathering of a large number of neighbours and had less durable contractual ties.

The first fence forms, crudely constructed with materials cleared off the land, were an obvious expedient in the backwoods situation, but the subsequent fences in all study areas had ample antecedents either in the New World or in the homeland. Wooden fences were rare in early nineteenth century Ireland but the forms found in Peterborough and Miramichi had local antecedents and were, moreover, widespread in the wooded areas of eastern North America in the eighteenth century. The snake, worm, or zigzag fence-type existed in late seventeenth century New England,[22] and two centuries later was the dominant style in

22 H.F. Raup, "The Fence in the Cultural Landscape," *Western Folklore* 6 (1947): 1-7. Raup suggested the snake fence was either of Indian provenance or was an early development in New England or the Middle Colonies. The snake fence has been reported from Tirol and Kniffen suggests a European origin for the type in America (Fred Kniffen, "Folk Housing: Key to Diffusion," *Annals Association American Geographers* 55 (1965):549-77.

America, especially in the more recently settled midwestern and far western states.[23] No doubt the type was transferred to Upper Canada by American Loyalists and spread with the frontier to the Peterborough region. Snake fences, although wasteful of both wood and space, required little labour and were adapted to frontier settlement in well-wooded areas. By contrast the traditional straight-log fence in Miramichi required considerable labour to construct; although probably related to the post-and-rail type that normally succeeded the snake fence in New England, the use of isolated wooden blocks and pairs of mortised posts may be a local innovation. In New England and Quebec, as in the Avalon, posts were usually embedded in the soil. In the former area the posts were bored and the rails pushed through but in Quebec the vertical posts were set in pairs, as in Miramichi, and strips of wood used to suspend the long narrow split rails between the paired posts.[24] In the Avalon, by contrast, a single post was used and the "longers" tied with *gads*. *Gad* is a Gaelic term and *gads* were widely used for tying in Ireland, but the "stake and longer" fence appears to be a Newfoundland creation. Wattled or "wave" fences existed in Ireland in the seventeenth century and the concept of interlacing pliable rods was popular in Irish vernacular architecture early in the nineteenth century. The "wave" or "riddlin" fences of the Avalon may be an adaptation of this distinctive technique or may have developed independently in the study areas.

There are definite homeland antecedents for the stone walls found in all three areas of the New World. The art of drywalling in Ireland goes back to prehistoric times but most of the contemporary walls were built during the century predating the migrations. Three types of wall were common: (a) walls only a single stone in width, found in areas where stony moraines and drift boulders occur; (b) neatly built field walls with a base of small stones, topped off with large boulders; (c) a broad, double wall containing a neatly built outer skin and a middle filled with small stones. The last type was reproduced in the New World.

Double stone walls are believed to be the oldest type and are frequently found around old house clusters, enclosing private gardens.[25] Single-stone walls usually enclosed former openfields, away from the cluster, while the carefully built wall with a heavy superstructure was a landlord introduction, confined chiefly to demesnes. Walls were restricted, in both the homeland and New World, to areas of stony soils. In Miramichi and especially Peterborough, however, stone walls were comparatively rare, even where the land was stony. Building with stone was a time-consuming and back-breaking task. Wood was the first

---

23 Mamie Meredith, "The Nomenclature of American Pioneer Fences," *Southern Folklore Quarterly* 15 (1951): 109-51. Because of its numerical dominance in the nineteenth century, the snake fence was regarded as the national type.

24 Wilbur Zelinsky, "Walls and Fences," *Landscape* 8 (1959): 14-20.

25 Sigurd Erixon, "The Age of Enclosures and Its Older Traditions," *Folklife* 4 (1966): 56-63.

material cleared off the land and, as noted, was ideal for fencing on the frontier. Stones unearthed with cultivation were carelessly thrown along the base of wooden fences, or piled over a rock or a large stump in the field. Labour was much too valuable to invest in practices such as walling. Time could be more profitably spent clearing land for crops. However, the stone wall was more durable than timber fences, but this does not explain its occurrence even on the most stony soils. In the final analysis aesthetic preferences and the force of cultural tradition appear to be the main factor in the building of stone fences in the study areas.

A ditch of sod and stone, the characteristic fence type of the homeland, was introduced to the New World by only a handful of immigrants. Like the stone wall, its construction required immense toil, and sods were better used in the fields. Improving landlords introduced the pleated hedgerow to the clayey lowlands of Ireland and some peasants incorporated these into the native sod ditches; neither this hybrid type, nor the hedgerow proper, was reproduced in the New World.

Although the spade was the dominant cultivation implement of the peasantry in pre-migration Ireland,[26] ploughs were used on larger farms and had a continuous history since early Celtic times. By the early nineteenth century the more primitive type, frequently consisting of a log shod with iron and attached to a crooked stick, was replaced by improved wooden ploughs, with mouldboard and coulter, prototypes of the iron ploughs that spread throughout the country later in the century.[27] Although light wooden homemade ploughs were used in both Peterborough and Miramichi, there is not enough evidence about them to allow a comparison with homeland types. Local Irish immigrant blacksmiths also manufactured ploughs but factory-produced ploughs were available in all three study areas from the beginnings of settlement. In both Peterborough and Miramichi the frontier technique of ploughing with oxen was adopted, but in the Avalon only the horse was used. The absence of ploughs along the Cape Shore and near St John's illustrates their unimportance in the cultural baggage of the Irish immigrants. To be sure, only an acre or so of ground was cultivated each year on the Cape Shore, but ploughs could have been advantageously used on the alluvial flats. In Freshwater, however, some Irish superstitions related to ploughing were transferred, suggesting the use of ploughs since the first generation of settlers.

26 Caoimhín Ó' Danachair, "The Use of the Spade in Ireland," in Alan Gailey and Alexander Fenton (eds.), *The Spade in Northern and Atlantic Europe* (Belfast: Queen's University Press, 1970), pp. 49-56. Ploughs were expensive but were also considered by the peasants as extremely wasteful implements of cultivation.
27 E. Estyn Evans, *Irish Folk Ways* (London: Routledge & Kegan Paul, 1957), pp. 130-31.

The spade was the most ubiquitous of peasant Irish cultivation implements. Because of its long history and the fact that it was locally made, a rich diversity of styles existed in the nineteenth century. Underlying this diversity were two basic types: (a) the one-sided spades of the south and west (Fig. 19G, H, I) and (b) the two-sided spade of the north and east (Fig. 19J). Since the early nineteenth century the latter type has spread slowly southwards, displacing the older one-sided spade, or producing hybridized forms. But even today most of the farmers in the south and southwest employ only the one-sided spade.[28]

With some minor modifications, the southern spade (Fig. 19H) was reproduced in the Avalon and Miramichi. In the homeland the long narrow blade was either wider towards the centre, or splayed with the mouth sometimes concave or fishtailed. Because the New World spades are old and work-worn, it is difficult to determine the original shape of the mouth, but the sides of the blade were normally parallel. In every other detail the southern Irish spade was identical to the Avalon and Miramichi type. The Peterborough Irish brought spades with them, and these almost certainly were one-sided, but they did not endure. Some of the immigrants received spades from the government on arrival, but the main reason for change appears to be that the two-sided spade of the Ulster-Scots, Scots, and English around Peterborough predominated and gradually spread through the Irish settlements. This spade type, available in the stores, was similar to the short-shafted, T-handled, two-sided spade of northern Ireland.

Although associated mainly with potato cultivation at the time of the migrations, ridges or "lazy-beds" existed long before the potato was introduced and were used for all root and grain crops throughout the country. The art of ridgemaking is practiced today only in western Ireland but in the early nineteenth century it was the dominant form of cultivation even in the southeast. Although ridges 18 feet wide have been recorded, ridge and furrow were normally no more than one "spade" (spade length) wide, or less than 5 feet, and the spade was the main implement of ridge making. The method of making "lazy-beds" in the New World was identical to Ireland, but the ridges of the New World were narrower.

There were three methods of planting potatoes on ridges in Ireland. Potato sets were left on top of the ridge in all areas but in the midlands a special wooden dibber, known as a *steeveen, gugger,* or *kibbin,* resembling a hand-rake, was used by the women to make holes in the ridge for the potato sets. In the south the narrow spade was thrust into the heart of the ridge and the sets were dropped in behind the blade as it was levered forward. This Munster mode of

28 For distribution and diffusion of spade types in Ireland see Evans, *Irish Folk Ways,* pp. 130-31; Caoimhín Ó'Danachair, "The Spade in Ireland," *Béaloideas* 31 (1963): 98-114; Alan Gailey, "The Typology of the Irish Spade," in Gailey and Fenton, *The Spade,* pp. 35-48.

planting "with the back of the spade" was reproduced in all three study areas, but was never as popular as leaving the seeds in the ridges.

The absence of the Munster spade and the "lazy-bed" in Peterborough is not easily explained. To be sure, the government gave the immigrants some spades, on arrival, which were probably of the improved, two-sided variety. They were also given hoes for planting potatoes, and advised not to use the spade.[29] However, other Irish immigrants arriving later did not, according to tradition, retain the one-sided spade or "lazy-bed" technique. It is likely that the two-sided spade was used widely, probably exclusively, by the English, Scots, and Ulster-Scots and that the southern Irish minority conformed to the popular pattern, buying this type in the store. Moreover, the spade was needed less in Peterborough because the pattern of crop rotation there meant that there was little ley land to cultivate. The early introduction of the plough also hastened the decline of the spade as a cultivation tool. By contrast, the Irish in the Avalon used the spade for cutting sods for building purposes as well as for ridge-making and digging potatoes. Sods were not used for construction in Miramichi and potatoes were not usually sown on ley ground; consequently the spade was not as important a work tool by the end of the last century as it was in the Avalon. Moreover Munster spade blades were exported to St John's and probably were also available in the stores in Miramichi and this was an important factor in their survival in both areas.

Although functionally interconnected initially, the "lazy-bed" outlasted the spade at least in the Avalon. In the homeland, where land was scarce and expensive, the "lazy-bed" technique according to Irish peasant opinion yielded one-third more potatoes per acre than did plough cultivation. This intensive form of cultivation appears almost anachronistic in the New World, where land was cheap and labour expensive. Its introduction and retention in the Avalon can be partially explained by the cost of ploughs, the continual cultivation of ley, and the small area of arable, but in both Avalon and Miramichi cultural preferences or tradition appear to be an important factor. Lazy-beds were also made with ploughs in Ireland, at least on large farms, but the frontier hilling technique was less labour-intensive and better adapted to arable (as opposed to ley) ground and so became ubiquitous in Peterborough and popular in Miramichi in the nineteenth century.

Another distinctive Munster tool, the *grafán*, was introduced to all study areas and is still the major cultivation tool on the Cape Shore. Although at

29 Great Britain, Colonial Office Correspondence, Upper Canada (MSS in National Archives, Ottawa), Series Q, May 17, 1823. Peter Robinson to William Horton: "For cultivating newly cleared land and planting Indian corn and potatoes, a strong hoe is preferable to a spade and is the principal implement that will be required initially; each family should have at least two."

present restricted to the far southwest of Ireland it was widely used in south-eastern Ireland before the migrations.[30] As well as a farming and digging tool, the *grafán* was used in the Avalon for mixing compost, "raising" bog, cutting sods after the plough (in Freshwater), and for land clearing.

In the more extensive arable agriculture of Miramichi and Peterborough the *grafán*, like the spade, became outmoded and it is significant that in the latter area there is no memory of its Gaelic name. It should be noted that this tool was widespread, not only in Atlantic Europe but in many parts of the New World, and was used near the study areas before the Irish came.

At the time of the migrations, grain was broadcast not only in the homeland but all over Europe and in the New World. The seed was normally carried in a basket or bag strapped around the shoulder. Before harrowing was introduced, the Irish in the homeland buried their seed in the ridges but this practice had virtually disappeared by the nineteenth century and there is no record of it in the New World. The Irish in Peterborough did bury their grain with hoes in the stump-littered fields where harrows could not be easily worked, but this tech-nique is less an example of cultural transfer than of frontier expediency. Little is known of traditional Irish harrows and it is likely that many Irish peasants relied on the *grafán* or improvised bush harrow to level the ridges, as on the Cape Shore. An improved rectangular harrow with a slightly tapered front was intro-duced in Scotland late in the eighteenth century and may have spread to Ireland; at any rate the St John's harrow resembles this type.[31] The triangular harrow used in Peterborough was known in western Europe in the middle ages, and survived in marginal areas there up to the nineteenth century. It was also found in many parts of colonial North America.[32]

Haymaking became popular in peasant Ireland only in the century prior to the migrations, with the introduction of timothy and clover by pastoral-minded landlords. Wild grasses had been used instead of winter feed. Hay was made or "saved" in 6 stages, the first 5 taking 3-4 days in fine weather.[33] Apart from Peterborough, where hay was often taken directly from the "coils" or

30 A.T. Lucas, "Paring and Burning in Ireland," in Nicholas Stephens and Robin E. Glasscock (eds.), *Irish Geographical Studies in Honour of E. Estyn Evans* (Belfast: Queen's University Press, 1970), pp. 99-147. It was used with the spade for sod cutting or paring and for cultivating probably since prehistoric times in Ireland and the West Country; as in the New World, the Irish *grafán* sometimes had a separate cutting edge.
31 Ian Whitaker, "The Harrow in Scotland," *Scottish Studies* 2 (1958): 149-65.
32 Henry Glassie, *Pattern in the Material Folk Culture of the Eastern United States*, University of Pennsylvania Monographs in Folklore and Folklife No. 1 (Philadelphia: University of Pennsylvania Press, 1969), pp. 200-203.
33 The practice of leaving hay out in field cocks to season was criticized by Arthur Young in the 1770's, who stated that the Irish were generally two months "making or marring their hay" (Young, *A Tour in Ireland 1776-1779*, vol. 2. [Shannon: Irish University Press, 1970] p. 246).

"handshakin's" — words of Ulster origin — to the yard, these 6 stages were repeated in the New World. The dry warm weather makes field cocking unnecessary in the New World, yet in the Avalon this anachronism was perceived only in the present century, by the third generation of settlers. Initially, the 4 stages of the Irish grain harvest — sheaf, stook, field-stack and yard-stack — were also practiced by some settlers, but generally the two latter stages were omitted. The final hay heap or grain stack in the barnyard was usually round, although hay "reeks" were built in Peterborough and Miramichi. Both styles were common in the homeland. Irish stacks in the "haggard" or "reek-yard" were more carefully made and were thatched, a tradition not recalled in the New World. Unlike Ireland, where mild winters permitted outside storing, much of the hay and grain in the study areas was stored in barns. Elaborate stacking took time, and the discomfort of collecting and transporting fodder from yard to barn in the bitterly cold winters of the New World discouraged stacking outdoors.

The tools of haymaking and harvesting were similar to those used in the homeland, but these tools were widely used not only elsewhere in Europe but in the New World. At the time of the migrations the toothed or serrated sickle dominated the homeland grain fields, but the heavier smooth-edged reaping hook was also used.[34] While the scythe was the dominant hay-cutting tool, it was not introduced into the grain harvest until the mid-nineteenth century, and like the plough was considered a wasteful implement when compared to the meticulous husbandry of the sickle. In the New World both sickle and reaphook were replicas of homeland farming but the Irish used a long, straight or "poled" scythe sned in the homeland and changed to a "hooped" sned in the New World.[35]

The displacement of the sickle by the scythe in the New World grain fields was far more rapid than in the homeland, even in the Avalon where the amount of grain grown per farm was less than in Ireland. Cutting by sickle was a far more labour-intensive technique than by cutting with the scythe although the scythe required more ancillary workers for linkage operations such as assembling and binding and "stooking" sheaves. In Ireland an over-supply of labour and a shortage of land prolonged the life of the sickle in the grain fields. Because conditions were the reverse in the New World it is surprising that the sickle was used at all, beyond those rough acres in the clearings where the scythe might be inoperative. To be sure, the scythe wasted more seed and straw, but unlike

34 E.J.T. Collins, "Harvest Technology and Labour Supply in Britain, 1790-1850," *Economic History Review* 22 (1969): 453-73.
35 Both "poled" and s-shaped sneds were common in England in the eighteenth century and the latter type was dominant in the New World when the Irish arrived (see E.J.T. Collins, "Labour Supply and Demand in European Agriculture, 1800-1880," in E.L. Jones and S.J. Woolf [eds.], *Agrarian Change in Economic Development: The Historical Problems* [London: Methuen, 1969], pp. 61-94).

Ireland this loss could be easily compensated by clearing more land and expanding the area under grain. This was the reaction, by and large, of the Peterborough-Irish, who relied on grain for a livelihood, but the retention of the sickle in Miramichi, for example, is in part related to aesthetic or cultural preferences derived from the homeland. The early demise of the sickle in the Avalon is partly related to the fact that oats were often cut green, for fodder, and as a crop was not distinguished from hay, which was invariably cut with the scythe.

Although elaborate cradles of wood and finely wrought iron were attached to the harvest scythes of southeastern Ireland, this occurred after the migrations and the Peterborough cradle was almost certainly a local borrowing. It was not introduced to the study area during the first two decades of Irish occupance, but was widespread in the older settled parts of Upper Canada. Its introduction to Peterborough and later to Miramichi was an important technological advance and reflects the degree of commercial grain cropping in these areas. Similarly, the introduction of home-drawn machines for cutting hay and grain and horse-drawn rakes reflected the growing commercialization of the farm, especially in Peterborough. Both hand-rakes and two-tine pitch-forks were similar to those of the homeland, but the three-tine hay-fork of Peterborough was yet another local borrowing.

The techniques of cutting hay and grain, and especially the division of labour in the fields, were transferred. Adult males cut hay with the scythe and women and children shook out the freshly sown grass and later made small hay heaps. In the harvest fields both men and women wielded the sickle, and the ancillary operations of binding and "stooking" were usually performed by both sexes. Despite the transfer of tools and techniques of the Irish harvest, few of the folk customs or beliefs associated with it were evident in the New World. In the Avalon a sudden whirlwind rushing across a hayfield was regarded as an ill-omen, indicating that the fairies were out to destroy the crop, but a fistful of hay, cast in the direction of the swirling hay, would appease them. Both in Avalon and Miramichi the last sheaf of harvest was referred to as the "hare" or "rabbit," but there were no end-of-harvest Irish ceremonies within living memory. In Irish folk-tradition, the last handful of standing corn in a field was twisted into a three-stranded plait and the reapers threw their sickles at it until it was severed. The triumphant slayer was then feted and made guest of honour at the harvest supper, where the last sheaf (*cailleach* or "hare") would be waked, like a corpse. It was usual in Miramichi and Avalon for a reaper to say "we'll get the hare out of it to-day" to hasten the last day's reaping, but in Peterborough there is no mention of even this vestige of Irish folk custom.

Because they were made on the farm, flails offer a wide range of styles and there are some striking examples of Irish regional types preserved in the study areas. The St John's flails are found only in the east and southeast of Ireland (Fig. 20J, K), the source region of the Avalon immigration. Its distribution in the east and southeast and the probably middle-English origins of the jointing terms — cap and middle-band — suggest that this flail type came to Ireland with the Normans, or later, with the establishment of monasteries.[36] Despite the correlation between the immigrant source area and the type of flail, there is another possible route of diffusion to the Avalon. The cap flail appears to have evolved in medieval times in northern France and to have spread westwards into England and Ireland, and eastwards into Germany, Bohemia, Hungary, Poland, and the Ukraine. One can readily dismiss the possibility of an east — or indeed continental — European provenance for the St John's flail since none of these areas had any close connection with the Avalon. But the cap flail was known in the West Country and could have been transported by the English settlers near St John's before the Irish arrived. It may be significant that the middle-band, an extra loop or linking piece uniting the two caps lashed over the heads of the flail sticks (a distinctive Irish innovation) did not appear in the Avalon. But certainly the grooved cap flail, used in the homeland, was a direct transfer. In the final analysis, it seems that both groups introduced independently the prevailing flail-type of their homeland to the St John's area, and this pattern of diffusion may have obtained for several other technical items in the St John's area.

The homeland of the Miramichi and Peterborough immigrants lay generally west of those going to the Avalon and was outside, or on the fringe of the cap-flail province. In these westerly areas the double-loop flail dominated (Fig. 20I) and it was this type that prevailed in Peterborough and Miramichi. Outside western Ireland the double-loop form is found only in Scandinavia and southern Europe; elsewhere it seems to have been displaced by the spread of the cap-flail in medieval times. There seems little doubt that the double-loop flail was carried by the Irish immigrants to their homes in the New World.

Finally, the hole flail found in Peterborough was not used in Ireland outside Ulster (Fig. 20H, L) but was spread over Scotland, the Hebrides, Shetlands, west Norway, south Sweden, the east Baltic, and southern France. This peripheral distribution suggests that it is the oldest type, yet its distribution in Ireland points to a Scottish introduction in the early seventeenth century. Certainly it was the Ulster-Scots who carried this type to the Peterborough area, and transmitted it to their southern Irish neighbours.

In Ireland lashing and stick threshing were usually associated with subsistence grain-growing or were special techniques used for separating seed-oats for spring sowing. The first sheaves of the harvest were also lashed, in keeping with ancient custom, and the winnowed grain ground in a quern and boiled for the reapers' ceremonial breakfast.[37] Along the Cape Shore the absence of the flail is

36 Caoimhín Ó'Danachair, "The Flail and Other Threshing Methods," *Journal of the Cork Archaeological Society* 60 (1955): 6-14 *et seq.*
37 Evans, *Irish Folk Ways*, p. 160.

explained by the weak grain-growing tradition. In a crop rotation where oats were sown only with timothy to convert the arable to ley, periods occurred when grain was not sown at all. During these interludes the old flailing craft probably perished. The variety of threshing techniques on the Cape Shore is a reflection of the intermittent threshing tradition. Where grain was grown continually, as around St John's, flailing survived.

The technique of flailing on an outdoors wooden platform and the method of placing the sheaves with heads overlapping, common to all study areas, were identical to old Irish practice. The mode of winnowing was also similar, although in some areas a shovel or bucket replaced the traditional winnowing tray.[38] In Peterborough, where commercial grain growing predominated even before the mid-nineteenth century, these archaic practices were generally displaced far earlier than in Miramichi. In the Avalon, traditional winnowing practices survived into the present century although along the Cape Shore the intermittent nature of grain production resulted in some local innovations for winnowing as well as threshing.

It has been suggested that the opposite doors in Old World peasant houses originated because the breeze blowing through winnowed the chaff more effectively. Indoor threshing or winnowing was rare in Ireland, however, and the use of the barn floor with its opposite doors in Peterborough and Miramichi was a local borrowing on the frontier, where it had been imported from Europe. The English near St John's transferred this tradition but it was never adopted by their Irish neighbours.

Transport implements used in pre-migration Ireland reappeared in the New World and preserved many of their antecedent forms. Perhaps the most characteristic was the "streel-car" and *kish*, recorded only on the Cape Shore, where it retained its Gaelic name and form. Folk-basketry, using straw or withes, was an archaic but ubiquitous practice in peasant Ireland; in the New World, outside the Avalon, it was associated mainly with the Indians rather than the Irish. Wood replaced straw as a material for boxes and baskets and other containers in use around the farm.

The absence of the "streel-car" outside the Cape Shore is best explained by an early introduction elsewhere of wheeled vehicles. Over rough ground and on steep hills the "streel-car" had better braking powers than did the wheeled cart and in Ireland lingered on after roads and wheeled carts were introduced. The forked slide, although the prototype for wheelless Irish vehicles, was not a distinctively Irish transfer to the Peterborough area, since other cultural groups used this type of vehicle before the Irish arrived. Similarly, the flat sledge used in all three study areas had been introduced before the Irish migrations.

38 For a description of Irish winnowing techniques, see *ibid.* p. 213.

It was only late in the eighteenth century under the supervision of improving landlords that an extensive network of roads was laid out in Ireland. Wheeled vehicles were subsequently adopted by the peasantry. The first carts had solid wooden wheels, two feet in diameter, with iron hoops; they were attached to a rotating axle and wheels revolved inside the shaft, under the cart.[39] The body of the cart was raised on uprights to give clearance. Because there are no surviving examples of the block-wheeled cart-type in the New World, it is impossible to compare forms, but it is likely that at least some of the details of the Irish type were reproduced. This two-wheeled Irish cart was the prototype of the better known Irish jaunting car, which was evolved after the migrations, and may be related to a cart-type in the St John's area called the "jingle."

Spoke wheels, although in use in Ireland since early Celtic times, only became widespread in peasant farming after the migrations. From the mid-nineteenth century onwards factory-made products gained a stronger foothold on the small Irish farm; one of these, the box-cart, with its spoke wheels, spread quickly from Scotland through Ireland, displacing the native block-wheeled types. The flat one-horse cart with projecting rear shafts or "trams," was an Irish adaptation to the mass-produced box-cart. A similar type was used in the New World, especially for carting hay and grain and wood. In both Peterborough and Mira-michi this cart had four wheels, an idea borrowed from neighbouring groups.[40] The wagon was capable of taking more than the two-wheeled dray-car and was better adapted to the larger farms in the two latter areas.

In Ireland, the various tasks of seedtime and harvest often began and ended on traditionally appointed days and were accompanied by fixed folk festivals. Little of this folk tradition crossed the Atlantic. To be sure, the same rhythmic quality of the farming year with its seasonal rush and weeks of leisure re-appeared in all three study areas, but much of its Irish character was lost through the rearrangement of the agricultural calendar. In Irish folk-tradition May 1st and November 1st marked the completion of sowing and reaping and were quarter days in the Celtic year. Of the numerous folk customs associated with May-Day, only the planting of the May-bush (Avalon and Miramichi), the gather-ing of May-flowers (Miramichi), and the blessing of cattle and children (Peter-borough) have been recorded. The May-bush, gaily bedecked with multi-coloured ribbons, was placed beside or on top of the garden fence on May 1st and remained there for the month. This custom was practised until very recently in the Avalon, but disappeared at the turn of the century in Miramichi. It was a

39 *Ibid.*, pp. 174-75, *et seq.*
40 Ireland shares the two-wheeled cart with Scotland and Norway, southern France, Spain, and Italy, and the Mediterranean. The 4-wheeled wagon is traditional in England, Holland, Denmark, Germany, Central Europe, and Russia (see Kevin Danaher, *In Ireland Long Ago* [Cork: Mercier Press, 1962], p. 111).

folk custom of regional significance in Ireland, confined largely to the southeast, the source of the Newfoundland-Irish immigration. Although parallels existed in Britain and other parts of Europe, it is undoubtedly of Irish provenance in the Avalon. Both in Miramichi and the Avalon the May-bush was connected with the cult of the Virgin Mary, which in Irish tradition finds its roots in the medieval world, but its origins stretch back to pre-Christian times and are linked to the ancient agricultural calendar. Spring-sown crops were in by this date, and the cattle driven to the hill pastures. In the New World, the round of spring sowing began about this time.

Saints' days were also observed in Ireland as a time to commence certain farm tasks. St Bridget's day (February 1st) saw the beginning of work in the fields and St Patrick's (March 17th) the sowing of gardens. Neither of these dates was observed in the New World, but Saints' days were commonly referred to by informants when asked when certain tasks were begun. Although Halloween could not be properly regarded as the end of the farming year in the New World, since some root crops still in the ground, many of the folk customs associated with this festival were transferred. In the Avalon the Gaelic word *caulcannon* describes the traditional meal of white vegetables – potatoes, white cabbage, and turnips – eaten on this night. Symbolic objects – a piece of wood, a wisp of straw, a button, a coin, a ring – were concealed in the meal. Each object symbolized some future event in the finder's life. Similar divination rites were characteristic of Halloween in the homeland. Various tricks such as switching farm tools and implements to confuse their owners, throwing cabbages at the doors or salt at the window, were common to all three areas and were practised in southern Ireland. Halloween customs have long since been urbanized, but up to the end of the last century the customs of this festival practised in the areas of Irish rural settlement may be regarded as transplants of an ancient folk tradition.

VI
Farm outbuildings

Farmsteads in the homeland traditionally comprised a number of buildings housing animals, fowl, crops, and farm equipment. These "out-offices" or "outhouses" were usually arranged around a rectangular space, forming a U-shaped courtyard or farmyard. The farmhouse frequently formed the base of the flagged or cobbled courtyard plan, with the outbuildings ranged on either side, at right angles to the front corners of the house. Sometimes the rear of the dwelling house might face the yard, or one wing of outbuildings be placed directly in front of the house, with a connecting line of buildings ranged on one side, but the basic pattern of three-sided courtyard formation remained. The midden was placed traditionally in the centre of the courtyard. This farmstead tradition coincided with the manorialized region of Ireland and it is possible that this arrangement was introduced by medieval colonists or by later English farmers.[1]

Many areas of Leinster and east Munster preserve the courtyard form, and the pattern extends as far west as Galway and into Ulster, but in western areas generally it yields to a linear arrangement of outbuildings. Forming a continuous

1 Caoimhín Ó'Danachair, "Irish Farmyard Types," *Studia Ethnographica Upsaliensia* 11 (1956): 6-15; R.H. Buchanan, "Rural Settlement in Ireland," in Nicholas Stephens and Robin E. Glasscock (eds.), *Irish Geographical Studies in Honour of E. Estyn Evans* (Belfast: Queen's University Press, 1970), pp. 146-61. Medieval monks may have influenced the formal courtyard style in Ireland but it is also possible that its antecedents are rooted in the agricultural revolution in Britain when the layout became popular there.

row and sometimes sharing a single roof, the outbuildings ran parallel to the long axis of the rectangular farmhouse but were placed a short distance from it. Sometimes this row of outbuildings was attached to the gable of the dwelling house, but in either case the various compartments did not have any inside communication. The use of separate compartments – cow house, calf pen, sheep house, pig sty, and barn – is shared by both linear and courtyard farmstead traditions and is mentioned in ancient Irish law tracts. Perhaps the oldest form of housing livestock in Ireland was the longhouse, where animals and humans shared one compartment, with the livestock located at one end of the dwelling. At the time of the migrations the longhouse was confined to the north and west of Ireland but even in the southeast domestic fowl were kept in boxes or coops under the kitchen table, in the lower half of the dresser, or along the kitchen walls.[2] Separate poultry cabins also existed, and like Irish pig sties were often built with cobble stone and were architecturally similar to the monastic huts or ᐧ *clochauns* of the early Irish Christian era.

Vegetables were usually stored out-of-doors in shallow pits and covered with straw, sods, and clay. Sometimes vegetables were stored in the barn or in *clochauns*. Subterranean storage was widespread in pre-medieval Ireland and examples of stone-lined cellars used as milk houses in the *boolies* in the last century are recorded, but the Irish cellar tradition flourished in unsettled times when wars threatened livestock and crops. The barn functioned mainly as a granary and in the south straw-rope granaries, shaped like a haystack, were sometimes erected in the haggard.[3] This latter feature was found in every farmstead for in the mild Irish climate hay and grain were stacked outdoors, close to the outbuildings.

THE NEW WORLD

Linhays

The most important outbuilding on the great majority of farmsteads north of St John's up to the end of the last century was a rectangular shed or "linhay" built on to the rear of the house or, occasionally, to one of the gable ends. The "linhay" walls were formed with closely set vertical posts or "studs," never more than 8 feet long and about 10 inches in diameter. These poles were faced or hewn only on their abutting sides, leaving no interstices (Fig. 22A). The exposed surface of the wall comprised a row of rounded spruce or fir poles, which frequently were not "rinded" (i.e., stripped of their bark). Originally the poles were driven directly into the ground, but folk memory recalls only a few

2 Ó'Danachair, "The Combined Byre-and-Dwelling in Ireland," *Folklife* 2 (1964): 58-75.
3 A.T. Lucas, "An Fhóir: A Straw-Rope Granary," *Gwerin* 1 (1956-57): 68-77 and "An Fhóir: Further Notes," *Gwerin* 2 (1958-59): 2-20.

examples without sills. Hewn spruce sills were usually placed on a shallow stone foundation to form the base of the shed. These members were joined in a half-notch at the corners, and holes about two and a half inches in diameter, were chiselled out of the top surface of the sill, into which the studs were mortised or "joggled." Sometimes square or V-shaped notches were bored to take the vertical studs. Usually only every third or fourth stud was mortised in this way, the intervening poles merely resting on or nailed to the sill. Overhead, the studs were mortised into a wallplate, on top of which the main roof timbers were placed. The "linhay" roof sloped gently from the rear wallplate of the dwelling.

The rafters, usually round, slender spruce poles, were mortised into the wallplates a foot or so apart and covered with strips of bark which were sometimes nailed with "trunnels." Grassy sods were cut in strips 8 feet long and over a foot wide and were rolled around a stick, carpet-like, and carried on to the roof where they were unrolled, and stretched from the rear wall of the "linhay" to the eave of the house. Sometimes smaller sods were used and board sheeting often replaced bark. The roof was "renewed" every few years by stripping away the old sods and replacing them with a fresh layer. The old sods were usually mixed in the compost heap. By the late nineteenth century shingles had replaced sods on most of the St John's "linhays."

Normally 10 feet wide and 6 feet high at the rear (Fig. 22B), the "linhay" extended the entire length of the dwelling house, about 40 feet. The floors, like the walls, were made of closely set poles and a plank or stone channel separated the animals' compartments from the walkway at the rear. All the livestock of the farm – cows, calves, horses and goats – were frequently housed in the "linhay." Their stalls or "pounds" were arranged along the back wall of the house so that they faced the farmhouse compartments, and the animals were secured by wooden "bales." Vertical posts or standards were placed about 2 feet from the rear of the wall of the dwelling house, inside the "linhay," and about 4 feet apart. A pole, running the full length of the "linhay," was nailed to these upright posts, about 5 feet from the ground. Another vertical post was set a few inches from each standard and could be adjusted to allow the animal's head to pass through to the stall. A tie of withe rods or *gads* was passed around both standard and adjustable pole, over the neck of the animal, securing it in the stall.

A door connecting the "linhay" with the farm kitchen existed in only 12 of the 49 examples recorded in the settlements north of St John's, and in all other cases a single door, placed at the gable end, was the only entry to the "linhay." A manure shutter was located in the back wall of the "linhay" and the building was drained by a flagged tunnel placed underneath the shutter. Ideally, the "linhay" was sited on a slope to facilitate the drainage of refuse, but this type of site was not always available. Sometimes, part of the floor-space was filled with hay, and in "linhays" where all the floor-space was occupied by livestock, a

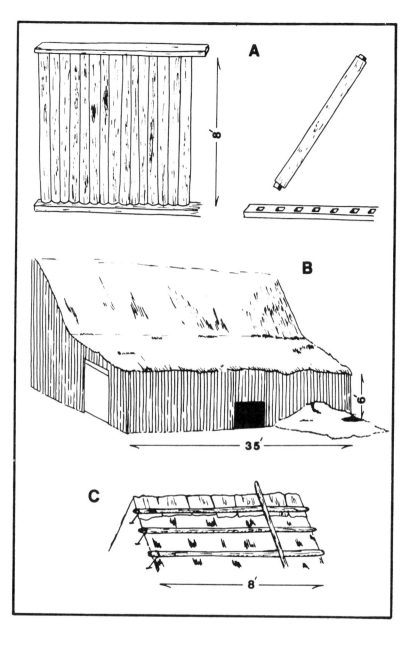

Figure 22
A – Studded wall, Avalon. B – Linhay, Avalon. C – Thatched root cellar, Cape Shore.

121

narrow loft was usually inserted where hay, hand-operated work-tools, and some fishing gear were stored.

Both the ubiquity and antiquity of the back "linhay" are attested to in field evidence, in local folk tradition and folk memory, and in documents.[4] In 1819 Anspach reported that "tilt-backs or linneys are sheds made of studs and covered either with boards or with boughs, resembling the section of a roof, fixed to the back of the dwelling, towards the wind."[5] Of the 58 houses examined north of St John's, 44 had back "linhays," 5 had "linhays" attached to the gable end of the house, and 9 had detached stables instead of "linhays." Local tradition maintains that the "linhays" were built with the dwelling houses, almost all of which were built before the mid-nineteenth century (see following chapter). Studding is itself an old building technique which was little practised at the end of the last century.

Barns and Stables

Separate stables or barns were introduced to several St John's farmsteads for the first time within living memory and the recent origins of others are confirmed by their frame walls. Yet detached outbuildings apparently were numerous in the mid-nineteenth century. North of St John's, where 92 houses but only 51 farmers were recorded in 1857, there were 47 "stores, barns and outhouses."[6] Fifteen separate barns of nineteenth century origins were examined. One side of the rectangular floor-plan was occupied by livestock, and the other reserved for hay and implements. A double door gave admission to the tool shed where carts, farm implements, and boats were stored. On another side, a single door led into the stable. Livestock were tied in their stalls in "bales" and all animals were housed together, as in the "linhay." Sometimes two "linhays" were added to the long sides of the barn; these housed livestock and tools while the main or original barn was used for hay and grain.

4 One of the earliest references uncovered in the St John's area was in 1808 when James Hayes petitioned "to extend the linnay at the back of his house by making it two feet wider" (Great Britain, Colonial Office Correspondence, Newfoundland [MSS in Provincial Archives, St John's], Series 194, Vol. 27, October 1, 1808). Five years earlier John Kennedy was permitted to repair his dwelling house and extend it 15 feet for a cowhouse (C.O. 194/27, May 4, 1803).

5 Lewis A. Anspach, *A History of the Island of Newfoundland* (London: Published for Author, 1819), p. 463. Newspapers reveal the widespread distribution of linhays in the early nineteenth century, but were often appendages to stables or fish stores and did not always house livestock.

6 Newfoundland, Department of Colonial Secretary, *Census of Newfoundland and Labrador, 1857* (in Memorial University Library, St John's), Appendix 27, p. 269. It can only be assumed, however, that these buildings were separate. Since every house had need of some place for storage, and linhays were widespread, it is highly unlikely that these latter were included in the count. It is also unlikely that some of the farmers had more than one outbuilding.

None of these detached outbuildings north of St John's was studded. Their distinguishing features were framed walls and a steeply pitched or "saddle" roof, with hay-lofts over the animals' quarters, and a tool shed. Round rafters rested on the wallplates and were secured by a half mortise joint with a single wooden peg at the roof ridge or "saddle." Boards were nailed on to the couples and then shingled. In the present century these peaked roofs were displaced by the now ubiquitous "whaleback" or flat roof style, with a full hay-loft and upstairs hatch to "pike" the hay through from outside.

In Freshwater almost all houses had an attached "linhay" at the rear but within living memory only a few were used for stabling livestock. By the late nineteenth century all Freshwater farmsteads had separate barns, most of them with studded walls, suggesting they were older than the framed barns north of the city. As early as 1834 James Neill, one of the first Irish settlers in the valley, willed to his son "all the ground on the north side of the road, commonly called Mair River road in St John's, on which stands the dwelling house, stabling, and outhouses."[7] Each of the 6 barns examined in Freshwater had hay "linhays." Most of the floor-space of the main barn was used for livestock with a portion partitioned off at the end for wagons and other farm equipment. Behind the horses the harness was hung on forked sticks called by their Gaelic name *bacán.* Above the livestock and tool sheds was the hay loft,[8] which opened on to the "linhay" at the rear. Hay was forked in through a gable-end hatch to the loft, and fed through another hatch to the cattle below. In all other details the Freshwater barns resembled those north of St John's.

Along the Cape Shore, barns (locally called stables) were similar in form to those in Freshwater. In the former area, however, the hay "linhay" was absent. Hay was stored at one end of the long stable, in an area referred to as the "bulk" which opened onto a loft over the animals' quarters. As in Outer Cove, side "linhays" were sometimes attached to the main stable to house pigs and sheep. A single door, centrally placed on the front side of the stable, with a brightly painted circle in the centre,[9] led directly into the main "body" of the building, where the animals were kept. In summer the hay was forked through this door and later transferred to the adjoining "bulk" and connecting hay-loft. Some stables over 80 feet long were built as part of a joint farm and were shared by more than one family.

7 Newfoundland, Supreme Court, *Registry of Wills* (MSS in Courthouse, St John's), "Will of James Neill, Freshwater," 1834.
8 Cow houses and stables with hay-lofts were recorded in the late 1820s on the Southern Shore (*Public Ledger,* St John's, April 27, 1837; March 28, 1828 [in Provincial Archives, St John's]).
9 The origin and meaning of this symbol are not clear. The painted circle is found especially on Newfoundland-English barn doors, and is apotropaic. It is found in all three Avalon study areas but is regarded as a decorative rather than a hex sign or charm.

Twenty-five Cape Shore farmsteads were examined in detail. Only one had a "linhay" attached to the house and in another livestock had been housed within the dwelling itself.[10] In 1857 there were 54 farmers, 54 dwelling houses, and 88 "stores, barns, and outhouses" along the Cape Shore.[11] None of the stables examined was built within living memory and local tradition asserts that some predate the mid-nineteenth century. All the walls of these stables were studded.

Cattle were secured in their "pounds," not by "bales," but with a rope fastened around the horns or neck of the animal and tied to a small ring or loop which in turn encircled a vertical post or standard. This small ring, traditionally fashioned from withe rods or *gads* was called a "traveller" because it ran up and down the standard as the animal raised or lowered its head in the stall. The rope was threaded with a smaller rope and an eye notched at each end. This secondary rope was then drawn over the cow's horns and secured with a short piece of wood, or toggle, with a V-notch or groove to hold the rope ends in place.

There is little evidence that sod roofs existed along the Cape Shore but within living memory shingles replaced thatch on some of these old stables. Thatched root cellars still survive and it is likely that early in the nineteenth century thatch was the common roof cover. Rushes rather than straw were used for thatching; they were closely sheared with the scythe to procure as long a stem as possible. As with shingling, the first "course" of thatch ran horizontally along the base line of the roof, covering the eave; a long stick or "lislonger" was superimposed to hold the thatch in place. This timber was tied with *gads* to "trunnels" embedded in the rafters at each end (Fig. 22C). Subsequent tiers were all pinned down to the bark undercover in this manner and the rushes forming the top or "saddle course" were bent over the roof ridge and further secured by placing a course of heavy sods on top. The sods straddled the roof ridge and effectively threw off the rain. As in St John's, most of the older studded stables with their peaked roofs were replaced early in the present century by a flat-roofed, two-level barn type with a full hay-loft.

The oldest remembered barn in both Peterborough and Miramichi was a two-bay log structure, separated in the centre by a wide threshing floor with opposite double doors. In Peterborough many of these barns are still in use, although two-level frame barns were introduced in the final decades of the last century. Log barns have not survived in Miramichi, but some were still in use at the turn of the century and are remembered by most informants.

10 During the first decade or so of settlement, the practice of keeping animals within the dwelling house may have been widespread. Edward Wix, who visited some Irish settlements in Placentia Bay in 1835 stated that "every hole and corner in the cabin ... that was not taken up by human inmates, was occupied by pigs, ducks, fowls, sheep or dogs ..." (Edward Wix, *Six Months of a Newfoundland Missionary's Journal* [London: Smith, Elder and Co., 1836], p. 21).

11 *Census of Newfoundland and Labrador, 1857*, pp. 352-53.

In both areas cedar logs were placed horizontally, one above the other, to form the walls. The logs were notched at the corners so that the timbers on one wall always lay half a thickness above or below those of the adjoining walls. In Miramichi a full dovetail and in Peterborough a simple square notch were employed to secure the logs at each corner. Logs measured up to one and a half feet in diameter, and a wall was usually about 10 logs high. Poles 6 inches in diameter were used as rafters. These rafters were mortised into the top log or plate and were joined at the ridge in a half-mortise notch held fast by a single wooden peg, usually of juniper. Alternatively the rafter ends were shaven, fitted flush, and secured by a peg. In Peterborough the opposite butt of the rafter was notched in rounded or V-shaped form and fitted over the log plate.

A space 15 feet wide and up to 12 feet high was cut out of the front and back walls where the double doors were placed. Two low log walls were built to divide the "mows" from the central threshing floor. Through the double doors a cart-load of hay or grain could be drawn and forked directly onto the "mows." In Miramichi and sometimes in Peterborough a portion of one "mow" was reserved for livestock, farm implements, and a granary. Hay or grain was stored in the loft or "scaffel" overhead. Livestock were admitted through a single door on the front corner, and their stalls were usually placed along the interior log partition, dividing the "mow" from the threshing floor. "Bales" were used in Miramichi. Adjustable poles were secured by inserting pegs into holes bored in the "scant-ling" or cross-timber in contrast to the rope-tie of the Avalon. In both Peterborough and Miramichi the horn-tie, already described for the Avalon, was also used. On many Peterborough farms until early in the present century cattle were allowed to run loose about the farmyard.

Although Catherine Parr Traill described Irish shanties in Peterborough as "reeking with smoke and dirt, the common receptacle for children, pigs and fowl,"[12] there is little evidence that livestock and humans ever shared the same roof in either Peterborough or Miramichi; even outbuildings connected to the dwelling house were rare. In Miramichi only one example of a connecting stable and dwelling house has been recorded. Small log stables probably preceded the big barn. It is difficult to date accurately the introduction of the two-bay barn to the Irish settlements but they certainly were built on some farms before the middle of the nineteenth century.[13] There was little point, however, in building such a barn until the farmer produced enough grain to fill it. Late in the last century in Peterborough, the two-bay barn was often reserved exclusively for

12 Catherine Parr Traill, *The Backwoods of Canada* (Toronto: McClelland & Stewart, 1968), p. 444.
13 In the 1851 census log barns and sheds are mentioned on Peterborough-Irish farms (Canada, *Census of Canada, 1851* [MSS in National Archives, Ottawa], RG31, Townships of Emily, Ennismore and Douro).

hay and grain, and livestock and implements were housed in small log stables set at right angles to the front corners of the barn (Fig. 23A, B). The carefully planned U-shaped courtyard usually facing the rear of the dwelling house located some distance to the south was a common feature of the cultural landscape in Peterborough up to 1900. Sometimes the smaller log stables, instead of flanking the main barn, were ranged at right angles to the barn on one side only, forming an L-shaped barnyard. Less frequently the Peterborough outbuildings were disposed linearly, or scattered haphazardly around the farm house. There is no evidence that the U-shaped courtyard ever existed in Miramichi; an omnibus structure served within living memory to house livestock, implements, and farm produce.[14]

When building these barns a good deal of man-power was required to hoist the heavy logs up the walls, and usually, as in so many other pioneer tasks, labour was pooled. Barn-raising "bees" or "frolics" are still remembered by informants in both Peterborough and Miramichi, but only in connection with the raising of frame barns, which began to replace the two-bay log barn late in the nineteenth century.[15] While the frame barns of Miramichi retained the layout of the two-bay log structure, the frame barns of Peterborough were two-level structures, with a stone-wall base. Livestock were housed on the ground floor compartments and the upper level, divided into two "mows" by a threshing floor as in the former log barn, was reached by a ramp of earth and stone, built on at the back.

Root Cellars

Potatoes, cabbages, turnips, and other vegetables were stored underground in cellars in all study areas. Cellars were rarely less than 15 feet square and 7 feet deep in the settlements near St John's. Some had clay walls, frequently lined with stone, and the stone wall projected about a foot above the ground. On this stone base a ceiling or "bed" was built out of cross-beams, "longers," birch bark or "rind," and sod. "Rind" was often purchased by the quintal in St John's and the sods, cut with the spade or *grafán*, were placed with the clay side upwards to complete the "bed." A hatch was located in the centre and a ladder led down to the cellar's earthen floor. A wooden shute was also inserted through this hatch, and different root-crops were packed into separate compartments, or "pounds," below. The thick covering of "longers," bark, and sod ensured a frost-free cellar. The hatch was fitted with a lid or door, but a saddle roof covered the cellar

14 Both barns and stables existed in early days, however; in 1826 the great fire destroyed 303 houses, 135 barns, and 66 stables (*The Mercury*, Newcastle, February 28, 1826 [in University of New Brunswick Library, Fredericton]).

15 "In raising a log house or barn," wrote Strickland, "a bee is absolutely necessary" (Samuel Strickland, *Twenty-Seven Years in Canada West* [London: R. Bentley, 1853], p. 37).

126

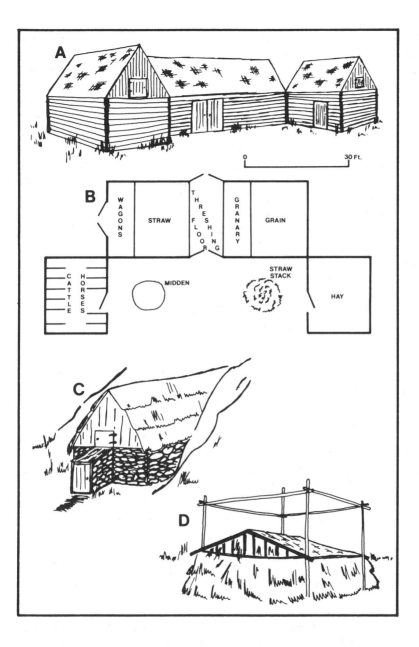

Figure 23
A, B – Two-bay barn and stables, Peterborough. C – Root cellar, Freshwater.
D – Hay barrack, St John's.

"bed" to give extra shelter. Shingles were sometimes used to roof the cellar, but in the late nineteenth century sod roofs were more common.

In Freshwater cellars were usually built into a steep knoll in such a manner that the entire front was exposed. Whereas in Outer Cove one entered through the half-door to the "cockloft" (the peaked section of the cellar), and then down the hatch, the Freshwater cellar had a full door on its exposed side, an external porch with studded walls, an inside hall, and another door at the end of this interior hallway (Fig. 23C). Alternate tiers of flags and "bog-sods" were used for walling and the peaked roof was sodded over to ensure a draught-proof compartment. In both Freshwater and Outer Cove early cabbages were usually stored in this upper, "cock-loft" section of the cellar.

Along the Cape Shore the "porch" cellar also dominated but the walls were frequently built with horizontally placed poles rather than stone. Until recently, the roof was thatched. Otherwise, the formal and functional features of the Cape Shore cellar were similar to those in Freshwater. The Cape Shore cellar type was also built in Peterborough and Miramichi. Part of the root house was used as a milk house or dairy in Peterborough, where milk and butter were stored during the warm summers. A double log-wall with interstitial filling or "grouting" was erected to ensure more even temperatures; this wall sometimes projected several feet above the ground.

Root cellars were essential in the continental climate of the New World, and it is likely that the cellars were among the first buildings on the pioneer farm.[16] Frost-proof cellars were frequently mentioned in farm sale advertisements in all study areas since the time of initial occupance. Although the detached cellar appears to have been predominant in all study areas during the nineteenth century, and is at present the only type in the Avalon, cellars located beneath the kitchen were introduced to Peterborough and Miramichi during the initial occupance stage. Along the Miramichi, houses with frost-proof cellars were advertised during the pioneer period[17] and even in the Avalon there is an early reference to a kitchen cellar.[18] Samuel Strickland relates how in Peterborough a bear forced an entrance into a pioneer kitchen and "the woman and her three

16 One year after initial settlement, one of the Peterborough-Irish stated that he had 300 bushels of potatoes in his cellar, and 100 bushels of wheat in his barn, besides peas, oats, and Indian corn (Great Britain, Colonial Office Correspondence, Upper Canada [MSS in National Archives, Ottawa], MG11, Series Q, vol. 345, pp. 392-4, Alex MacDonnell to R.W. Horton, No. 345, March 6, 1827).
17 *The Gleaner and Northumberland Schediasma*, Chatham, March 23, 1830 (in University of New Brunswick Library, Fredericton). A 4-roomed house with a good frost-proof cellar beneath the dwelling, plus barns and outbuildings were offered for sale.
18 C.O. 194/25, September 10, 1751. Hay was stored in a cellar under Margaret Penny's house in Bay Bulls, south of St John's. The kitchen cellar was never a traditional feature of the farmsteads in the Avalon study areas, however.

children had barely time to get into the potato cellar and shut down the trapdoor."[19] By the end of the nineteenth century in both Peterborough and Miramichi kitchen cellars had virtually displaced the detached unit.

Pens and Coops
Separate outbuildings for pigs and fowl were built in all study areas, although sometimes pigs and fowl were housed in stables with the livestock. Small log pens for pigs still survive in both Miramichi and Peterborough, but in the latter area pigs were often kept in a special compartment beneath the corn-crib in the barnyard. In the Avalon pigs were frequently kept in huge molasses puncheons, placed near the dwelling house in a small pound. Alternatively separate pig pens with studded walls and sod roofs were used.

Small log or studded structures were also built to shelter poultry, ducks and geese, but in the Avalon hens were kept in the farmhouse kitchen. Nesting boxes with wooden slats were placed below the fireside settles on the Avalon hearth, each side of the fire, and were concealed by a long door, hung horizontally, and secured at the bottom by a latch. During winter the hens were kept in these "coobs" and were put outdoors for the summer. It was believed that they laid better beside the warmth of the fire. Straw was used for bedding and ashes from the fire were added as a detergent. Kitchen "coobs" were widely used in all study areas of the Avalon throughout the last century.[20]

Hay "Barracks"
The scarcity of barns in the coastal settlements north of St John's is partly explained by the presence of the hay "barrack," a structure not found in the other study areas. Four posts, up to 20 feet long, were stuck in the ground in square formation; each of these vertical members was braced by two shorter posts. The main posts were sometimes further secured by 4 horizontal timbers placed near the top. Each vertical post was equipped with a block and tackle on to which a "saddle" or pyramidal roof, made of clapboard, was attached (Fig. 23D). By using ropes the light wooden roof could be lowered and raised over the hay stack, set between the posts. The "barrack" floor, covering approximately 300 square feet, was normally made of "longers." While hay was the characteristic crop stored in this distinctive outbuilding, fodder (green oats) was often placed on top of the hay. A well-drained slope near the farmhouse provided an ideal site for the barrack, but in a few cases the structure was located out in the

19 Strickland, *Twenty-Seven Years in Canada West*, p. 46.
20 Anspach, *A History of Newfoundland*, p. 463. "Under these benches they manage convenient places for their poultry, by which means they have fresh eggs during the most severe winters. ..."

meadow, away from the farmstead. As far back as local memory extends, the majority of settlers north of St John's owned at least one "barrack."[21]

Few elements of the southeast Irish farmyard tradition ever crossed the ocean. All major components of the farmyard – the number of outbuildings, their form, disposition and the materials of construction – were radically altered. Most new forms or ideas about outbuildings were borrowed from pre-existing local New World traditions and the factors influencing change were environmental and economic. As the operational centre of the farm, the farmyard complex reflected the patterns of farm production and was sensitive to their changes; it was also an important indicator of the immigrants' adaptation to a new physical environment.

In the West Country a separate shed with a peaked roof is called a "linhay." One long side of the rectangular "linhay" is open, and the roof on this side is supported by a series of wooden posts or stone pillars. The "linhay" shelters various animals, fowl or equipment but was used most commonly as a cow house.[22] Above the "linhay" was a small hay loft or "tallet" with access to feed racks below. The word "linhay" is also used in the southeast of Ireland and is called in Gaelic *lann-iotha* (corn-house).[23] It has been described as a lean-to shed attached to a house or other outbuildings and used for the storage of tools and crops. As far as is known, however, such an outbuilding is rare. Whether the "linhay" in the St John's study areas is based on Irish antecedents or was borrowed from a Devonshire tradition there remains a vexed question, but it is certain that the placing of this building along the rear of the farmhouse does not have any Irish, or indeed English, antecedents. The physical separation of dwelling house and outbuildings was a feature of southeast Irish farmsteads, as noted, but even in the west and north, where such connections were numerous, the addition was invariably to the gable end of the house rather than on the rear. The "back-linhay" was an adaptation to the cold Newfoundland winters, where

21 A barrack capable of containing 20 tons of hay was recorded on an Irish farm near Freshwater in 1836 (*Public Ledger*, St John's, April 26, 1836).
22 N.W. Alcock, "Devonshire Linhays: A Vernacular Tradition," *Devonshire Association, Report and Transactions* 95 (1963): 117-30. Sometimes there were several linhays on the farm and these might be dispersed or clustered around a courtyard (see N.W. Alcock, "A Devon Farm: Bury Barton, Lapford," *Devonshire Association, Report and Transactions* 98 [1966]: 105-31).
23 P.W. Joyce, *English as We Speak it in Ireland* (London: Longmans, 1910), p. 287. The word is also spelled "linnie," "linney," or "linny" and in Ireland is apparently found only in the southeast.

the placing of hay and livestock along the rear of the house, rather than on either of its narrow ends, afforded extra shelter for the household. Internal communication and the storing of hay above the animals greatly reduced the farmer's trips outdoors during winter, but the Irish displayed a sense of some separation of humans and livestock by rarely establishing any internal entrance to the "linhay." In the final analysis, the absence of the "linhay" on the Cape Shore, where the Irish were isolated from the English, suggests that in the St John's study area the "linhay" was borrowed from English neighbours.

The antecedents of the hay "barrack" in the St John's area is even more puzzling. Although this item has been recorded in continental Europe since medieval times it was never part of the peasant tradition of Britain or Ireland.[24] German and Dutch immigrants brought the barrack to the New World, especially to Pennsylvania and New Jersey. The conditions or circumstances of its importation to the St John's area are unknown, but if it is of American provenance it is likely that the idea came in through commercial contact with New England. The "barrack" did not spread far beyond the vicinity of St John's and never gained a foothold in Freshwater where the Irish either adopted the notion of storing hay in the barn or "linhay" loft or continued the homeland technique of open stacking outdoors.

In the pastoral economy of the Avalon the barn was unimportant but it came to dominate the farmstead in Miramichi and especially in Peterborough. Before the Irish migrations the two-bay barn was widely distributed not only in North America but in Europe as well. Like the "barrack" it was not used, however, in Ireland. Although frequently referred to as the "English" barn in North America, it is likely that more than one European group transferred this type across the Atlantic. It appears that the two-bay barn came first with the Puritans to New England and spread west through the Great Lakes country from this secondary hearth.[25] The two-bay barn was also known in Scotland, Germany, and France, and it is likely that at least the two latter groups also introduced it to

---

24 Alfred L. Shoemaker, "Barracks," *Pennsylvania Folklife* 9 (1958): 3-11. The diffusion of the barrack in Europe has been associated with the spread of Germanic culture and at the time of the Atlantic migrations the outbuilding was spread from France to the Ukraine. The idea did reach England via Holland but never became popular (see Nigel Harvey, *A History of Farm Buildings in England and Wales* [Newtown Abbott: David and Charles, 1970], pp. 89-90).

25 Fred Kniffen, "Folk Housing: Key to Diffusion," *Annals, Association American Geographers* 55 (1965): 549-77. It was predominantly as a frame rather than a log structure that the English barn spread westwards, with remarkably little change in form. It was introduced into Upper Canada late in the eighteenth century by the Loyalists and other American settlers, and possibly directly from Britain by post-Napoleonic immigrants.

their respective areas of settlement in the New World.[26] In the Irish settlements of Peterborough and Miramichi this barn became the exclusive type, but, like many other mainland North American frontier features, neither the two-bay barn nor horizontal log construction reached the Avalon.

The two-bay barn was ideally suited to the storing of hay, and especially the storing and threshing of grain. The loaded wagon could be drawn into the barn, and the sheaves pitched directly on to the mows. Stacking, a time-consuming task, was avoided. Where grain cropping was a commercial enterprise, it was important to get the grain stored away as quickly and as efficiently as possible. Threshing – either by flail or "horse-power" – could be performed indoors on the threshing floor; part of one mow was normally reserved as a granary. In the cold North American winters this arrangement was far superior to outdoor stacking and outdoor granaries. The absence of the two-bay barn in the Avalon is perhaps more related to the nature of the farm economy than to isolation from mainland North America. Some of the Westcountrymen were probably familiar with this barn type in their homeland but the two-bay barn was associated primarily with a grain economy, using the broad central passage as a threshing floor. Neither Irish nor English immigrants became commercial grain farmers in the Avalon and although the two-bay barn was a more effective structure for storing hay quickly, this was apparently insufficient reason for its introduction.

One of the major contrasts between homeland and New World stabling systems was in the number of buildings used. With the exception of sheep and pigs, all livestock were housed collectively in a single main room without compartments in the New World, in contrast to the multiple units of the homeland. During the first few years of occupance the immigrants acquired a cow or two, a few pigs, an ox or a horse, some calves, and occasionally some sheep or goats. Given the immigrants main objective – to clear enough land to have a commercial farm in operation as early as possible – it was more practical to house this small, varied collection of livestock in a single structure. Unlike their stone and mud counterparts in the homeland, one log building was constructed much more quickly than two small ones; the extra cutting and notching for each additional building took time. Nor were logs long enough in either Peterborough or Miramichi to reproduce the longhouse or sometimes lengthy wing of outbuildings characteristic of Irish farmsteads. Such constraints were not inherent in the studded architecture of the Avalon, and although early documents suggest the existence of cow houses and stables, the construction of several separate

26 Henry Glassie, "The Pennsylvania Barn in the South," *Pennsylvania Folklife* 15:2 (1965-66): 8-19; 15:4 (1966): 12-25; see also John Fraser Hart's review of Robert-Lionel Séguin, *Les granges du Quebec du XXVIIe au XIXe siècle* (Ottawa: Musée Nationale du Canada, Bulletin No. 192, 1963) in *Geographical Review* 55 (1965): 424-26.

buildings or the internal division of a long outbuilding into separate compartments with separate entrances was rare in living memory. In Peterborough it was the grain barn that came to dominate the farmyard, and when the grain economy was superseded by a pastoral one, livestock were housed in the lower level and hay and other feed in the upper level of the new barn type. The housing of livestock and feed together in a single omnibus structure was a feature in Miramichi and to a lesser extent in Freshwater since at least the mid-nineteenth century. In all areas the premium initially was on time, and livestock were not as well housed as on the better peasant farms in the homeland. Mainly because they were time consuming tasks, the laying of flagged or cobbled yards or the construction of large stone walls around the farmstead were also avoided. In the harsh North American winters multi-purpose structures were functionally superior to the homeland arrangement. In Ireland mild winters permitted the farmer to stack all his hay and grain outdoors in the haggard; the barn functioned only as a granary and even granaries were sometimes erected outdoors. Much time was wasted carrying feed during winter from the haggard to the various animals' quarters but outdoor stacking eliminated the need for large barns or hay lofts. Although some of these outdoor stacking techniques crossed the Atlantic, they generally yielded to the dominant North American practice of indoor storage. Even in the smaller structures, such as the "linhay," studded stable, or log stable, a hay-loft was often introduced or part of the floor-space reserved for hay. The proximity of livestock and fodder was not only a labour-saving device but eliminated much outside travelling in the bitterly cold winters of the New World; the concentration of animals in one compartment helped, moreover, to combat the cold. Hay and grain also afforded extra shelter. Although the Irish continued to stack some of their hay and grain outdoors, it is significant that the dialect word "haggard" (hay-gard), referring to the area in the yard where stacks were made, was not part of the farmyard terminology in any of the New World areas.

Climatic factors were mainly responsible also for the adoption of root cellars either outside or under the farmhouse. The mild winters of the homeland permitted the storage of crops in shallow pits outside. As in the case of stabling techniques, the root cellar tradition was either borrowed from earlier settlers or a product of independent adaptation.

Some elements of traditional Irish stabling techniques were reproduced in the New World. The methods of tying cattle in their stalls, for example, were adapted from homeland practice. "Bales" were and still are confined to the southeast of Ireland and may have been originally imported from the continent or Britain; the term is widely used in England and Scotland. The use of "bales" in all three study areas suggests direct transfer from the homeland. The technique of securing livestock with a rope tied around the neck or horns most likely represents an older Irish form, dominant today only in the west. It is difficult to

133

explain the exclusive use of the horn-tie along the Cape Shore and the "bales" north of St John's. It may be that the first form introduced was copied by later southern Irish arrivals who may have used the alternative method in the homeland. One interesting adaptation to the horn-tie along the Cape Shore was the substitution of withe rods or *gads* for ropes of grass, straw (*sugán*), or horsehair.

In the Avalon the centrally placed chimney, with its porch and hallway entrance (see chapter vii) did not easily admit livestock to the dwelling and, as in southeast Ireland, livestock were never housed in this house type. Even in Peterborough and Miramichi, where the western Irish house form was reproduced, there is no evidence of the combined byre and dwelling sometimes associated with this house type in Ireland. This is understandable when one considers that the longhouse was confined to the north and west of Ireland at the time of the migrations. In the New World, rural poverty or the exigency of a pioneer situation, more than ethnic inheritance, explains the few cases where animals and humans shared one roof. The keeping of domestic fowl in the kitchen is, however, a transfer of old Irish practice but the placing of the coops beneath the benches beside the fire was an adaptation to the colder winters of the Avalon.

Apart from a few Freshwater farmsteads, the compact courtyard or the linear range of buildings, both widespread in Ireland, never crossed the Atlantic (Fig. 24). It is tempting to see the Peterborough courtyard as a transfer of the Irish form, but there were fundamental differences in lay-out. The barn took the place of the dwelling house in Peterborough, at the base of the three-sided complex and the farmhouse was usually located a considerable distance from the barnyard.[27] Apart from St John's and the Cape Shore this isolation of farmhouse and outbuildings was a common characteristic of the New World farmsteads. Fire hazards were far greater than in the Old World where the thatched roof was the only highly combustible material. Wooden buildings were frequently burned, and the hay and straw in them were an added risk; by placing his outbuildings well away from the dwelling house, the immigrant minimized the dangers of losing the entire farmstead in a fire.

In exchanging mud and stone (the traditional Irish building material) for wood, the immigrants were compelled to either invent their own techniques of wood construction or to borrow local methods. The origins of studding in the Avalon are obscure. Vertical post construction, without interstices, was widespread in western Europe in pre-medieval times and an example still survives in

27 This U-shaped farmyard open to the south, with detached dwelling, was the most popular farmstead pattern in Britain during the Agricultural Revolution (Harvey, *Farm Buildings*, pp. 77-82).

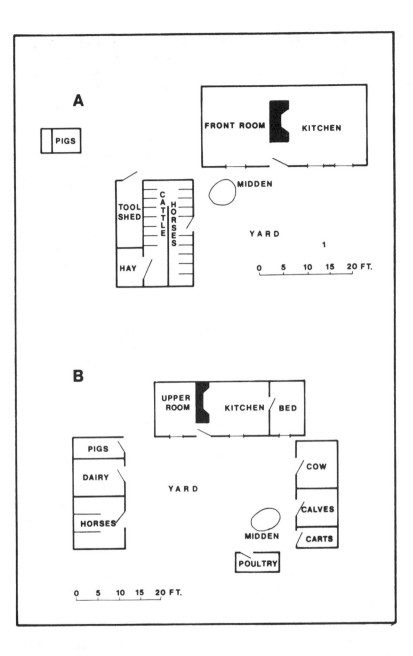

Figure 24
Farmstead layout: A — Freshwater. B — Southeast Ireland.

135

an Old Saxon church in Essex.[28] In England the vertical half logs were tongued and grooved, between sill and plate, on adjoining edges, to produce a tight fit; in the Avalon the abutting poles were "stogged" with moss to ensure draught-proof walls. In Ireland palisaded walls were used in folk housing and to enclose Celtic forts and farmsteads, but had long since disappeared at the time of the migrations. The French carried vertical post construction — *poteaux en terre* or *pieux en terre* — to North America, but usually left interstices, about the width of each post, which were filled in with clay and other materials.[29] It is possible that this building technique was used in Placentia by the French, and later adapted by the Irish, but an English origin for Newfoundland studding seems more plausible. The English were the dominant group in the Avalon in the seventeenth and eighteenth centuries; moreover, the widespread distribution and similarity in form suggest that studding spread from a single source. English settlers around St John's utilized vertical post construction before the Irish came and in the St John's Irish settlements this technique was certainly a local borrowing. Whether the Irish of the Cape Shore borrowed the technique from earlier French or from English settlers, or whether it was independently evolved is, however, difficult to determine.

The horizontal log work in Peterborough and Miramichi was equally alien to Irish tradition, but the similarity in form, especially the techniques of notching, to pre-existing, local methods points clearly to cultural borrowing. Like vertical posts, horizontal log construction was carried to America by more than one cultural group[30] and was undoubtedly the dominant mode of construction in Peterborough and Miramichi when the Irish arrived.

Framing was an improved and perhaps a more expensive form of construction, and was apparently the predominant technique in the English and Dutch settled parts of the seaboard settlements of North America; it spread slowly into the areas where the Irish settled and, apart from Miramichi, did not become common among the Irish until the end of the last century. In the latter area the numerous sawmills, associated with the lumber industry, provided cheap lumber and possibly influenced the early conversion to frame barns along the Barnaby.

28 Fred Kniffen and Henry Glassie, "Building in Wood in the Eastern United States: A Time-Place Perspective," *Geographical Review* 56 (1966): 40-66, quoting Martin Shaw Briggs, *The Homes of the Pilgrim Fathers in England and America, 1620-1685* (London: Oxford University Press, 1932), pp. 56-57; June A. Sheppard, "Vernacular Buildings in England and Wales: A Survey of Recent Work by Architects, Archaeologists and Historians," *Institute British Geographers, Transactions* 40 (1966): 21-37.
29 Kniffen and Glassie, "Building in Wood," p. 47.
30 *Ibid.*, pp. 50-65. It appears that at least the Swedes and Germans introduced horizontal log construction independently to America, but Moravia, Silesia, and Bohemia is now regarded as the important source-region for North American notching forms. American immigrants transplanted these techniques to the Miramichi and the area south of the Peterborough district in the late eighteenth century.

As noted earlier, a few of the Irish immigrants became professional sawyers. There were no sawmills along the Cape Shore and timbers had to be cut with a pit saw, a laborious and backbreaking task. Unhewn posts remained predominant until the end of the century. Sawmills were rare in the Peterborough-Irish settlements. In Downeyville the immigrants had to go to the Orange town of Omemee 5 to 10 miles away to obtain sawn lumber and other Irish settlers in the area depended largely on the town of Peterborough. The more cheaply and easily constructed log barns persisted in the Irish settlements into the present century, and many are still in use.

VII
The dwelling house

Irish peasant houses of the early nineteenth century may be divided into three basic types: the central chimney style of eastern tradition, the western gable hearth house, and single-roomed cabins. Over 40 per cent of the latter existed in 1841 and were located mainly in the west and north.[1] Predominantly the homes of cottiers and labourers whose members increased dramatically in the first half of the nineteenth century, most of these cabins disappeared with this social class after the famine. One-roomed houses were least numerous in the southeast, but certainly existed there at the time of the migrations. Their major characteristics were a square floor plan with sides usually around 15 feet, puddled mud floors, thatched roof, a chimneyless open hearth, small windows, walls of stone, sod or mud and, of course, no internal divisions.

Walls and Roof
Many of the architectural features of the Irish cabin were also apparent in the more traditional 2- to 4-roomed Irish peasant house. Techniques of walling and flooring, for example, were similar. In the southeast tempered clay, and to a

---

1 Ireland, *Report of the Commissioners Appointed to take the Census of Ireland for the year 1841* (Dublin: Queen's Printer, 1843). Thirty-seven per cent of Irish houses had 2-4 rooms.

lesser extent wattles and daub or dry stone were used for external walls.[2] Mud walls were made from a mixture of damp red clay and chopped rushes or straw and were at least 20 inches thick. Mud floors were widespread, but flags were also common.

The frame of the roof was the only part of the traditional Irish house where timber was widely used. There were two basic types of framing. A roof might be carried on 3 or 4 purlins, resting on the gable walls between eaves and ridge and spanning the length of the dwelling. A purlin patchwork was sometimes substituted, the individual members resting on the partition walls. Ultimately the gables carried the weight of the roof and gable walls were often built of stone or tough, heavy sod for this purpose. The purlin framing offered the advantage of extending the house longitudinally but was confined almost exclusively to northern Ireland.[3] The other basic type was a roof supported by pairs of inclined timbers (couples) extending from sidewalls to ridge. The space between the individual rafters, called a "bay," was a standard unit of measurement, a house being so many "bays" or couples in length.

Two coupled roof types are still recognized in Ireland. In the west, couples do not usually meet but are joined near the apex by a short, wooden collar (tie-beam or yoke) which helps carry the overhead ridge purlin. Alternatively the couples are notched into the ridge purlin and are further secured by wooden pegs. Either of these jointing techniques produces a roof pitch without a perceptible ridge, and such a roof is especially well adapted to the more exposed, stormy western districts, as it is nicely rounded against the wind. In the southeast, by contrast, a steeply pitched roof is characteristic. Couples meet and sometimes cross, are notched into one another and fastened with a single wooden peg. Campbell believed the distinction between the rounded and sharply angled roof ridges was fundamental. The former, associated with hay-rope thatching in Ireland, was part of Atlantic fringe tradition; the latter, associated with *scollop* thatching, was on continental European origin.[4]

One of the diagnostic features of traditional Irish houses is the shape of the roof. It is either gabled or hipped. In the former type the gable walls extend vertically to the roof ridge. There are only two surfaces on the roof, front and back. Hipped roofs are four sided, having part of the gable ends sloping to the ridge, with the roof resting on inclined rafters. The hipped roof is an integral feature of the central chimney house type in Ireland and is found mainly in the south and east; the gable roof belongs to the western Irish tradition. Some scholars regard the latter tradition as indigenous and the hipped roof as a

2 C. Ó Danachair, "Materials & Methods in Irish Traditional Building," *Journal Royal Society Antiquaries Ireland* 87 (1957): 61-74.
3 E. Estyn Evans, *Irish Folk Ways* (London: Routledge & Kegan Paul, 1957), p. 48.
4 Åke Campbell, "Notes on the Irish House," *Folkliv* 1 (1937): 207-34.

continental importation possibly of Anglo-Norman origins, but it has also been suggested that the gable roof is a borrowing from landlord or town houses in the early modern period and that the hipped roof is a survival in the east of an older, native tradition once dominant in Ireland.[5] Whatever the type of framing or the shape, the Irish peasant roof was usually covered with an undercoat of sod and an overcoat of straw thatch pegged to the roof frame or sod with *scollops* or pliable sally rods.

Hearth and Chimney

In Irish tradition the hearth was the focal point for the household group. Prior to the introduction of chimney flues around the sixteenth century the fire lay on an open hearthstone at the centre of the house, and the smoke escaped through a hole in the roof. By the time of the migration hearths and chimneys were widespread, and wattle and daub was probably more popular than stone construction. Ashes from the open fire were stored in a special pit beneath one of the stone or wooden benches beside the fire. The two benches flanking the fire were fully beneath the open canopy and were honoured places for the older folk; seating arrangements around the fire were fixed by custom.[6] In Irish tradition the size of the hearth is typologically significant. Over most of the country a shallow hearth of less than 3 feet prevailed and was the only type in the north and west. In the southeast a deeply recessed hearth appears, possibly derived from English traditions in Ireland in the early modern period.[7] The breast or front of the chimney was usually supported by a solid wooden beam, brace-tree, or mantle that spanned the fireplace about 5 feet above the hearth, but stone lintels resting on stone corbels or stone-arched mantles were also found.[8] Where wattled hearths occurred the brace-tree usually spanned the kitchen, resting on the exterior walls.

In the wattled chimneys of Munster utensils were hung over the fire on a stout stick or iron bar set transversely into the throat of the chimney flue, at varying distances above the fire. An iron chain or bar was suspended from this horizontal member and was equipped with teeth or holes to carry the various pot hooks which in turn carried the pots and pans and other cooking vessels.

5 See F.H.A. Aalen, "The Evolution of the Western Irish House," *Journal Royal Society Antiquaries Ireland* 96 (1966): 47-58.
6 Conrad M. Arensberg and Solon T. Kimball, *Family & Community in Ireland* (Cambridge: Harvard University Press, 1940), p. 126.
7 Aalen, "Furnishings of Traditional Houses in the Wicklow Hills," *Ulster Folklife* 13 (1967): 61-67. Kevin Danaher, Irish Folklore Commission, has shown the writer illustrations of Munster hearths 7 feet in depth, but 4-5 feet was more usual in the southeastern Irish peasant house.
8 Ó Danachair, "Hearth & Chimney in the Irish House," *Béaloideas* 16 (1946): 91-104. The notion of arches may be borrowed from medieval castles.

Like many other facets of the Irish hearth and house, the adjustable pothook is a culture element of Atlantic European tradition. The iron crane was introduced before the migrations, its spread associated with the distribution of stone chimneys.

The major cooking vessel in Irish tradition was a huge three-legged iron pot which was ideal for boiling and prolonged stewing. Potatoes were the dietary staple at the time of the migrations, but cabbage and bacon were also boiled in this large vessel. Food for animals and for domestic fowl was prepared in the iron pot. Baking was done in a large bake-oven or bastable, suspended over the fire. Thin oat cakes and potato bread, a mixture of flour and potatoes, were popular. Bread was also baked on a griddle, often just a flat stone which rested on an iron trivet.

Floor Plans

In Ireland the location of the hearth within the dwelling is an all-important criterion distinguishing house types. The fundamental distinction was between centrally placed and gable-end hearths. At the time of the migrations the central hearth location was dominant over much of the east and south of Ireland, and became less common to the north and west. The hipped roof and jamb-wall entrance were associated with the central chimney, but in the west and north gabled houses sometimes had centrally placed chimneys.[9] The entrance door of the jamb-wall tradition led in directly in line with the main hearth and was separated from it by the projecting hearth wall. A door at one end of this vestibule or hallway led into the "front" room and the entrance at the opposite end was sometimes open and led directly into the combined kitchen-living room. In the southeast this hallway extended outwards beneath the thatched eaves to form a small outside porch where the front door was placed. The jamb wall provided a draught screen as well as a dignified entrance, associated with the inclusion of a parlour at "the other end." The Irish sense of curiosity was satisfied with the existence of a "spy-hole" above the bench in the jamb wall, through which the fireside residents could observe the inside hallway and front door. The earliest examples of jamb walls in Irish houses date from the early seventeenth century,[10] although it has been suggested that they are lineal descendants of the wattled partition in the early Irish house.[11]

9 Ó Danachair, "Some Distribution Patterns in Irish Folklife," *Béaloideas* 25 (1957): 108-23.

10 S.P. Ó Ríordáin and C. Ó Danachair, "Lough Gur Excavations: Site J. Knockadoon," *Journal Royal Society Antiquaries Ireland* 77 (1947): 39-52.

11 A.T. Lucas, "Wattle and Straw Mat Doors in Ireland," *Studia Ethnographica Upsaliensia* 11 (1956): 29-32. Campbell regarded the jamb wall as a continental importation, probably in medieval times (Campbell, "Notes on the Irish House," p. 221).

The western Irish house, by contrast, had its entrance at the far end of the kitchen, away from the fire; it provided ready access to the large kitchen and the hospitality of the open hearth. Unlike the southeastern house there was no porch and hallway and no parlour. The western Irish house had 2 or 3 but rarely 4 rooms. Wherever in the west the fireplace partition occurred, the room at the back of the fireplace – the "room above" – was occupied by the grandparents or parents and a body of folk belief relates to this room. In the 4-roomed peasant houses of the southeast the parlour or "upper room" is probably borrowed from the aristocracy in the early modern period; it was used only on important social occasions and for important visitors. Apparently there is no connection between the "special" rooms in the western and eastern Irish house.

Lofts were common to both Irish house types, but rarely extended the full length of the dwelling. The kitchen loft or *thallogue* was located between the brace-tree and rear wall of the fireplace and was used for storing domestic utensils, farm tools, and sometimes vegetables. A loft, used as a children's bedroom, was also placed over the bedroom or rooms opposite the fireplace. It might be noted that the Irish preferred the low house, and there was little space in the Irish loft. Two-storey dwellings were rare in Irish folk tradition. In the northwest the single bedroom in the typical two-roomed dwelling was augmented by a bed outshot recessed into the sidewall, beside the fire.

The centrally-placed front door in the western house was flanked by two small windows, one on each side. In the central chimney type the door was off-centre and there were usually three windows in front. Both house types had a window in the peaked gable to admit light to the sleeping loft. Windows were taxed and therefore were inordinately small. They were sometimes absent in the Irish house. A major characteristic of the western house was the opposing doors. It is possible that this feature was introduced to regulate the draught in the old chimneyless houses when the fire lay in a free-lying position towards the centre of the dwelling, or was related to the Celtic pastoral tradition when cows were housed with humans under one roof. The use of opposite doors did decline after the introduction of flues and the demise of the long house. In the southeast a draught was provided by a fire bellows, built into the hearth, but this may be of post-migration origins.

Kitchen Furniture

In the combined kitchen-living room of the Irish house the furniture was ranged along the walls, leaving the central space free. Wooden settles that opened into box-beds were widespread, especially in the western kitchens, where the loft was extremely small and sometimes absent. The most outstanding feature of Irish peasant furnishings was the large wooden dresser with its bottom doors, and shelving on top. The dresser became popular in peasant Ireland only in the decades before the migrations, and as elsewhere in Atlantic Europe it was descended from the court sideboards of an earlier aristocracy.[12] Its place in the Irish kitchen varied regionally but was often located directly opposite the fire, forming part of the partition between kitchen and bedrooms.[13] Finally the kitchen table was traditionally located beneath the window, by the wall, a tradition that has been contrasted with the centrally-placed table of continental Europe, where the table and not the fire was the social focus of the house.[14]

THE NEW WORLD

Initial Dwellings

Immigrants settling virgin lands usually went through a phase during which a crude dwelling formed out of the most immediately available material served temporarily as a shelter. Folk memory and folk tradition recall little of this initial stage in the Avalon, which perhaps is indicative of its brevity there. Both near St John's and along the Cape Shore the first dwelling was called a "tilt," and according to oral tradition these were one-roomed single-storied structures, rarely more than 14 feet square. There is a tradition that north of St John's "tilts" had mud or sodded walls. The "dug-outs" still widely remembered may be survivals of these embryonic dwellings. Built in against a bank down by the seashore in Logy Bay, Outer and Middle Cove, they comprised a single room, with a clay floor, a single door, and sod walls without windows. The peaked roof was usually covered with sods, giving the entire dwelling the appearance of a root cellar. An open fire was placed on a hearthstone at one end, the smoke escaping through a hole in the roof. Benches, beds, and other furnishings were ranged along the walls, leaving only a small area in the centre of the floor free. These crude huts were used only during the summer season, when some families left their farms to live close to the sea.

At least some of the first dwellings were studded. J.B. Jukes, travelling through Logy Bay in 1839, noted the scattered wooden huts used by the fishermen and describes a "tilt" near Flatrock, just north of the study area:

This was formed of trunks of trees placed upright on the ground, close together, with larger ones for the corner pieces, and a good strong gable-end roof formed of a frame of roughly squared beams. The corner pieces and beams were nailed together and the rest driven in tight with wooden wedges wherever necessary. The interstices of those trunks which formed the walls were filled up with moss,

12 Sigurd Erixon, "West European Connections and Culture Relations," *Folkliv* 2 (1938): 137-72. It was preceded by simple wall shelves and racks and the diffusion of the dresser has been linked with the widespread adoption of tea (see Evans, *Irish Folk Ways*, p. 91).
13 Alan Gailey, "Kitchen Furniture," *Ulster Folklife* 12 (1966): 18-34.
14 Campbell, "Notes on the Irish House," p. 234.

tightly rammed between them; and the roof was covered by long strips or sheets of birchbark, laid tile-like over one another, and kept down by poles or sticks laid across them. A space for a door is left in the middle of one side and a fireplace is built up with stones and boulders against one end, over which is a space in the roof, and some boards nailed together for a chimney. In this way a tolerable room, 12 or 14 feet by 8 or 10, sufficiently compact to keep out wind and weather to a certain extent ... was built.[15]

A "tilt" of somewhat similar proportions and construction was photographed in Logy Bay in 1886 and is sketched in Figure 25A. Local folk tradition along the Cape Shore asserts that the first dwellings were studded huts with thatched roofs. This tradition is substantiated by Wix's description of "tilts" around Placentia and across the Bay.[16]

No documentary data on the first dwelling in the Irish settlements in Miramichi have been found. Informants refer to this building as a "camp" but outside the fact that it seemed to be a small building with walls of horizontally placed logs there is no knowledge of its form. Over one hundred miles west of Miramichi the first dwelling in the Irish settlement of Johnville was described as a dugout type, with a clay floor, log walls, a roof of split poles covered with bark, branches, and sods.[17] A stone fireplace was built at one end. Figure 25B, showing a typical New Brunswick "shanty" or "camp" is based on several illustrations in the provincial museum at St John. It is likely that the Barnaby dwellings were similar to these.

The Peterborough-Irish built temporary huts where the town now stands, and from there the immigrants dispersed to their farm lots in the surrounding townships. Frances Stewart reported that these huts "look very odd, being made with poles standing up, boughs or branches of trees interwoven and mud plastered over this; they live in these until log shanties are ready for their families in Douro."[18] The "shanties" were erected either by neighbouring settlers accustomed to building with wood, who were paid £10 for each completed building, or

15 J.B. Jukes, *Excursions in and about Newfoundland in the Years 1839-40* (London: John Murray, 1842), p. 70. The cottages in Placentia had roofs of rind and studded walls in 1729, shortly after the French settlers there had been replaced by Irish and English immigrants (see B. Lacy, *Miscellaneous Poems Compos'd at Newfoundland on Board H.M. Ship "The Kinsale"* [London: The Author, 1729], pp. 1-20).

16 Edward Wix, *Six Months of a Newfoundland Missionary's Journal* (London: Smith, Elder and Co., 1836), pp. 21-22, 44, 58. One "tilt," on Isle Valen, west of Placentia, was only 12 feet by 10, yet accommodated 15 persons. In some "tilts" around the Bay even the chimneys were built of studs.

17 William P. Kilfoil, *Johnville: The Centennial Story of an Irish Settlement* (Fredericton: Unipress, 1962), pp. 24-25.

18 Frances Stewart, *Our Forest Home* (Montreal: Gazette Printing and Publishing Co., 1902), p. 84.

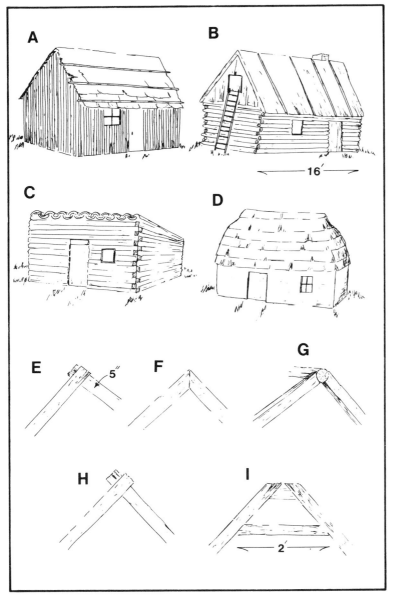

Figure 25

A – Tilt, St John's. B – Camp, Miramichi. C – Shanty, Peterborough. D – Cabin, Ireland.
Rafter joints: E, F – Avalon. G – St John's. H – Eastern Ireland. I – Western Ireland.

145

by the immigrants themselves under government supervision and assistance. Many of the immigrants added an outside skin of sods to the horizontally laid logs for extra warmth and covered the roof frame with sod, and mud and bark.[19] Wild grass and balsam boughs were also used as a roof cover. Others plastered their walls on the outside with a thick coating of mud.

According to local folk tradition, these log "shanties" were one-roomed dwellings with a single slope on the roof. Only one example survives in Downeyville. It is almost square in form, with dimensions of 14 by 12 feet and has a single door, centrally located on the front or high wall of the building (Fig. 25C). In this latter wall there was a single window. There are no traces of a fireplace, but old-timers claim that it was usually placed on a hearthstone set in the clay floor at one end of the cabin, the smoke passing out through a hole in the roof. A wall of stone or bank of clay protected the log wall from the fire. Basil Hall visited an Irishman's "shanty" in Douro in 1827 and reported that it was 20 feet by 12, and that the log walls were 7 feet high.[20] The interstices were chinked with mud and moss, and the roof was covered with logs split longitudinally, hollowed and laid out with the concave and convex sides alternately upwards, overlapping like long tiles and sloping from ridge to eave so that each alternate log formed a gutter to carry off the rain. Local tradition confirms that this kind of roof cover was widespread in the Irish areas and in Peterborough generally.[21]

The "shanty" phase lingered on in Peterborough until the second half of the nineteenth century. In Ennismore and Douro, where the southern Irish dominated, 39 and 32 per cent respectively of the total dwellings in 1851 were "shanties." A decade later all but a few of them had disappeared. Where the southern Irish were less prominent, as in Otonabee, Asphodel, and Smith Townships, the proportion of "shanties" in 1851 was as low as 16, 28, and 6 per cent respectively. A closer investigation of each township confirms the impression that the southern Irish retained the "shanty" longer than other neighbouring groups. In Douro 84 per cent of the "shanties" were occupied by southern Irish in 1851, 93 per cent in Ennismore, 74 per cent in Otonabee, 67 per cent in Emily, 50 per cent in Asphodel, and 39 per cent in Smith where the Irish comprised less than 12 per cent of the total population. A decade later, with a few exceptions, the "shanty" had been replaced in all of these townships by a more substantial house.

19 P.G. Towns, "Early Life in Douro," *Peterborough Daily Examiner,* May 15, 1925.
20 Basil Hall, *Travels in North America* 1 (Edinburgh: Carey, Lea & Carey, 1829), p. 291 *et seq.*
21 Catherine Parr Traill, *The Backwoods of Canada* (Toronto: McClelland & Stewart, 1968), pp. 44-45, 57-60.

The Second House: Avalon
Walls and roofs — In the Avalon this house was far more substantial than the "tilt" and generally survived from its construction in the 1830s and 40s well into the present century. Some of these traditional houses are still in use. The house plan was rectangular, in contrast to the almost square "tilt." Larger houses measured 25 feet in width and over 40 feet in length, but houses were sometimes as small as 16 by 26 feet. The walls were studded. Unlike outbuilding walls the studs were faced on all sides or, alternatively, were split or sawn longitudinally, with the rounded sides exposed on the outside. Each pole was "squatted" on a timber stand, barked and trimmed, then sawn lengthways with a pit-saw, or split with hammer and wedges. As well as abutting more closely, hewn studs were less difficult to board inside than were the rounded poles. The abutting edges of the studs were "stogged" or "chintzed" with moss, using a sharply pointed wooden implement called a "shem." Strips of bark covered the moss, producing an almost draught-proof wall. Not all house walls were clapboarded, even in living memory. Local timber was unsuitable for this purpose and imported hemlock sheeting was expensive. In older houses every stud was mortised into sill and wallplate, but more commonly every third or fourth stud only was jointed, the intervening timbers merely resting on or nailed to the sill. Occasionally along the Cape Shore, but more especially in the St John's settlements, studded walls evolved into a frame structure when the intermediate, loose-fitting members were omitted. The frame was covered inside and out with clapboarding and sometimes shingles were added. Building with studs was slow, especially when all members were mortised into wall-plate and sill. The poles seldom exceeded 12 inches in width and at least 100 were needed for the average Avalon dwelling.[22]

House walls were low, rarely exceeding 7 feet, and were crowned by a peaked — "coupled" or "saddled" — roof with a low pitch. Round poles, usually about 6 inches in diameter, were used as rafters. They were either nailed to or crowfooted on the wallplate and inclined towards the ridge of the house, where each couple was joined in an open mortise joint and secured with a "trunnel," as in barn couples (Fig. 25E, F). In the settlements north of St John's the settlers sometimes used a ridgepole, or "strongback," which ran the length of the house, onto which the rafters were mortised, one on each side (Fig. 25G). Couples were placed about 3 feet apart along the sidewalls and were further supported by a "collar-beam" or brace set a foot or so beneath the apex or ridgepole. The brace was secured to the two opposing rafters with wooden pegs. The ridgepole was supported by two uprights or studs, one at the centre of each gable wall, and was

22 In 1803, 120 studs, "sufficient to build a cook-room" were shipped from Placentia to Paradise (Great Britain, Colonial Office Correspondence, Newfoundland [MSS in Provincial Archives, St John's], Series 194, vol. 23, letter to John Whelan, March 1803).

sometimes reinforced by an upright embedded in the stone chimney. Occasionally the ridgepole was cut by the centrally placed chimney, but it more frequently formed a continuous member from gable to gable.

All the houses north of St John's and all but 4 in Freshwater were gabled, but over a dozen dwellings along the Cape Shore had a 4-sided or hipped roof, locally called a "bell" or "cottage" roof.[23] One or more inclined timbers rested on the gable-end wallplates and were mortised into the end couples, producing a secondary slope or pitch at each end of the house.

Strips of spruce bark and long sticks were placed over the rafters, or hemlock sheathing, purchased in St John's or Placentia, was used. Along the Cape Shore thatched roofs were older than shingle roofs but less than a dozen thatched homes, most of them in St Brides, survived to the end of the last century. The form of thatching was similar to that on the root cellar. It is likely that in the settlements close to St John's sodded roofs were fairly common, but within living memory sod was reserved for the "linhay" and other outbuildings. From the middle of the nineteenth century shingles probably dominated as a roofing material in all Avalon study areas. The first papers published in St John's list shingles for sale and in 1816 four stores specialized in selling shingles and other lumber.[24] Long before the Irish spread along the Cape Shore, shingles were used in Placentia: in 1788, for example, shingles, ships' masts, bowsprits, square oak balks, and inch boards were imported from Quebec.[25] Shingles were manufactured locally along the Cape Shore as far back as folk memory extends. Pine or oak-beams, salvaged from a shipwreck or purchased in Placentia, were cut into blocks about 16 inches long and split into thin slabs with an iron wedge or hammer. Each slab of wood was fashioned into a shingle by shaving it with a drawknife. Placed on a wooden bench or "shaving horse" the piece of wood was secured by a wooden or iron bolt which passed through the bench and could be operated underneath by foot. Shingles varied in size but rarely exceeded 5 by 15 inches. Like many other tasks along the Cape Shore, shingling was a specialized craft and an expert could manufacture over 1,000 shingles a day.

23 The eighteenth century Catholic church in Placentia was described as a "little low building with a cottage roof" (Monsignor Flynn, "The Parish of Placentia," *Newfoundland Quarterly* 36 [1936]: 29-32). In Freshwater the 4-sided roof was referred to as a "bee-hive" roof.
24 *Royal Gazette & Newfoundland Advertiser,* St John's, July 16, 1816 (in Provincial Archives, St John's).
25 Newfoundland, Letter Book of Saunders and Sweetmans, Placentia (MSS in Arts & Culture Library, St John's), May 12, 1788. In the following year lumber and shingles were imported from St John's and in 1790, 22,000 shingles were requested to cover the houses in Placentia.

Hearth and chimney – The hearth and chimney of the Avalon house were located towards the centre of the rectangular floor plan, forming a partition between the kitchen-living room and the "front" or "upper" room. The chimney complex lay fully inside the studded sidewalls. Using local stone, walls from 2 to 3 feet in thickness were built up on 3 sides to a height of 6 feet. The rear wall of this 3-sided structure measured up to 14 feet in length (Fig. 26A). Two projecting walls, averaging 7 feet each, surrounded the hearth floor and were linked by a 10 by 10 inch oak beam or balk to complete the basic architecture of the hearth. A fourth wall rested on this wooden member to form a stone chimney that tapered upwards from the level of the balk to a summit measuring not more than 3 square feet. Lime and sand were the ordinary mortar ingredients, but along the Cape Shore a sticky white clay or daub was also used. Wattled or "rodded" chimney stacks were built instead of stone in the latter area, especially in the thatched houses in St Brides. A light framework of "longers" or sticks extended from the hearth walls and back to the roof ridge and withes were woven through these slender uprights in the same fashion as described for the *kish*. The structure was plastered over with mud, both inside and out, and a special wooden box was fitted over the roof ridge to form a chimney crown. In the St John's settlements the crown was sometimes built with brick.

The hearth floor, covering an area up to 50 square feet, was paved with wide flags that extended out into the kitchen; in a few houses brick was used instead of flags. A huge hearth stone, on which the fire was placed, was located close to the rear hearth wall, and was sometimes surrounded by a low, protecting wall. Directly above the fire, at the level of the balk, an iron bar or "bolt" spanned the chimney canopy and was embedded in the walls on either side. From this bar the iron crooks and adjustable pot-hangers, suspended over the open fire, carried the various cooking vessels including a round-bellied three-legged iron pot or bake-oven, an iron kettle, and frying pan. The adjustable hanger or cotterel was bored or had sharply angled teeth on to which the crooks were fitted. A number of variously sized crooks were also used for the adjustable hangers, especially along the Cape Shore, or two or three bars were set at different levels over the fire. Apart from Freshwater, the moveable iron bar or crane (an improved form of hanging) was rarely used. The crane was pivoted on a stone spud placed towards the centre, but more usually at one side of the hearth floor, and could swing in, gate-like, over the hearthstone.

A notable element of hearth furnishings was the "dogirons," a crude iron grate used to carry the log fire. In some houses along the Cape Shore, however, the fire was placed on the open hearthstone. The hob was another salient item of the hearth complex; it was usually a stone seat or ledge either behind or beside the fire, but in some cases the space between the hearthstone and sidewall, or rearwall, has been called the hob. Whatever its form, its function was clear: pots and pans and other fireside gear were left on it when not in use. Elaborate

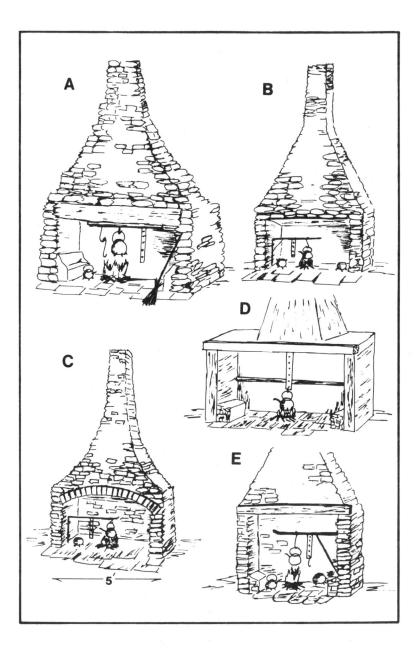

Figure 26
Hearth and chimney: **A** — Avalon. **B** — Miramichi. **C** — Peterborough. **D** — Southeast Ireland. **E** — Western Ireland.

wooden benches were built into the two projecting walls to flank the fire. Along the Cape Shore the fireside settle was often a moveable stool or bench under which boots and shoes, rather than domestic fowl, were kept. Above the benches small alcoves, called "catholes," were incorporated into the architecture of the hearth walls and were used for storing tobacco, pipes, mitts, socks, knitting equipment, and kitchen paraphernalia. The alcove was also the repository for the powder horn, used to ignite the fire. Traditionally the cod-oil lamp was suspended from a nail driven into the hardwood beam and illuminated the entire hearth area.

The massive stone hearth was the focal point of the whole house, and in Branch, where an extra bench was placed along the rear wall, as many as 15 people could sit around the centrally-placed open fire. Indeed some settlers regarded the "chimney corners" almost as a separate compartment within the kitchen-living room.

Floor plans – In the Avalon the dominant floor plan consisted of an outside porch leading into a short hallway or vestibule, in line with the hearth, and on into the kitchen on one side and into the "front" or "upper" room behind the fireplace, on the other (Fig. 27A). At the other end of the rectangular unit, off the centrally-placed kitchen, were two small bedrooms with their doors facing the fireplace. Along the Cape Shore 26 of the 48 houses investigated had this 4-room layout, while a dozen houses, all in Branch and Patrick's Cove, had their bedrooms along the back of the dwelling, behind the kitchen and front room. In the settlements north of St John's 11 of the 58 houses examined had back bedrooms, evolved from the "linhay." In Freshwater 10 of the 12 houses surveyed were also of this latter plan, while only two had the central kitchen plan, compared to 24 houses in the settlements north of St John's. Only 8 of these Avalon houses had no bedrooms on the ground floor. All but 15 houses had the porch-and-hallway entrance, 8 along the Cape Shore, and 7 north of St John's, and all of the houses with a hallway or "entry" had a "front" room. The house entrance was placed directly in line with the chimney in all but 8 houses, and only in 7 cases (6 in Outer Cove and one in Freshwater) was the chimney located at the gable end rather than towards the centre of the dwelling. There was no "front" room in gable-hearth houses. Freshwater aside, only in a few cases were these traditional dwellings more than one storey high, but all had a sleeping loft running the length of the building. The loft floor was supported on ceiling joists resting on the sidewalls of the house, and the loft space was subdivided by the stone chimney stack. The loft was used as a bedroom, principally by the children. Light was admitted through small windows on the side gables, or, in the one and a half storey homes, through a row of half windows along the front wall. The ladder or stair giving access to the loft was usually located between the stone chimney and back wall in the Cape Shore, between the hallway and stone

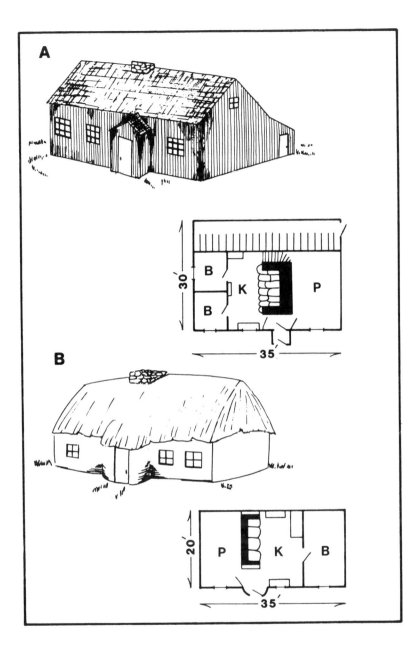

Figure 27
Floor Plan: A — Avalon. B — Southeast Ireland.

chimney in Freshwater, and in the front corner (across from the kitchen door) in the settlements north of St John's.

Within living memory all floors were boarded. Local timber was normally used, although pine boarding was available in St John's and Placentia. On Saturday women carried sand from the beach and sprinkled it on the kitchen floor where it was often left overnight and in some cases for several days before being swept up. The householders often amused themselves by drawing decorative patterns on the sanded floor.

Kitchen furniture – The disposition of kitchen furnishings outside the hearth itself was fixed by custom. On the Cape Shore the dominant location of the dresser was along the partition wall dividing the kitchen from the bedrooms, but it was sometimes placed in a corner against the back wall, an arrangement predominating in the St John's settlements. Traditionally in all three Avalon settlements the kitchen table was placed under the front window, with a settle bed located along the opposite wall. Dressers were home made. The upper section of the dresser had three shelves, where the large willow patterned plates were stacked, all standing on edge and facing out towards the kitchen. Lustre jugs were hung on pegs, and the top of the dresser was often carved into attractive designs. Below these shelves there was a drawer for cutlery while the base of the dresser was used to store pots and pans and other kitchen utensils (Fig. 28A). Part of this equipment might also be stored under the "stillen" or wooden bench in the porch, where buckets of water, boots and sometimes dairy produce were kept.

The settle or "stretcher," often with carved back and arm rests or "pumbles," was used only as daytime seats in the Avalon kitchen. They were less common than the fireside benches, especially near St John's. Another characteristic item of furniture was the "rocker," usually reserved for the older members of the family (Fig. 29C). A cruder rocking chair, fashioned out of a puncheon and furnished with two runners underneath was common to all three settlements, and was especially popular along the Cape Shore (Fig. 28D). More elaborate furnishings – tables, chairs, couches – were kept in the "upper" or "front" room of the Avalon house. This room was used only on special occasions – the "times" (dances) at the end of the fishing season, wakes or weddings, or whenever important visitors arrived. Bedrooms were sparsely furnished, but the feather bed had a special status as part of the daughter's dowry.

Survivals – After 1870 this single-storied structure evolved in some cases into a two-storey dwelling, with all the bedrooms located either upstairs or in the "linhay." Otherwise the raised house preserved all the elements of the central-hearth form and lay-out. The central chimney type was gradually replaced at the

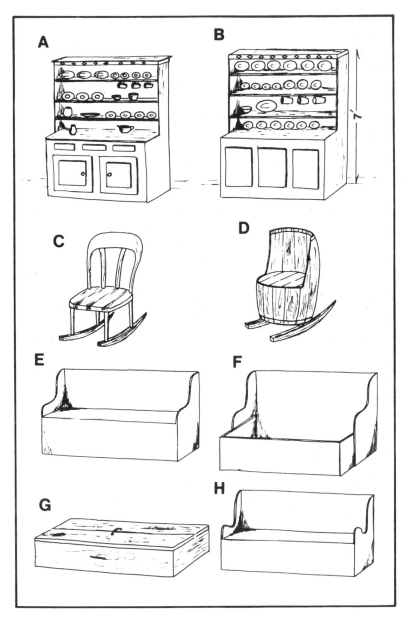

Figure 28
Kitchen furniture: Dressers. A — New World. B — Ireland. C — Rocking chair, Avalon. D — Barrel chair, Avalon. E, F — Miramichi settle-bed. G — Peterborough bunk-bed. H — Settle, Ireland.

end of the century, by a two-storey, flat-roofed frame building that is the characteristic contemporary house. The shallow roof developed concurrently with the "whaleback" barn roof and afforded more sleeping room upstairs. A square rather than rectangular floor plan was associated with the flat-roofed house type, the central hearth-and-chimney was replaced with a stove, a much more effective heating device. Certain characteristics of the old layout pattern were transferred to the new dwelling: the front room and large kitchen, the porch and entry, and furniture items such as the settle, rocking chair, and dresser were retained. But other diagnostic elements of the older house – the studded walls, the coupled roof, the central hearth and chimney, the ground bedrooms, the sleeping loft – disappeared.

No other item of material culture in the Avalon was surrounded with so many folk beliefs and superstitions as the individual house. It was unlucky to build a house on the site of a previous one, or across a path, for in doing so one might disturb the souls of the dead. Moreover, bad luck would follow if the material of an old house were used to build a new dwelling. When building a chimney, the hearth could be protected from evil spirits by inserting a coin somewhere in the chimney wall, or by placing seashells on the hearth. Once built, it was unlucky to raise the roof of a house, or, if adding to it, to build the extension to the same height as the dwelling. The fire itself was a symbol of good luck: embers flying from the hearth were taken as a sign of impending improvement in the household's material welfare and a firebrand or "flanker" taken from the fire and thrown over the roof protected the home from destruction by fire. Flankers were also placed under the churn if evil spirits were interfering with the churning. A visitor should always leave by the same door as he entered, otherwise bad luck might follow for the household. Floors should be swept from east to west, and it was considered extremely unlucky to sweep out a wake room while the corpse was still there.

Peterborough and Miramichi
Walls and roofs – In both Peterborough and Miramichi the second house was a one-storey log building with a peaked roof (Fig. 29A, B). Like the Avalon house, these log buildings had a rectangular floor plan, but were considerably smaller. The average dimensions of the loghouse were 22 feet by 16, with walls around 8 feet high. Cedar logs were popular, but pine and hemlock were also used. Logs were hewn to approximately 12 inches by 6 in Miramichi, the narrow side forming the thickness of the wall; in Peterborough they were almost square in section. Stone foundations were rarely built; the log sill was placed directly on the soil. Both walling and roofing techniques and materials were similar to the log barns, and the walls were often whitewashed. For this latter purpose limestone was burned for several days in a kiln and then mixed with water to provide the wash.

155

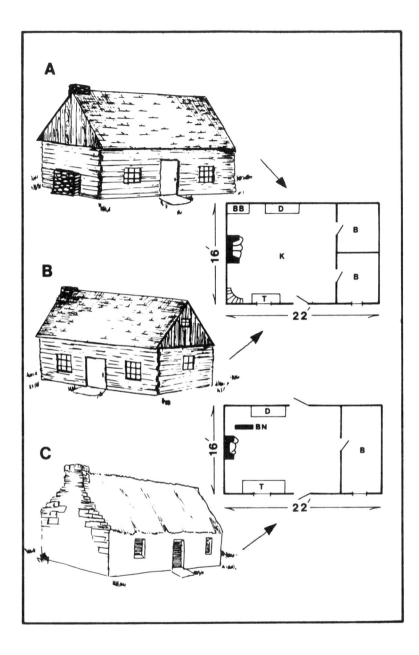

Figure 29
Gable chimney houses: A — Peterborough. B — Miramichi. C — Western Ireland.

156

In both areas the front wall of the log dwelling had a centrally placed door with a window on each side, about half way between the door and the corners of the house. The door was originally composed of a single slab of cedar, later of jointed boards, and was closed with a latch or hasp. Nine to 12 pane windows were usual. Frequently there were one or two extra windows at the gable ends or back of the dwelling and one or two smaller windows admitted light to the sleeping loft.

Hearth and chimney – Many of the loghouses were built about the middle of the last century, after stoves had become locally popular. The stone hearth and chimney appeared only in 9 of the 17 loghouses examined in Miramichi and in 14 of the 28 Peterborough houses. In all cases the hearth-and-chimney complex was located at the gable end and was a much smaller structure than in the Avalon. Flags some 5 by 3 feet, and 6 to 9 inches in thickness, taken from the bed of the Barnaby river, were used to construct the Miramichi hearth. Two of these flags were placed with their longer sides upright, about 5 feet apart, facing each other just inside the gable wall. Another larger flag was placed behind them, abutting the end wall and protecting it from the open fire. The two projecting flags in this 3-sided figure were linked by a long, stone mantle, functionally analogous to the wooden balk of the Avalon hearth. A narrow supporting wall was built on the outside of all three slabs. The interior hearth space was 5 feet wide, 5 feet high, and 3 feet deep (Fig. 26B). A fourth wall rested on the mantle piece, to complete the chimney stack which tapered upwards to about two square feet at the summit. Sometimes the supporting wall at the back of the fireplace was wholly within the loghouse, sometimes exposed externally as high as the wallplate. Two holes were bored into one of the projecting slabs and crane fitments inserted. The hearth floor was formed with a few flat flags, on one of which the fire was placed. Fire-irons or andirons, so widespread in the Avalon, were rarely used in Miramichi.

The Peterborough hearth was equally shallow. As in the other study areas the settlers used local stone or rubble, cemented with lime and sand, but instead of the stone mantle or wooden beam a narrow iron bar usually supported the mantle wall. On this bar, sometimes slightly arched over the hearth floor, rested a row of wedge-shaped stones, standing on their thin edges to form a decorative mantle (Fig. 26C). In all other architectural details the Peterborough hearth was similar to that of Miramichi. Wherever the open fire existed in these two study areas, the fireside area and culinary traditions were usually similar to the Avalon. Because the hearth was not deeply recessed there were no benches on the Peterborough or Miramichi hearth floor, and in the latter area intramural keeping-holes could not be incorporated because of the stone slabs that surrounded the open fire. In Peterborough alcoves were also absent.

Floor plans — In both areas the floor-space was subdivided into three compartments; a big kitchen, occupying more than half the house, and two small bedrooms at one gable end, whose doors faced the fireplace. All floors were boarded, usually with pine. As in the Avalon, access to the loft was gained by a ladder or boxed-in kitchen stairs. Formally and functionally the loghouse loft resembled the Avalon type, but in the later one and a half storey dwellings in Peterborough a low "knee" wall existed, above the loft floor, against which beds could be placed.

Kitchen furniture — A box-bed, or settle-bed, usually placed along the back wall, was a characteristic item of kitchen furniture in both study areas. They were more numerous in Miramichi where they survived up to the present century. The form of the settle-bed resembled the fireside benches of the Avalon. A hinged seat opened out and formed a shallow rectangular space where the children slept (Fig. 28E, F). During the day it was folded and used as a bench. The Peterborough "bunk" was similar, but did not possess the high back (Fig. 28G).

The kitchen table in both study areas was placed beneath the front window while the dresser or cupboard, similar in design to the Avalon type, was normally beside the settle. When not in use pots and pans were sometimes stored beneath the kitchen stairs, in the "pothole." As in the Avalon one or two rocking chairs, reserved for the old timers, were located close to the fire.

Survivals — The clear predominance of loghouses in both study areas is amply demonstrated in the 1851 census. Of the 104 houses in mid-nineteenth century Miramichi 83 were of log and 21 of frame construction. Frame or plank buildings were confined almost exclusively to Nowlanville, an area more immediately tributary to Nelson and the main river settlements. Ten of these houses survived into living memory, and were identical in layout to the loghouses. All had gable-end chimneys and stone fireplaces. From 1860 onwards a different house style evolved which by the close of the century had largely replaced the loghouse. The basic proportions and external form of the loghouse were preserved in this new type. Inside, a central hall and stairway divided the kitchen from the front room, and bedrooms were ranged along the back of the dwelling. Alternatively, the two front rooms were reserved as a parlour and a bedroom and kitchen added on to the back of the house to form a T-shaped plan. Less frequently, a kitchen was added to one side of the dwelling. The walls were framed and the house sometimes raised to one and a half stories, but the steeply pitched roof of the loghouse remained. A stove replaced the stone hearth, and the chimney, made of brick, retained its traditional location at the gable end.

Log dwellings were even more dominant in Peterborough in the middle of the last century and yielded more slowly to frame or brick structures than did those in Miramichi. All but one of Ennismore's houses were log in 1851 and even a decade later there was only one stone and one frame dwelling. All but 7 of the Ennismore loghouses were one-storey dwellings in 1861. The southern Irish retained the loghouse longer than neighbouring groups. In Otonabee, for example, the southern Irish ranked lowest, proportionally, in the lists of families occupying frame and stone houses, but headed the shanty and loghouse list in the mid-nineteenth century. Only Protestant immigrants occupied stone and frame dwellings in Douro in 1851, where the southern Irish were numerically dominant; by 1861 the Protestant minority owned 74 framed and 4 stone houses, the Irish only 17. Building with logs declined in the Scots-Irish settlement of southern Emily between 1851-1861, and between 1856 and 1860 there were more frame dwellings than log erected in the first two concessions of the township.[26] By contrast, the Catholic Irish in north Emily continued to build almost exclusively with logs. By 1861 the Catholic Irish, although comprising 38 per cent of the total population of Emily occupied only 12 per cent of buildings in the township that were not made of log.

The frame, brick, and stone dwellings introduced by Scots-Irish, Scots, and English immigrants were eventually diffused into the southern Irish settlements. Almost all of these houses had a central hallway, dining room and parlour and had most of the sleeping rooms upstairs. This improved house became widespread in the southern Irish townships only in the present century.

The dialect words describing the first dwelling differed in each study area and, with one possible exception, had no southern Irish antecedents.[27] Certainly the log walls and trough roof of the Peterborough "shanty" were local borrowings; indeed some "shanties" there were built for the Peterborough-Irish by neighbouring pioneers. Similarly, the walling techniques adopted in the Avalon and Miramichi were widespread in those areas before the Irish settled and were undoubtedly copied. However, some elements of homeland construction were introduced to this first dwelling. In Peterborough there is evidence of the use of wattle and daub, while sod walls and sod roofs and the use of thatch are probably of Irish provenance. It might also be argued that the small square floor plan, mud floors, small windows, single-room lay-out and chimneyless open hearth of

26 Canada, *Census of Canada, 1861* (MSS in National Archives, Ottawa), RG 31, C-1076, Emily Township. The dates of construction for all but "shanty" dwellings were collected for some Emily concession lines in this census.
27 Eugene O'Growney, *Simple Lessons in Irish* 3 (Dublin: M.H. Gill, 1936), p. 25, suggests that the word "shanty" is derived from the Gaelic *sean-ti'*, an old house. There is considerable controversy among dialectologists over the etymology of this term. It was widely used in Upper Canada before the Peterborough-Irish arrived.

these pioneer dwellings were important characteristics of the Irish cabin (Fig. 25D).[28] As in Ireland these units were built in difficult times, under emergency conditions, and did not endure very long. In the New World they were more the mark of pioneer expediency than a transfer of a tradition and other ethnic groups, coming from areas where perhaps the one-roomed cabin was unknown, resorted to this type on the frontier. The relative longevity of the "shanty" amongst the Peterborough-Irish may reflect cultural preferences or inertia, especially since the cost of building a more substantial three-roomed loghouse was minimal. Construction materials could be taken off the land when clearing it, labour could be pooled and almost everything in a loghouse could be home-made. Yet many of the Peterborough-Irish, at least, remained in the "shanty" for a generation.

Walling materials and techniques appear as the least transferable of the various components of Irish vernacular architecture. Building with mud, sods, wattle and daub, or stone, was a time consuming task and such walls afforded poor insulation in a Canadian winter. As previously argued, timber was far more practical for building on the frontier, and log or studded walls were less costly and required fewer skills than frame construction. The framing of the New World roof, however, differed little from homeland tradition. Apart from some dwellings in the St John's study areas, where the ridgepole was introduced, the jointed couple technique of southeast Ireland was used (Fig. 25H). This type of rafter joint, where blades are pinned together diagonally at the apex in an open mortise notch was widespread in colonial North America and in Europe.[29] In western Ireland a ridgepole helped carry the heavy roof-load of sod and thatch (Fig. 25I) and its use in St John's may extend back to the days when sod roofs were common, but it became an anachronism when the lighter and more steeply pitched shingle roofs were introduced. Ridgepoles could not, of course, be easily supported by the frail frame of the loghouse gables, whereas the gable studs of the Avalon house gave ample support to this member. Collar beams, used in Ireland to brace the couples and reduce the outward thrust of the rafters on the wallplates, were also unnecessary on the Peterborough or Miramichi roof, but in the Avalon where roofs were both heavier and wider, collar beams were common. The intensified thrust on the roof was to some extent diminished in the Avalon by the introduction of the hipped roof; the thrust was spread on all four walls and reduced the danger of collapse. This was partly the rationale for

28 Evans, for example, regarded the Scots-Irish log cabin in America as a reproduction, in a novel medium, of the space relations of the single-roomed, gable-chimney house of mud or stone that was probably the dominant type in Ulster in the eighteenth century (E.E. Evans, "Cultural Relics of the Ulster Scots in the Old West of North America," *Ulster Folklife* 11 [1965] : 33-38).

29 Henry Glassie, "A Central Chimney Continental Log House from Cumberland County," *Pennsylvania Folklife* 18 (1968-69): 33-39.

hipped roofs in the homeland. A gabled roof although stylistically less attractive was architecturally simpler and offered more space in the sleeping loft; and even in the Avalon the gable roof was predominant. Instead of laths and a sod undercoating, strips of bark were used to cover the rafters in the study areas, and this latter technique was widespread in eastern North America. Shingling techniques were also borrowed from neighbouring settlers, and their absence in some Cape Shore settlements reflects cultural isolation.[30] But even here the technique of thatching was adapted to North American pioneer traditions: the rushes were placed directly on the wood or bark and were pinned down by horizontally placed poles as on the bark roofs.

The central chimney, jamb-wall complex of southeast Ireland was reproduced in the Avalon with a few modifications. Whereas stone flues were a minority in the homeland, in the New World they became the norm. Wattled chimney canopies were an obvious fire hazard in wooden dwellings. In 1803, for example, inhabitants of Placentia were ordered to build flues of stone or brick for this reason,[31] and the literature on the backwoods abounds with warnings of this kind. Despite the danger, wattled flues were introduced and survived on the Cape Shore up to the present century. The white clay used as mortar in the stone and wattled chimneys of the New World was similar to the daub or tempered clay used in the homeland. Beneath the canopy, the deeply recessed Avalon hearth is possibly of southeast Irish derivation (Fig. 26D), but it is also likely that the Westcountrymen transferred a similar tradition. Richard Bonnycastle describes the "capacious stone chimney, with a deep recess, like those of the old farm houses in Buckinghamshire, where benches and chairs are placed and where old people sit. ..."[32] The huge stone hearth and chimney of the traditional Devonshire farmhouse, normally located with its back to the central passage and byre, resembled the Avalon complex and it is likely, moreover, that the West Country was an important source area for the southeast Irish massive hearth.[33] The ubiquity of these massive hearths on the Cape Shore, however, suggest direct transfer from Ireland. Certainly the use of keeping holes and hobs and the placing of benches beneath the chimney hood, beside the fire were all

30 Shingling was common in medieval Ireland and survived in Armagh, for example, up to the eighteenth century (see W.H. Crawford, "The Woodlands of Brownlow's Derry," *Ulster Folklife* 10 [1964]: 57-64).
31 Newfoundland, Surrogate Court Records, Placentia (MSS in Arts & Culture Library, St John's), March 3, 1803.
32 R.H. Bonnycastle, *Newfoundland in 1842: A Sequel to the "Canadas in 1841"* (2 vols; London: H. Colburn, 1842), pp. 126-27.
33 For West Country house types see Bruce W. Oliver, "The Devonshire Cottage," *Devonshire Association, Report and Transactions* 81 (1949): 27-45; M.W. Barley, *The English Farmhouse and Cottage* (London: Routledge and Kegan Paul, 1961), pp. 108-13, 164-68, 221-24; N.W. Alcock, "Devon Farmhouses," *Devonshire Association, Report and Transactions* 100 (1968): 13-28.

part of the homeland hearth tradition; but the Avalon Irish never transferred the ash pit, which in Ireland was placed beneath one of the benches. The disappearance of the "spy-hole" is in part related to the difficulty of incorporating such a feature in the rough dry-wall of the Avalon jamb-wall and the fact that during the long winters the closed doors reduced the attractions of such an observation point.

It was largely because of adverse winters, too, that the exterior porch was extended in the Avalon and a network of doors established; an inrush of cold air always accompanied the opening of these doors in winter. It should be noted also that the "stillen" in the Avalon porch is of Irish provenance. Some of the immigrants in Peterborough and Miramichi would have been familiar with the outside porch in the homeland and it was, perhaps, log architecture that precluded its reproduction in these areas. It would have been extremely difficult to incorporate either this feature or the outshot into a log wall, as it would involve considerable cutting and notching to construct projecting walls. By contrast, these items were easily added if studding were used, but the southeast Irish had no outshot tradition.

Both in western Ireland and in Peterborough and Miramichi the hearth was too shallow and narrow to admit seats beneath the chimney, although in the western Irish tradition small stone hobs were sometimes built on either side of the fire (Fig. 26E). The small hearth tradition may well reflect the source area of the Peterborough and Miramichi immigrants, outside the province of large fireplaces in the southeast, but shallow hearths were characteristic of pioneer folk housing near these study areas before the Irish came. Certainly there are no antecedents for the upright flags of the Miramichi hearth or the iron bar used to support the outer wall of the chimney stack in Peterborough; the stone lintels of the former and stone-arched mantles of the latter area, however, are recorded in Irish peasant houses.

In all study areas the homeland tradition of preparing food in vessels suspended over the open fire endured until the introduction of the stove. The fixed iron bar and the movable crane both reappear, but it is difficult to explain the ubiquity of the latter in the Peterborough and Miramichi areas, unless cranes came ready-made from the stores. According to folk tradition the three-legged iron pot, the bake-oven, the iron pan, and the kettle were among the few items of material culture that were carried physically across the Atlantic by the immigrants. These culinary items were probably the most prized possessions in the immigrants' baggage and were put to use immediately in the New World. In some cases they were stored away after they had been displaced by more modern cooking vessels and may still be produced as evidence of the family's connections with Ireland. Not all of the culinary gear used in the homeland was transferred, or if transferred, did not last long. There is no memory of the Irish griddle, sometimes just a flat stone on which bread was baked, or the trivet, on

162

which the griddle rests. The traditional Irish diet was maintained in the New World under the old open fire regime and only slowly gave way with the spread of stoves.

It is significant that the built-in bread oven, a fundamental feature of the hearth traditions in central and eastern Europe, and parts of western Europe, never took root among the immigrant Irish, despite its use by neighbouring groups in the study areas. Apart from the baronies of Bargy and Forth in south Wexford, where many other culture-elements of late-medieval English-planter origins survived, the built-in oven was rare in Ireland. The "dog-irons," another important feature of traditional English hearths, were not used in Ireland. In the New World, logs replaced peat as the standard fuel, and "dog-irons" were introduced to carry the logs. They represent one of the few intrusive elements in the immigrant Irish hearth-and-chimney complex.

In the New World the stove was a much more practical heating and cooking device than the open fire. More than one cooking vessel could be used concurrently, something much more difficult to manage over the open fire. The stove was an expensive item, yet its slow acceptance by the immigrants, especially in the Avalon, cannot be attributed to economic factors alone. To the immigrants and to many of their decendants, the open hearth was the social nucleus of the house, and a symbol of hospitality and family solidarity. In the Avalon, the displacement of the open hearth came in the middle decade of the last century, often with the change in Peterborough from "shanty" to loghouse and from log to frame construction in Miramichi. Building a stone chimney was a laborious task and the stove required only a light brick chimney stack, supported on wooden brackets high in the gable.

The most distinctive parallel that might be drawn between Irish and New World houses was in the floor plan. In the Avalon the 4-roomed, one-storey, central-chimney dwelling with hall and entry, parlour, and sleeping loft was identical to the southeast Irish house (Fig. 27B) while the smaller 2- or 3-roomed layout of the loghouses in Peterborough and Miramichi, with the gable-end fireplace and small loft was similar to the western Irish arrangement (Fig. 29C).[34] The latter type is of Atlantic European tradition and other British groups reproduced this layout in the Peterborough and Miramichi areas. In colonial America the central chimney is largely of German provenance, although this house type is found all over continental Europe; its origins in the Avalon are unquestionably southeast Irish and West Country, but it is impossible to determine to what extent the Irish in the study areas were influenced by the West

34 Glassie has argued that the rectangular, 2-roomed, gable-hearth house built by the Scots-Irish in the Old West is based on the western Irish house (Glassie, "The Types of Southern Mountain Cabin," in Jan H. Brunvand (ed.), *The Study of American Folklore* [New York: W.W. Norton, 1968], pp. 338-70).

Country tradition there. While it is highly unlikely that all Avalon emigrants had occupied the central chimney type in the homeland or all Peterborough and Miramichi Irish lived in the gable chimney type, the relative strength of either tradition in the homelands of the immigrants is manifested in the New World.

Other analogies with Irish styles were manifest in the form and disposition of kitchen furniture. In the New World the dresser and settle or box-bed resembled Irish styles (Fig. 28B, H). While the table was placed usually under the front kitchen window in all areas the dresser in the New World was normally located along the back wall of the kitchen, rarely along the partition wall facing the fire, as was the case in the homeland. There were, however, some innovations to the Irish kitchen plan. Whereas in the Old World a simple ladder often served as access to the loft, a boxed-in stairs came to dominate in the study areas. This feature was known in medieval English houses, and on the continent, but was never popular in the Irish peasant house. In the New World also, the abundance of lumber facilitated the inclusion of a full loft and boards replaced mud on the floor. There is no memory of the half-door in the immigrants' dwellings. Finally the external appearance of these two house styles, with their centrally placed front door, two or three front windows, white washed walls, single storey, and sloping roof retained the basic proportions of the houses in the homeland.

VIII
Transfer and adaptation: a summary

The patterns of transfer and adaptation of Irish material folk culture and other settlement traditions to the New World, described and interpreted in chapters iii-vii, are summarized in Figure 30. Generally, the movement of Irish across the Atlantic resulted in a rapid loss of cultural traits, but the rate of attrition varied between study areas. The extent of cultural transfer and the durability of transferred traits was greatest on the Cape Shore, where some homeland traits and trait complexes were readily reproduced and were slow to change, and least in Peterborough, where homeland traits were introduced less frequently, and when introduced did not normally last very long. Between these extremes Miramichi occupied a somewhat middle place, while the St John's settlements were culturally closer to the Cape Shore. Although it should also be noted that there were variations within each study area both in the rate of transfer of individual traits and the durability of transferred traits, for some traits and trait complexes the patterns of transfer and discard in all study areas were strikingly similar. Individual farm outbuildings and the lay-out of the farmstead, for example, was everywhere the least transferred of the trait clusters examined, but traditional Irish settlement patterns and associated open fields were only slightly more transferable. In all study areas traditional Irish field systems were less likely to be reproduced than was farm technology and there was a striking contrast in the extent of transfer of house interiors as compared with house exteriors.

Cultural change was no novelty to these immigrants. For a century or more prior to the migrations Irish peasant culture had been subjected to a variety of influences, both internal and external, that eroded much of its medieval heritage. Irish peasant culture had never been static, but the pace of change after 1700

165

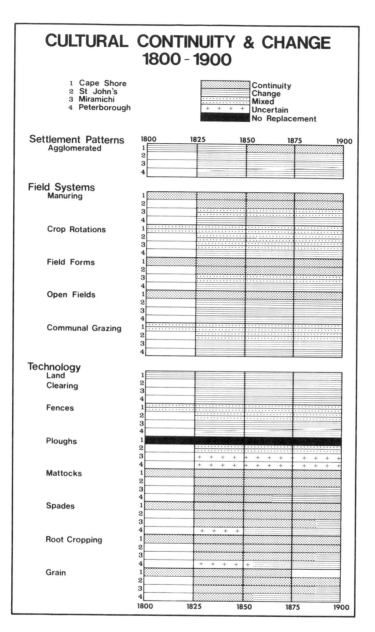

Figure 30

166

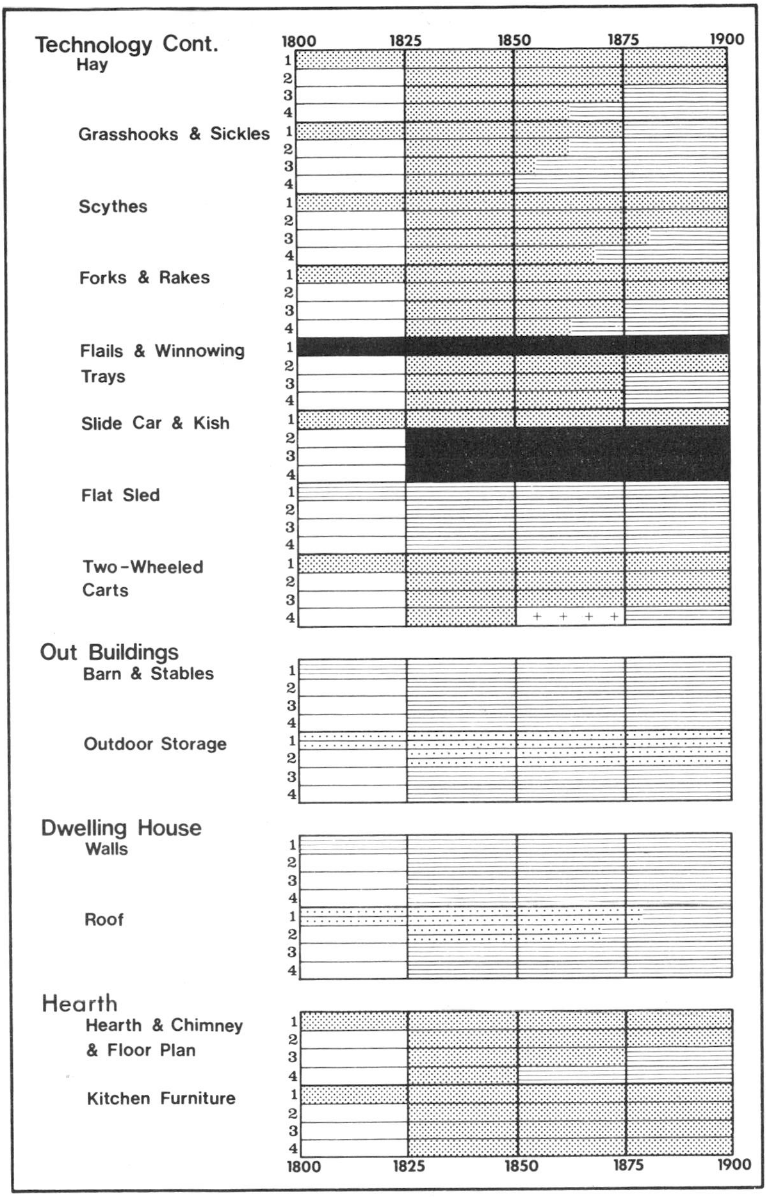

Figure 30 (cont'd)

was without precedent. In the eighteenth century the Gaelic tongue disappeared over most of Ireland; there was a revolution in agriculture, transportation, communication, and trade; and there was intense demographic and economic growth. As a result the Irish landscape was transformed. Many of these changes have been alluded to already, but it is important to view them in their broader European context. The currents of change reached into almost every nook and cranny of northwestern Europe in the eighteenth century, especially after 1750, and in many areas produced more revolutionary results than in Ireland. Industrialization and urbanization were making rural society more individualistic and rural culture more standardized and homogeneous. As urban demands for food grew, agriculture became more mechanical, more intensive, and more commercial. Generally speaking, the transformation of the countryside was less evident in the traditionally arable areas of lowland, northwestern Europe, where the manorial village and three-field system held sway, as in the pastoral regions of Atlantic Europe, where the hamlet and its infield/outfield ensemble yielded to the more intensive and advanced livestock husbandry of the "improvement." Few districts remained unaffected by the new farming at the close of the eighteenth century.

The medieval systems of settlement and agriculture were by no means entirely erased even in the pastoral parts of northwestern Europe before the dawn of the nineteenth century. After 1800, however, the pace of change quickened as the precipitous rise in population continued and food demands grew in proportion. Between 1750-1850 the population of Europe increased from 140 to 260 million and by the end of the nineteenth century had reached almost 400 million. Many of the vestiges of medieval European society that had survived the eighteenth century were erased and peasant culture lost much of its regional diversity.

Ireland was one of the regions most affected. Its population had almost doubled in the five decades before 1840 but unlike many other areas of northwestern Europe there was relatively little urbanization or industrial growth. Large industrial centers in Britain became major markets for Irish farm products and the landlords began to reorganize peasant agriculture and settlement. Land pressure became intense after the Napoleonic wars and there was little choice for the massive surplus population but to emigrate. During the first half of the nineteenth century the volume of Irish emigration exceeded that of any other European nation and they dominated the flow across the North Atlantic.

For all these changes in Irish peasant culture before the migrations, they were far less than those the Irish immigrants had to make – and almost instantaneously if they were to survive – once they found themselves in the unfamiliar setting of the New World. Once the Irish peasant had left his native townland he had said farewell to kin and neighbours and to almost everything that was customary and familiar. For the first time, perhaps, he faced the world virtually alone, as a stranger. To his eyes the novelty of the move must have appeared overwhelming. The journey to the coast, the sojourn in the Irish port, the crossing, the arrival in an alien city, and the subsequent search for a livelihood were all novel experiences. To be sure, his kindred and neighbours in the homeland had known some social dislocation, shuffled as they had been within their native townland or moved to another townland nearby, and considerable economic disruption; but the scale of dislocation and disruption bore little resemblance to that experienced by the immigrants. Despite resettlement the homeland survivors could maintain old social and economic ties and continue to some extent as a well-knit community, for the traditional network of friendship and kinship was rarely shattered completely.

In contrast, the emigrants were uprooted. The web of relationships and obligations that united them in the homeland was sundered and no similar social order could be reconstructed immediately in the New World. For those who settled in the city, moreover, there was little in the homeland experience or tradition that helped ease a painful and arduous adaptation. In the countryside, where the immigrants continued their age-old occupation, the trauma of transplantation was perhaps less severe, but the rural settler endured extreme isolation in the backwoods and had to contend with a novel physical environment.

To a greater or lesser degree, all European emigrants were uprooted in this manner. The majority came from the land, from the peasant heart of Europe. Whether they settled in city or country, in homogeneous clusters or not, the attrition of their cultural heritage was a continual and unrelenting process. Cultural change became more gradual once the initial shock of transplantation was over – indeed there was a reversion to homeland ways in some cases – but the general rate of change in nineteenth century North America probably equalled that of the more progressive parts of the Old World and the immigrants shared in these changes. The overriding factor in the demise or survival of homeland traditions in the New World was the structure of the economy in the area settled, but economic considerations were paramount in every phase of the emigrant's experience from the moment he left the homeland, and even before his departure.

The major stimulus of Irish and indeed European emigration to North America in the nineteenth century was economic distress in the homeland coupled with the economic opportunity that apparently beckoned in the New World. A precipitous rise in population resulted in extreme pressure on the land and in many parts of northwestern Europe there was insufficient industrial development to absorb the under-employed. North America, by contrast, appeared as a vast and empty continent, with virtually unlimited free land, growing industrial centres, and an insatiable demand for labour. Once settled on the land, the struggle for a livelihood led immigrants to discard homeland traits which impeded their economic progress. It was the primary aim of all to establish a commercially viable economy, but in the case of the Irish, the farming systems and especially the degree of agricultural commercialization varied between study areas, and these differences go far in explaining differences in the rates of transfer and survival of cultural traits. Farm fragmentation or *parcellément* in the crowded lands of Europe had resulted in extreme agricultural inefficiency and the suppression of the medieval patterns of rural settlement invariably had an economic rationale. The abundance and low cost of land in the New World meant that in any expanding agrarian economy, subdivision of farms was neither necessary nor profitable and *clachan* forms did not evolve, except on the Cape Shore, where the evolving pattern of settlement reflected an economic emphasis on fishing after 1850. Commercial livestock and subsistence arable farming persisted in this area but the sons of the immigrants became primarily fishermen. Fields closest to the sea were sometimes subdivided and worked in partnership by close relatives who also fished jointly and lived close together by the sea. Whenever commercial arable farming was practised, the communal restraints of joint farming inhibited commercial progress. In other parts of the New World, continental European immigrants – the Mennonites for example – reproduced village traditions of the homeland, but these settlements were gradually abandoned in the face of New World economic conditions, although they possessed far more centripetal characteristics than did the Atlantic European hamlet. Whereas the latter comprised only the houses of primary producers, the continental village (which was much larger) usually had some public buildings – church, castle or court, inns, stores – as well as artisans' dwellings located in the heart of the settlement.

The rate of land clearing, or the amount ultimately cleared, was governed partially by the nature of the economy and differences in the amount of land farmed influenced the rates of cultural transfer and survival, especially of field systems and farm technology. It was more economical to clear land quickly and farm it extensively on the frontier, especially if a grain economy dominated, as in Peterborough. A meagre soil, a marginal climate, and opportunities for alternate employment discouraged commercial arable farming in the Avalon and to some extent in Miramichi. Farms remained small and a more labour intensive agriculture evolved. Indeed the Avalon acres were probably worked as intensively as those in the homeland but pastoral husbandry, despite its commercial importance, was slovenly when compared to the labour-intensive transhumance traditions of the homeland. Settlers were too absorbed clearing the land or fishing to pursue intensive pastoral farming and stinting was not necessary where rough grazing acres were virtually unlimited. The change from an intensive to an extensive type of land use appears to be almost universal among European immigrants on the frontier, but as the backwoods disappeared and technology improved, more capital-intensive forms of agriculture appeared. Labour remained expensive and such labour-intensive Old World practices as building with stone, sod or mud, for example, were rarely transferred to the wooded regions of North America.

In the North Atlantic world of the nineteenth century increasing links with urban centres were significant in the growing standardization of farm technology. Factory-made implements were replacing homemade tools and a more "scientific" agriculture was developing, an extension of the agrarian improvements of the previous century. In the nineteenth century the rate of innovation was generally more rapid in North America than in Europe and the migration and settlement of Europeans usually resulted in an increase in the changing agricultural technology as they adapted to the farming systems of the New World. Shortage of labour was a powerful incentive to mechanize and the labour problem became acute as farms increased in size. Technological innovation and change were closely related to farm size. Once the area cultivated in Peterborough, for example, exceeded the homeland farm acreage, some traditional tools and techniques were discarded. Where farms were small, and especially where subsistence or near-subsistence arable agriculture existed, as in the Avalon, traditional technologies remained. There are few areas in the New World where technological stability is as evident as in the Avalon. Even in Europe, as farms were consolidated and enlarged, simple and intermediate technologies gradually waned; in several instances the Avalon-Irish actually reverted to an agricultural technology that was anachronous in the homeland before the migrations.

Whether material traits were transferred, borrowed, or invented, the process usually had an economic rationale. Ideas that eased the pain or quickened the process of adaptation and enabled a more profitable utilization of resources were embraced by the immigrants, whether these ideas originated within or outside the study areas or were based on homeland experience. The trait complex least affected by economic conditions was the farm house. To be sure, some architectural aspects of folk housing were modified to suit New World economic conditions, but interior lay-out and furnishings were the most uniformly transferable of Irish trait complexes to all study areas. Despite differences in the local economy of the Avalon study areas, houses differed slightly and house styles were almost identical in Peterborough and Miramichi. Outbuildings were more sensitive to economic conditions, but were still less influenced by them than field systems or farm technology.

Several traits were borrowed by the immigrants from pre-existing neighbouring groups. These groups had already adapted to the New World environment and possessed a range of material traits and ideas quite novel to the Irish. To prosper in a strange environment, all immigrants had to adapt to the pre-existing economic pattern and the rural economies eventually evolved by the Irish in the study areas frequently differed little from pre-existing local patterns. Borrowing was most evident in Peterborough, where agricultural change was most profound and least in the Avalon, where the agrarian system was closest to that practised traditionally in the homeland. However, the agrarian system evolved in the Avalon was little closer to homeland tradition than that of Miramichi, where a mixed small-farm economy prevailed, yet cultural borrowing on the Avalon was far more sluggish. In the latter area ethnic contacts and interactions were few, especially on the culturally isolated Cape Shore, and it is significant that the rates of transfer and survival were more manifest here than in any other study areas. The juxtaposition of Irish and Westcountrymen near St John's resulted in some borrowing by the former, notably of architectural styles; but the material traditions of both these groups did not differ markedly in the Old World and it is difficult to identify the relative rates of transfer and borrowing in such a situation. Even in the more ethnically diverse areas most cultural borrowings probably resulted less from direct contacts between Irish and non-Irish as from face-to-face dyadic contacts between incoming and previously settled heads of nuclear Irish families. However, when such contacts between Irish or Irish and non-Irish were made and the recently arrived family was confronted by a tradition that was part of its homeland heritage and in the new setting decided to adopt it, the distinctions between transfer and borrowing became blurred. Ireland shared in many of the traditions of Atlantic and to some extent of continental Europe and the problem of proving the "Irishness" of some items is common to all study areas; it is, in a more general way, a difficulty facing almost all such studies of ethnic settlements in the New World.

Whenever items occurred in the study areas that were unknown in the homeland or in the cultures of neighbouring New World groups, such items were independently invented. Invention *in situ* might have occurred during the first years of settlement in the isolation and novelty of the backwoods, but there is little evidence of inventiveness or individuality of style in the patterns of material folk cultural in any of the study areas. Almost all the material traits described were well known, either in the homeland or in the New World, and any trait that was distinctive or unique to a study area was usually shared widely within that area. Whenever considerable local variation in a cultural trait occurred, like threshing on the Cape Shore, some independent invention was likely, but such local variation was rare. Enduring independent inventions were a product of a few individuals.

The migration of unrelated nuclear families was important in the formation of dispersed farmstead settlement and compact farm units in all study areas. Because the Atlantic migration implied an abandonment of the old extended family structure, few of the communal ties that pervaded traditional Irish rural society and settlement pattern crossed the ocean. The isolated individual or nuclear family was the social dominant in the voluntary stream of European migration across the Atlantic and this was paramount in the creation of the dispersed settlement pattern that pervaded the frontier. Assisted or group migrations did occur, such as the Puritans of New England and German sects in

Pennsylvania, and although these groups formed villages in the wilderness much like those of their homeland, these villages lacked the character of their Old World analogues because initially most of their occupants were strangers to one another, drawn together by a common religious bond. In the Old World the patterns of rural settlement changed as agrarian individualism grew but, despite resettlement, much of the traditional social structure and communal consciousness remained; by contrast all the immigrants were uprooted and, with few exceptions, their individualism was reinforced by the economics of migration and later by the economics of the frontier.

The influence of the non-cultural environment on the patterns of cultural transfer and adaptation was both widespread and profound. Several items of the immigrants' traditional architecture, farmstead lay-out and cropping schemes were permanently affected by the change in environmental conditions; and the change or modification of these traits were largely the result of forest and climate. Wood was universally adopted as the principle material of construction because it was widely available and easy to use. The clearing of the forest was the first task in the creation of a farm on the frontier. Whether they came from the mud and stone traditions of Atlantic Europe or from the timber traditions of parts of continental Europe, the immigrants almost invariably opted for wood construction in the backwoods of eastern North America. The change from a temperate to a continental climate influenced all trait complexes, especially outbuildings. Storage problems were much more acute in the New World than in the Old World and the predominantly outdoor storage traditions of the homeland yielded to underground and barn storage in the study areas. Moreover, the use of wood for outbuildings influenced their form, lay-out, and location in relation to the dwelling house. Climatic factors compelled immigrants to synchronize their traditional annual round and several homeland festivals associated with seedtime and harvest did not survive the process. Finally, the rivers of New Brunswick and the seas of the Avalon influenced the location and pattern of settlement and many immigrants in the latter area, coming from inland locations in the homeland, changed their primary occupation, a change that in turn altered other aspects of their folkways.

For more than a century prior to the great migration, the patterns of material folk culture and settlement were continually changing but the movement across the Atlantic accelerated the tempo of change for all European emigrants. Traditions were transferred, however, and many survived the nineteenth century. The rates of cultural transfer and survival varied not only between ethnic groups but amongst a single group and this variability was the product of many factors. In the case of the handful of Irish in this study, the differences are explained not by the social and economic conditions of the migration since these did not vary greatly, but by contrasting conditions in the New World. Among these conditions the pattern of ethnic group settlement was more important than the physical environment but the differences in the rural economy between study areas were supreme in determining differences in the transfer and survival of homeland traits.

The Atlantic migrations and the transit of culture is a broad and complex theme that has received the attention of many scholars from different disciplines. In the past most studies have been too sweeping in scope and too general in their conclusions. There is a great need for more quantitatively-oriented micro-studies with a cross-cultural comparative emphasis before any synthesis of the character of this last great folk migration can be achieved.

Glossary[1]

Note: References to the occurrences of terms outside the study areas are in brackets. Occasionally, etymologies or occurrences are quoted from printed sources; these references are placed at the end of the article. Lexicographical sources consulted are: Wright, *English Dialect Dictionary*, 1905; Dinneen, *English-Irish Dictionary*, 1927; Onions, *Shorter Oxford Dictionary*, 1959.

The following abbreviations are used:

Am.: America; Av.: Avalon; Brit.: Britain; C.Sh.: Cape Shore; Cont. Eur.: Continental Europe; Dev.: Devon; Engl.: England; Engl. Dial. Dict.: English Dialect Dictionary; Frw.: Freshwater; Ger.: German; High.: Highlands; Irl.: Ireland; Ir.: Irish; Lan.: Lancashire; M.E.: Middle English; Mir.: Miramichi; O.E.: Old English; Pet.: Peterborough; Scot.: Scotland; Sc.G.: Scottish Gaelic; Sh.O.D.: Shorter Oxford Dictionary; St J.: St John's; Swd.: Swedish; W. Con.: West Country.

Dialect Terms Used In Study Areas

ANDIRONS. Two iron bars with short legs and ornamental heads, placed on hearthstone to support log fuel. Mir. (Eng., N.Am.).

---

1 Thanks are due to Dr. R.B. Walsh, Department of Phonetics, University College, Dublin, who assisted with the glossary.

BACÁN. (1) A gate hinge, Av. (Irl.); (2) a forked stick for hanging horse harness in stable, Frw. From Irish *bacán*, a hinge or hook.

BALE, BAIL. A wooden frame to which cattle are tied in the byre or stable, Av., Mir., Pet. (Brit., S.E. Irl.).

BARRACK. A roof sliding on four posts, under which hay is kept, St J. (Cont. Eur., N.E. N.Am.). From Dutch *bargh.*

BARRENS. (1) land burnt over, in stage of recolonization by plants; (2) an unimproved, treeless tract in the forest, Av., Mir. (N.Am.).

BEE. A co-operating neighbourhood work-group, Mir., Pet. (N.Am.).

BONE, BOWAN. An uncropped strip of ground, C. two feet wide, dividing different crops in a field, Frw. (Irl.) Ir.

BOW, BOWING. Scythe cradle, Mir. (N.Irl.).

BULK. A pile of material, especially fish or hay, Av. cf. Sh.O.D., belly, trunk or body, 1713. *Dial. Dict.*, a pile of sorted fish (Cornwall).

BURN BAITINGS. Sod pared off ground, placed in heaps and burnt, St J. (High. Brit., Irl.).

BURNBRUSH. Meaning same as BURN BAITINGS q.v., C.Sh.

CAULCANNON. All Hallows' Eve meal of potatoes, turnips, cabbage, and other white vegetables, Av. cf. *Engl. Ir. Dict.* CÁL CLEANNFHIONN, white-headed cabbage (S.E. Irl.).

COCK-LOFT. An area enclosed by peaked roof and ceiling, St J. cf. *Dial. Dict.,* area over the garret, 1589. (W. Con.).

COILS. Small hay heeps in field. Pet. (N.Irl.).

COLLAR-BEAM. Member supporting couples, Av.

COMMONS. Crown land, used for open grazing, Av., Mir., Pet. (Brit. Is.).

COOB. A hen-coop, Av. (W. Engl., Irl.).

DOG IRONS. Same as ANDIRONS. Av.

DRAY. (1) a stoneboat, Frw.; (2) a heavy slide, Av.; (3) a long flat hay-cart, without sides, C.Sh. cf. Sh.O.D. a low cart, without sides, used for carrying heavy loads, especially used by brewers, 1581. *Eng. Dial. Dict.* a sledge (W. Con.); a long cart (S.E. Irl.).

FLANKER. Burning piece of wood or sparks from fire, St J. (W. Con.).

FROLIC. Same meaning as BEE q.v. Mir.

GAD. Withy, Av.; Ir. gad.

GRAFÁN. A mattock, Av., Mir.; Ir. GRAFÁN.

GRUFF. Same meaning as GRAFÁN, q.v. C.Sh.

HAMPER. A pair of baskets or sacks slung across horse's back, Av. cf. Sh.O.D.; a large basket with a cover, generally used as a packing case, M.E. *Eng. Dial. Dict.,* a measure of six pecks (Cheshire).

HANDSHAKIN'S. Same as COILS. Pet. (N.Irl.).

JINGLE. A light, two-wheeled cart or car, N. St J.; *Engl. Dial. Dict.* (1) a covered two-wheeled car; (2) a gentleman's jaunting car 1830 (S.Irl.).

JUMPER, JUMPSLED. Slide or sled, Pet., Mir.

KISH. A basket, made of withies, Av., Ir. Cis.

KNEE. Naturally curved tree-root, Av.

LAZY-BED. Potato ridges, Av., Mir. (High. Brit., Irl.).

LEA, LEY. Arable land, under grass, Av., Mir. (Brit., Irl.).

LINHAY, LINNEY, LINNY. A lean-to studded shed attached to rear of dwelling house, for livestock, St J. (W. Con., S.E. Irl.).

LISLONGERS. Long poles used to pin down thatch on traditional Cape Shore roof.

LONG-CART. Same meaning as DRAY, q.v. St J.

LONGER. Pole, Av.

MÁILÍN. A bag for carrying seed when sowing, Av., Ir. MÁLA.

MOW. Unit for hay or straw in two-bay (mow) barn, Pet., Mir.

PIKE. A hay-fork, Av. (W. Con., S.E. Irl.); cf. Sh.O.D., a hay-fork or pitch-fork, M.E.

PLANCHON. Board or plank, Av. (W. Con.); cf. Sh.O.D., planks, late M.E.

POUND. Small enclosure, Av. (High. Brit.); cf. Sh.O.D., a pen, late M.E.

PRONG. A manure fork, Av. (W. Engl., Irl.); cf. Sh.O.D., an instrument with two or more tines, 1492.

RED GROUND. Ploughed land, St J. Cf. *Engl. Dial. Dict.,* red land. (Scot.).

REEK. Rectangular grain or hay stack in yard. Pet., Mir. (Brit. Irl.).

SADDLE. Peaked roof, Av.

SAVE-COCKS. Hay piles in field, up to seven feet high, C.Sh.

SETS. Potato seeds, Av., Mir., Pet. (Brit., Irl.).

SETTLE. A fireside bench, Av., Mir. (Brit., Irl.); cf. Sh.O.D., a chair, bench, stool; O.E., a long wooden bench, usually with arms and high back, with locker or box under seat, 1553.

SHANTY. A crude, temporary dwelling in backwoods, Mir., Pet.; cf. Sh.O.D. from French *chantier;* possibly from Ir. sean-ti' old house.

SHAVING-HORSE. Implement for holding unfinished shingles. (N.Am.).

SHEM. (1) sharply pointed wooden artifact, like trowel, used for packing moss in between studs in house walls, and for stripping bark off trees; (2) a wedge, Av.

SHOCK. Two rows of barley sheaves standing in field, Pet.

SOUPLE. Leather joining two flails, Pet. (Scot., N. Engl., N.Irl.).

SPRONG. Same meaning as PRONG, Av. q.v.

SQUARE. (1) a kin-group house cluster, C.Sh.; (2) small area of land, St J.; cf. Sh.O.D., a square or rectangular piece of ground, especially a garden plot of this shape, 1615.

STANCHION. A wooden upright, Av.; cf. Sh.O.D., late M.E.

STANDARD. Meaning same as STANCHION, q.v.; cf. Sh.O.D., an upright timber, 1480.

STILLEN. Wooden stand or bench, on which milk pails and water cans were placed, C.Sh., (S.E. Irl., Lan.).

STRONGBACK. Ridge pole, Av.

STOG. To stuff, to pack, Av.; cf. *Engl. Dial. Dict.,* to stab, to pierce (Scot. Irl.).

STOOK. Two rows of standing sheaves of grain in field, Pet., Mir. (Irl. High. Brit.).

STREEL, STREELIN. To drag along ground, Av.; from Ir. straoill, a sloven.

SÚGÁN. A rope of hay or straw, Av., Mir., Pet., Ir.

SWARTH. Row of mown grass, as it falls from scythe, Av., Mir., Pet. (Brit. Irl.).

TILT. Same meaning as SHANTY, Av.; cf. *Engl. Dial. Dict.,* "to totter" (N. Dev.).

TRUNNELS, TRENNELS. Wooden pins, Av. (Brit.); cf. Sh.O.D., tree-nails, M.E.

WHALEBACK. Flat roof, Av.

WINROW, WINDROW. Row of mown grass or hay, Av., Mir., Pet. (Brit. Irl.).

Terms Not Used in New World Study Areas

BLOCKFLUR. Regular shaped fields, Ger.

BOOLEY. Summer dwelling of herders in mountain pastures, Ir. buaile.

CAILLEACH. Last sheaf of harvest, Ir.

CAOIL-FHÓD. Unploughed or unworked strips between individual plots in open field, Ir.

CHANGEDALE. Periodic exchange of infield plots among co-tenants, N. Engl. Irl.

CINEADH. Kin-group, Ir.

CLACHAN. A farm-cluster or hamlet occupied by conjoint tenants, frequently blood relations, Sc.G., Scot., N. Ir.

CLOCHAUNS. Bee-hive huts, originally early Christian monastic sites in Ireland. Architectural similarities in modern Irish buildings and in Mountain Booleys, Ir.

COLLOP. The proportional relationship of stock to grazing land, Ir.

COORING. Labour pooling, Ir. CABHRAÍOCHT.

CRICH. Same meaning as CAOIL-FHÓD, Ir.

CUIBHREANN. Individual family plot or share in openfield, Ir.

EINZELHOF. Isolated farmstead, Ger.

GAVELKIND. Irish rule of land inheritance involving equal shares to male heirs, Engl.

GUGGER. Sharp pointed wooden tool used to set potato seeds in lazy-beds, Ir.

HAGGARD. Part of farmstead where hay & grain stacks are built, Brit. Irl.

HARE. Same meaning as CAILLEACH, Irl.

KEELOGUES. Same meaning as CAOIL-FHÓD, Ir.

KIBBIN. Same meaning as GUGGER, Ir.

LÁNN-IOTHA. Linhay, Ir.

MACHAIR. Same meaning as BOOLEY, Ir.

MEARINGS. Same meaning as CAOILFAOID, Brit. Irl.

MEITHEAL. A co-operating work-group, often kin, Ir.

MORROWINGDALE. Same as CHANGEDALE, Eng. Irl.

RÍ. Village headman or king, Ir.

RIBS. Same meaning as CAOILFAOID, Brit., Irl.

RODDENS. Same meaning as CAOILFAOID, Irl.

RUNDALE. Conjoint landholding system in infield-outfield agriculture, Irl.

SCOLLOPS. Rods used to pin down thatch on Irish roof, Irl.

SOUM. Same meaning as COLLOP, Scot., N.Irl.

STACÁN. Same meaning as CAOILFAOID.

STEEVEEN. Same meaning as GUGGER. Ir.

TALLET. Hay loft above linhay, W. Con.

THALLOGUE. Sleeping loft in Irish house, Ir.

TRAMS. Rear shafts or Irish cart, Brit. Irl.

Appendix 1

Surname diversity among immigrants*

	No. Surnames	No. times surnames are repeated			
		1 (once)	2	3	4
N. St John's	41	2	2	–	–
Freshwater	28	–	–	–	–
Cape Shore	34	3	1	1	–
Miramichi	90	3	–	–	2
Downeyville	95	8	2	–	–
Ennismore	45	6	–	–	1

* Canada, *Census of Canada, 1851* (MSS in National Archives, Ottawa); church records; interviews.

Appendix 2

Farm size*

	−10 acres	10-30	30-60	+60
Wexford 1841	28%	35	24	13
Kilkenny 1841	31	33	25	11
Waterford 1841	29	25	23	23
Tipperary 1841	36	36	14	16
Cork 1841	29	36	23	12

* Report of Commissioners, *Census of Ireland, 1841* (Dublin, 1843).

NOTE: Bourke's revised figures for the Census of 1841 are used (P.M. Austin Bourke, "The Agricultural Statistics of the 1841 Census of Ireland. A Critical Review," *Economic History Review* 18 [1965]: 376-91).

Appendix 2 (cont'd)

Farm Averages**

	No. Farmers	Improved Acres	Wheat (acres)	Oats (acres)	Barley (acres)	Peas & Beans (acres)	Potatoes (acres)	Turnips (acres)
Cape Shore 1836	34	9	–	1bu.[a]	–	–	240bu.	–
Cape Shore 1857	54	15	–	1bu.	–	–	54br.[b]	–
N. St John's 1836	58	3(18)[c]	–	10bu.	–	–	139bu.	–
N. St John's 1857	81	4.3	–	3bu.	–	–	40br.	–
Miramichi 1851	91	15	11.6bu.	60.6bu.	1.7bu.	1.7bu.	139.4bu.	13.7bu.
Miramichi 1861	87	23	2.4(67)	3.4(86)	1(17)	1.1(6)	1.6(86)	.4(23)
Ennismore 1851	75	30	11(55)	4.5(52)	2(5)	4(52)	1.4(60)	1.4(12)
Ennismore 1861	50	45	14(37)	6.6(37)	3.4(8)	6(36)	1.5(36)	1.3(12)
Downeyville 1851	128	30	9(120)	6(108)	1.4(5)	2(66)	1.3(108)	–
Downeyville 1861	98	62.1	17.5(84)	10(80)	2.6(3)	4.5(69)	1.5(51)	1.4(37)

** Newfoundland, Department of Colonial Secretary, *Census of Newfoundland, 1836; Census of Newfoundland and Labrador 1857* (in Memorial University Library, St John's). Canada, *Census of Canada, 1851; Census of Canada, 1861* (MSS in National Archives, Ottawa).

a   bu = bushels;
b   br = barrels;
c   Numbers in parentheses indicate number of farmers involved.

Appendix 2 cont'd.

Farm Averages

Hay (tons)	Pasture (acres)	Butter (lbs.)	Cows	Cattle	Oxen	Horses	Sheep	Pigs & Goats
3.5	–	–	–	9	–	1	1.3	3.
15	–	182	3.4	8	–	1	5.4	3.7
1.1	–	–	–	.4	–	.6	–	–
3.2	–	44	1	2.3	–	.7	–	1.5
7	–	127	2.2	4	–	.8	5	1.6
6.5(86)	–	130(81)	2.3(78)	2.2(87)	2.2(15)	1.7(70)	6(81)	3.5(81)
6(52)	19(67)	230(58)	2.7(70)	3(68)	3(65)	2(44)	12(56)	9(60)
8.3(33)	14(39)	161(31)	2.5(34)	4.5(29)	2.6(16)	2.6(20)	10.2(29)	7.6(33)
5.2(65)	17(110)	100(75)	2.4(100)	2.5(78)	2.3(80)	2.2(60)	8(88)	6.6(104)
7.3(60)	24(91)	174(70)	2.8(70)	3.3(58)	2.6(24)	2.7(51)	10.2(56)	7.9(68)

Selected bibliography on European ethnic group settlement in rural North America

This is by no means a complete bibliography. Several works were omitted because of their brevity or poor quality of scholarship; and the author believes there are many important references he should have found. Information on the scope and objectives of this bibliography is contained in chapter i. References to citations in the text are listed in sections II, III, and IV of this bibliography.

I

Ander, O. Fritof. *The Cultural Heritage of the Swedish Immigrant: Selected References.* Rock Island, Ill.: Augusta College, 1956.

—. *In the Trek of the Immigrants.* Rock Island, Ill.: Augusta College, 1964.

Arensberg, Conrad and Solon T. Kimball. "American Communities." *American Anthropologist* 57 (1955): 1143-60.

Arnow, Harriette Simpson. *Seedtime on the Cumberland.* New York: Macmillan, 1960.

Bailey, Alfred G. *The Conflict of European and Eastern Algonkian Cultures 1504-1700: A Study in Canadian Civilization.* Toronto: University of Toronto Press, 1969.

Bailyn, Bernard. *Education in the Forming of American Society.* Chapel Hill: University of North Carolina Press, 1960.

Baltensperger, Brad. "Culture and Agriculture on the American Frontier." *The Monadnock* 45 (1971): 22-29.

Barbeau, Marius. "Island of Orleans." *Canadian Geographical Journal* 5 (1932): 154-171.

—. "A French Settlement on the Saint Lawrence." *The Dalhousie Review* 14 (1934): 77-84.

Bartz, Fritz. "Französische Einflüsse im Bilde der Kulturlandschaft Nordimerikas: Hufenseidlungen und Marschpolder in Kanada und in Louisiana." *Erdkunde* 9 (1955): 286-305.

Bennett, John W. *Northern Plainsmen: Adaptive Strategy and Agrarian Life.* Chicago: Aldine Publishing Company, 1971.

—. *Hutterian Brethren: The Agricultural Economy and Social Organization of a Communal People.* Stanford: Stanford University Press, 1967.

Bidwell, Percy W. and John I. Falconer. *History of Agriculture in the Northern United States 1620-1860.* Washington: Carnegie Institute, 1925.

Billigmeier, Robert H. (ed.) and Fred A. Picard. *The Old Land and the New: The Journals of Two Swiss Families in the 1820's.* Minneapolis: University of Minnesota Press, 1965.

Bird, J.B. "Settlement Patterns in Maritime Canada, 1687-1786." *Geographical Review* 45 (1955): 385-404.

Bjork, Kenneth O. *West of the Great Divide.* Northfield, Minn.: Norwegian American Historical Association, 1958.

Bjorklund, Elaine M. "Ideology and Culture Exemplified in Southwestern Michigan." *Annals, Association American Geographers* 54 (1964): 227-41.

Blegen, T.C. *Norwegian Migration to America.* Northfield, Minn.: Norwegian American Historical Association, 1940.

—. *Grass Roots History.* New York: Kennikat Press, 1947.

—. *The Land Lies Open.* Minneapolis: University of Minnesota Press, 1949.

—. *Land of Their Choice: The Immigrants Write Home.* Minneapolis: University of Minnesota Press, 1955.

Boke, Richard L. "Roots in the Earth." *New Mexico Quarterly* 11 (1941): 25-36.

Bressler, Leo A. "Agriculture Among the Germans in Pennsylvania During the Eighteenth Century." *Pennsylvania History* 22 (1955): 102-33.

Brewer, D.C. *Conquest of New England by the Immigrant.* New York: G.P. Putnam and Sons, 1926.

Bridenbaugh, Carl. *The Colonial Craftsman.* New York: New York University Press, 1950.

Brodeur, David B. "Evolution of the New England Town Common." *Professional Geographer* 19 (1967): 313-18.

Brunner, Edmund D. *Immigrant Farmers and Their Children, With Four Studies of Immigrant Communities.* Garden City: Institute of Social and Religious Research, 1929.

Bucher, Robert C. "The Continental Log House." *Pennsylvania Folklife* 12 (1962): 14-19.

—. "The Cultural Backgrounds of Our Pennsylvania Homesteads." *Bulletin of the Historical Society of Montgomery County, Pennsylvania* 15 (1966): 22-26.

—. "The Swiss Bank House in Pennsylvania." *Pennsylvania Folklife* 18 (1968-69): 2-11.

Buchkner, Urban D. *Study of the Lower Rio Grande Valley as a Culture Area.* Austin: University of Texas Press, 1929.

Buck, Solon J. *The Planting of Civilization in Western Pennsylvania.* Pittsburgh: University of Pittsburg Press, 1939.

Campa, Arthur L. "Cultural Variations in the Anglo-Spanish Southwest." *Western Review* 7 (1970): 3-9.

Caruso, John A. *The Mississippi Valley Frontier: The Age of French Exploration and Settlement.* Indianapolis: Bobbs-Merrill, 1966.

Clark, Andrew H. *Three Centuries and the Island: A Historical Geography of Settlements and Agriculture in Prince Edward Island, Canada.* Toronto: University of Toronto Press, 1959.

—. "Old World Origins and Religious Adherence in Nova Scotia." *The Geographical Review* 50 (1960): 317-44.

—. "Acadia and the Acadians: The Creation of a Geographical Entity." In J. Andrews (ed.). *Frontiers and Men: A volume in Memory of Griffith Taylor (1880-1963).* Melbourne: Cheshire Co., 1966.

—. *Acadia: The Geography of Early Nova Scotia to 1760.* Madison: University of Wisconsin Press, 1969.

Clark, S.D. *The Developing Canadian Community.* Toronto: University of Toronto Press, 1962.

Cobb, Douglas S. "The Jamesville Bruderhof: A Hutterian Agricultural Colony." *Journal of the West* 9 (1970): 60-77.

Comeaux, Malcolm L. *Settlement and Folk Occupations of the Atchafalay Basin.* Baton Rouge: Louisiana State University Press, 1972.

Commager, Henry Steele (ed.). *Immigration and American History: Essays in Honour of Theodore C. Blegen.* Minneapolis: University of Minnesota Press, 1961.

Connally, Ernest Allen. "The Cape Cod House: An Introductory Study." *Journal of the Society of Architectural Historians* 19 (1960): 47-56.

Connor, Seymour V. "Log Cabins in Texas." *The Southwestern Historical Quarterly* 53 (1949): 105-16.

Cozzens, Arthur B. "Conservation in German Settlements of the Missouri Ozarks." *Geographical Review* 33 (1943): 286-98

Culbert, James L. "Distribution of the Spanish-American Population in New Mexico." *Economic Geography* 19 (1943): 171-76.

Cummings, Abbott Lowell. *Architecture in Early New England.* Sturbridge: Society Preservation New England Antiquities, 1964.

Cybrinsky, Roman A. *Patterns of Mother Tongue Retention Among Several Selected Ethnic Groups in Western Canada.* Department of Geography Paper No. 5. State College: Dept. of Geography, Pennsylvania State University, 1970.

Dale, Edward E. *Frontier Ways: Sketches of Life in the Old West.* Austin: University of Texas Press, 1959.

Davis, Darrell H. "The Finland Community, Minnesota." *Geographical Review* 25 (1935): 382-94.

Dawson, C.A. *Group Settlement: Ethnic Communities in Western Canada.* Toronto: Macmillan, 1936.

Dawson, Nora. *La vie traditionelle a Saint-Pierre (Ile D'Orleans).* Les Archives de Folklore No. 8. Quebec: Les presses universitaires Laval, 1960.

Deffontaines, Pierre. "Le Rang: type de peuplement rural du Canada Français." *Cahiers de géographie* 5 (1933): 1-32.

Dégh, Linda. "Survival and Revival of European Folk Cultures in America." *Ethnologia Europaea* 2 (1968): 97-107.

Demos, John. "Notes on Life in Plymouth Colony." *William and Mary Quarterly* 22 (1965): 265-86.

—. *A Little Commonwealth: Family Life in Plymouth Colony.* New York: Oxford University Press, 1970.

Derrau, Max. "A l'origine du 'Rang' Canadien." *Cahiers de géographie de Quebec* 1 (1956): 39-47.

Donnelley, Thomas C. and Arthur N. Holcombe (eds.). *Rocky Mountain Politics.* Albuquerque: University of New Mexico Press, 1940.

Dornbusch, Charles H. and John K. Heyl. *Pennsylvania German Barns.* Allentown, Pa.: Schlechters, 1958.

Duncan, Kenneth. "Irish Famine Immigration and the Social Structure in Canada West." *The Canadian Review of Sociology and Anthropology* 2 (1965): 19-40.

Dunn, Charles W. *Highland Settler: A Portrait of the Scottish Gael in Nova Scotia.* Toronto: University of Toronto Press, 1953.

Durand, Loyal, Jr. "Dairy Barns of Southeastern Wisconsin: Relation to Dairy Industry and to Regions of 'Yankee' and 'German' Settlement." *Annals, Association American Geographers* 32 (1942): 112-3.

Ehlers, E. *Das Nordliche Peace River Country, Alberta, Canada.* Tübingen: University Tübingen, 1965.

Eichhoff, Juergen. "Wisconsin's German-Americans: From Ethnic Identity To Assimilation." *German-American Studies* 2 (1970): 44-54.

Evans, E. Estyn. "Old Ireland and New England." *Ulster Journal of Archaeology* 12 (1949): 104-12.

—. "The Scotch-Irish in the New World: An Atlantic Heritage." *Journal of the Royal Society of Antiquaries of Ireland* 95 (1965): 39-49.

187

—. "Culture and Land Use in the Old West of North America." *Festgabe für Gottfried Pfeifer: Heidelberg Geographische Arbeiten* 15 (1966): 72-80.

—. "Cultural Relics of the Ulster Scots in the Old West of North America." *Ulster Folklife* 11 (1965): 33-38.

—. "The Scotch-Irish: Their Cultural Adaptation and Heritage in the American Old West." In E.R.R. Green (ed.). *Essays in Scotch-Irish History.* London: Routledge and Kegan Paul, 1969.

Ferguson, Erna. *New Mexico: A Pageant of Three Peoples.* New York: Alfred A. Knopf, Inc. 1951.

Fife, Austin E. "Folklore of Material Culture on the Rocky Mountain Frontier." *Arizona Quarterly* 13 (1957): 101-10.

—, Alfa Fife and Henry Glassie (eds.). *Forms Upon the Frontier: Folklife and Folk Arts in the United States.* Logan: Utah State University Press, 1969.

Figate, Francis. *The Spanish Heritage of the Southwest.* El Paso: C. Hartzog, 1952.

Fischer, E. *The Passing of the European Age. A Study of Transfer of Western Civilization and its Renewal in Other Continents.* Cambridge: Harvard University Press, 1948.

Fitchen, John. *The New World Dutch Barn.* Syracuse: Clarendon Press, 1968.

Fletcher, Stevenson W. *Pennsylvania Agriculture and Country Life 1640-1840.* 2 vols. Harrisburg: Pennsylvania Historical and Museum Commission, 1950.

Fleure, H.J. "New England and Old." *Geography* 31 (1946): 105-10.

Forman, Henry Chandlee. *The Architecture of the Old South: The Medieval Style, 1585-1850.* Cambridge: Harvard University Press, 1948.

—. *Virginia Architecture in the Seventeenth Century.* Williamsburg: Virginia 350th Anniversary Celebration Corporation, 1957.

Francis, E.K. "The Adjustment of a Peasant Group to a Capitalistic Economy: The Manitoba Mennonites." *Rural Sociology* 17 (1952): 218-28.

—. *In Search of Utopia: The Mennonites in Manitoba.* Glencoe, Ill.: Free Press, 1955.

Gagliardo, J.G. "Germans and Agriculture in Colonial Pennsylvania." *Pennsylvania Magazine of History and Biography* 83 (1959): 192-218.

Galitzi, C.A. *A Study of Assimilation Among Roumanians in the United States.* New York: Columbia University Press, 1929.

Gellner, John and John Smerek. *The Czechs and Slovaks in Canada.* Toronto: University of Toronto Press, 1968.

Gentilcore, R. Louis. "The Agricultural Background of Settlement in Eastern Nova Scotia." *Annals, Association American Geographers* 46 (1956): 378-404.

—. "Vincennes and French Settlement in the Old Northwest." *Annals, Association American Geographers* 47 (1957): 285-97.

Gingerich, Melvin. *The Mennonites of Iowa.* Iowa: State Historical Society Iowa, 1939.

Glassie, Henry. "The Smaller Outbuildings of the Southern Mountains." *Mountain Life and Work* 40 (1964): 21-25.

—. "The Old Barns of Appalachia." *Mountain Life and Work* 40 (1965): 21-30.

—. "The Pennsylvania Barn in the South." *Pennsylvania Folklife* 15 (1965-1966): 8-19; *Ibid.,* 15 (1966): 12-25.

—. "The Types of Southern Mountain Cabin." In Jan H. Brunvand (ed.). *The Study of American Folklore.* New York: W.W. Norton 1968, pp. 338-70.

—. *Pattern in the Material Folk Culture of the Eastern United States.* University of Pennsylvania Monographs in Folklore and Folklife No. 1. Philadelphia: University of Pennsylvania Press, 1969.

—. "A Central Chimney Continental Log House from Cumberland County." *Pennsylvania Folklife* 18 (1968-69): 33-39.

González, Nancie L. *The Spanish-Americans of New Mexico.* Albuquerque: University of New Mexico Press, 1969.

Govorchin, Gerald Gilbert. *Americans from Yugoslavia.* Gainesville: University of Florida Press, 1961.

Graham, I.C.C. *Colonists from Scotland: Emigration to North America 1707-1783.* Ithaca: Cornell University Press, 1956.

Greven, Philip J. Jr. "Old Patterns in the New World: The Distribution of Land in 17th Century Andover." *Essex Institute Historical Collections* 101 (1965): 133-48.

—. "Family Structure in Seventeenth-Century Andover." *William and Mary Quarterly* 23 (1966): 234-56.

Gritzner, Charles F. "Log Housing in New Mexico." *Pioneer America* 3 (1971): 54-72.

Guillett, Edwin C. *Early Life in Upper Canada.* Toronto: The Ontario Publishing Company, 1933.

—. *Pioneer Farmer and Backwoodsman.* Toronto: The Ontario Publishing Company, 1963.

Hale, Richard W. "The French Side of the 'Log Cabin Myth.'" *Proceedings Massachusetts Historical Society* 72 (1960): 118-25.

Halich, W. *The Ukrainians in the United States.* Chicago: University of Chicago Press, 1937.

Hamilton, L *Canada: Landschaft und Volksleben.* Berlin: E. Wasmuth, 1926.

Handlin, Oscar. *Race and Nationality in American Life.* Boston: Little and Brown, 1957.

— (ed.). *Immigration as a Factor in American History.* Englewood Cliffs, N.J.: Prentice-Hall, 1959.

Hansen, M.L. *The Atlantic Migration.* Cambridge: Harper & Row, 1940.

189

Harris, Richard C. *The Seigneurial System in Early Canada.* Madison: University of Wisconsin Press, 1966.

—. "Of Poverty and Helplessness in Petite-Nation." *Canadian Historical Review* 52 (1971): 23-50.

Helm, June (ed.). *Spanish-Speaking People in the United States.* Seattle: American Ethnological Society, 1968.

Hindle, Brooke. *Technology in Early America.* Chapel Hill: University of North Carolina Press, 1966.

Hoffmann, Oscar. "Culture Change in a Rural Wisconsin Ethnic Island." *Rural Sociology* 14 (1949): 39-50.

Hoglund, A. William. *Finnish Immigrants in America, 1880-1920.* Madison: University of Wisconsin Press, 1960.

Hostetler, John A. *Amish Society.* Baltimore: Johns Hopkins Press, 1963.

Hummel, Charles F. "English Tools in America: The Evidence of the Dominys." *Winterthur Portfolio* 2 (1965): 27-46.

Jakle, John A. and James O. Wheeler. "The Changing Residential Structure of the Dutch Population in Kalamazoo, Michigan." *Annals, Association American Geographers* 59 (1969): 441-60.

Janson, Florence E. *The Background of Swedish Immigration, 1840-1930.* Minneapolis: University of Minnesota Press, 1931.

Johnson, Aili K. "Lore of the Finnish-American Sauna." *Midwest Folklore* 1 (1951): 33-39.

Johnson, H.B. "Germans in Minnesota." *Rural Sociology* 6 (1941): 16-34.

—. "The Location of German Immigrants in the Middle West." *Annals, Association American Geographers,* 41 (1951): 1-41.

Jones, Robert Leslie. "Agriculture in Lower Canada, 1792-1815." *Canadian Historical Review* 27 (1946): 33-51.

Jordan, Terry G. "Population Origins in Texas, 1850." *Geographical Review* 59 (1969): 1-28.

—. "German Houses in Texas." *Landscape* 14 (1964): 24-6.

—. *German Seed in Texas Soil: Immigrant Farmers in Nineteenth-Century Texas.* Austin: University of Texas Press, 1966.

Kaups, Matti. "Finnish Place Names in Minnesota: A Study in Cultural Transfer." *Geographical Review* 56 (1966): 377-97.

Kaye, Vladimir J. *Early Ukranian Settlements in Canada.* Toronto: University of Toronto Press, 1964.

Kenney, Alice P. *The Gansevoorts of Albany: Dutch Patricians in the Upper Hudson Valley.* Syracuse: Syracuse University Press, 1969.

Kimball, Fiske. *Domestic Architecture of the American Colonies and of the Early Republic.* New York: C Scribner & Sons, 1932.

Kniffen, Fred. "The American Agricultural Fair: The Pattern." *Annals, Association American Geographers* 39 (1949): 264-82.

—. "A Spanish (?) Spinner in Louisiana." *Southern Folklore Quarterly* 13 (1949): 192-99.

—. "The American Covered Bridge." *Geographical Review* 41 (1951): 114-23.

—. "The Physiognomy of Rural Louisiana." *Louisiana History* 4 (1963): 291-99.

—. "Folk Housing: Key to Diffusion." *Annals, Association American Geographers* 55 (1965): 549-77.

—. and Henry Glassie. "Building in Wood in the Eastern United States: A Time-Place Perspective." *Geographical Review* 56 (1966): 40-66.

—. *Louisiana, Its Land and People.* Baton Rouge: Louisiana State University Press, 1968.

Knowlton, Clark (ed.). *Indian and Spanish American Adjustments to Arid and Semi-Arid Environments.* Lubbock, Texas: Texas Technological College, 1964.

Knubel, Hans. "Die Hutterersiedlungen in Mittelkanada." *Geographische Rundschau* 19 (1967): 61-3.

Kolehmainen, John I. and George W. Hill. *Haven in the Woods: The Story of the Finns in Wisconsin.* Madison: University of Wisconsin Press, 1965.

Kollmorgen, Walter M. *The German-Swiss in Franklin County, Tennessee: A Study of the Significance of Cultural Considerations in Farming Enterprises.* Washington: US Department of Agriculture, Bureau of Agricultural Economics, 1940.

—. "A Reconnaissance of Some Cultural-Agricultural Islands in the South." *Economic Geography* 17 (1941): 409-30. "Agricultural-Cultural Islands in the South: Part II." *Ibid.*, 19 (1943): 109-17.

—. *The German Settlement in Cullman County, Alabama: An Agricultural Island in the Cotton Belt.* Washington: US Department of Agriculture, Bureau of Agricultural Economics, 1941.

—. *Culture of a Contemporary Rural Community: The Old Order Amish of Lancaster County, Pennsylvania.* Rural Life Studies No. 4 Washington: US Government Printing Office, United States Department of Agriculture; Bureau of Agricultural Economics, 1942.

—. "The Agricultural Stability of Old Order Amish and Old Order Mennonites of Lancaster County, Pennsylvania." *American Journal Sociology* 49 (1943): 233-41.

—. "Immigrant Settlements in Southern Agriculture." *Agricultural History* 19 (1945): 69-78.

—. "French-Speaking Farmers of Southern Louisiana." *Economic Geography* 22 (1946): 153-60.

Laatsch, William G. "Hutterite Colonization in Alberta." *Journal of Geography* 70 (1971): 347-59.

Landgraf, John L. *Land Use in the Ramah Area of New Mexico.* Papers Peabody Museum American Archaeology and Ethnology 42: 1. Cambridge: Harvard University Press, 1954.

Landing, James E. "The Failure of Amish Settlements in the Southeastern United States: An Appeal for Inquiry." *Mennonite Quarterly Review* 44 (1970): 376-88.

—. "Amish Settlements in North America: A Geographic Brief." *Bulletin Illinois Geographical Society* 12 (1970): 65-69.

Lawton, Arthur J. "The Pre-Metric Foot and Its Use in Pennsylvania-German Architecture." *Pennsylvania Folklife* 19 (1969): 37-45.

Lehmann, Heinz. *Zur Geschichte des Deutschtums in Kanada.* Vol. 1, Stuttgart, 1931; Vol. 2, Berlin, 1939: Ausland und Heimat Verlagsaktiengesellschaft.

Lemon, James T. "The Agricultural Practices of National Groups in Eighteenth-Century Southeastern Pennsylvania." *Geographical Review* 56 (1966): 467-96.

—. *The Best Poor Man's Country: A Geographical Study of Early Southeastern Pennsylvania.* Baltimore: Johns Hopkins Press, 1972.

Lengyel, E. *Americans from Hungary.* New York: Garden City Publishing Co., 1948.

Lewis, H.H. "Population of Quebec Province: Its Distribution and National Origins." *Economic Geography* 16 (1940): 59-68.

Lewthwaite, G.R. "Wisconsin Cheese and Farm Type: A Locational Hypothesis." *Economic Geography* 40 (1964): 95-112.

Leyburn, James Graham. *The Scotch-Irish: A Social History.* Chapel Hill: University of North Carolina Press, 1962.

Long, Amos, Jr. "Bakeovens in the Pennsylvania Folk-Culture." *Pennsylvania Folklife* 14 (1964): 16-29.

—. "Bank (multi-level) Structures in Rural Pennsylvania." *Pennsylvania Folklife* 20 (1970-1): 31-39.

Lynch, R.W. "Czech Farmers in Oklahoma." *Economic Geography* 20 (1944): 9-13.

Lynn-Smith, T. *Sociology of Rural Life.* New York: Harper & Brothers, 1947.

Mahr, August C. "Origin and Significance of Pennsylvania Dutch Barn Symbols." In Alan Dundes (ed.). *The Study of Folklore.* Englewood Cliffs, N.J.: Prentice-Hall, 1965.

Marcella, Gabriel. "Spanish-Mexican Contributions to the Southwest." *Journal Mexican-American History* 1 (1970): 1-15.

Marshall, Douglas G. "Nationality and the Emerging Culture." *Rural Sociology* 13 (1948): 41-7.

Mather, Cotton and Matti Kaups. "The Finnish Sauna: A Cultural Index to Settlement." *Annals, Association American Geographers* 53 (1963): 494-504.

Mattison, Ray H. "Early Spanish and Mexican Settlements in Arizona." *New Mexico Historical Review* 21 (1946): 273-327.

McDermott, John F. *Research Opportunities in American Cultural History.* Lexington: University of Kentucky Press, 1961.

—. *The French in the Mississippi Valley.* Urbana: University of Illinois Press, 1965.

—. *Frenchmen and French Ways in the Mississippi Valley.* Urbana: University of Illinois Press, 1965.

McLean, Robert M. and Grace Williams. *Old Spain in New America.* New York: Associated Press, 1946.

Mead, Robert O. *The Atlantic Legacy: Essays in American-European Cultural History.* New York: New York University Press, 1969.

Meinig, D.W. *The Great Columbia Plain: A Historical Geography, 1805-1910.* Seattle: University of Washington Press, 1968.

—. *Imperial Texas: An Interpretive Essay in Cultural Geography.* Austin: University of Texas Press, 1969.

—. *Three Peoples in Geographical Change, 1600-1970.* London: Oxford University Press, 1971.

Merrens, Harry Roy. *Colonial North Carolina in the Eighteenth Century.* Chapel Hill: University of North Carolina Press, 1964.

Meynen, Emil. "Das Pennsylvaniendeutsche Bauernland." *Deutsches Archiv fur Landes-und Volksforschung* 3 (1939): 253-92.

Miller, E. Joan Wilson. "The Ozark Culture Region as Revealed by Traditional Materials." *Annals, Association American Geographers* 58 (1968): 51-77.

—. "The Naming of the Land in the Arkansas Ozarks: A Study in Culture Processes." *Annals, Association American Geographers* 59 (1969): 240-51.

Montgomery, James E. "Three Southern Appalachian Communities: An Analysis of Cultural Variables." *Rural Sociology* 14 (1949): 138-48.

Mook, Maurice A. and John Hostetler. "The Amish and Their Land." *Landscape* 6 (1957): 21-29.

Munch, Peter A. "Segregation and Assimilation of Norwegian Settlements in Wisconsin." *Norwegian-American Studies and Records* 18 (1954): 102-40.

Myers, Sandra L. "The Spanish Cattle Kingdom in the Province of Texas." *Texana* 4 (1966): 233-46.

Nahimy, Vladimir C., and Joshua A. Fishman. "American Immigrant Groups: Ethnic Identification and the Problem of Generations." *Sociological Review* 13 (1965): 311-26.

Newton, Milton Jr., "The Annual Round in the Upland South: The Synchronization of Man and Nature Through Culture." *Pioneer America* 3 (1971): 63-73.

—. "The Darlings Creek Peasant Settlements of St. Helena Parish, Louisiana." *Southern Anthropological Society Proceedings* 4 (1971): 38-48.

Nielson, George R. "Folklore of the German-Wends in Texas." *Texas Folklore Society Publications* 30 (1961): 244-59.

Nostrand, Richard L. "The Hispanic-American Borderland: Delineation of an American Culture Region." *Annals, Association American Geographers* 60 (1970): 638-61.

Olsen, Stanley J. "Examples of Colonial Spanish Hoes." *The Florida Anthropologist* 21 (1968): 117-20.

Page, Evelyn. "The First Frontier: The Swedes and the Dutch." *Pennsylvania History* 15 (1948): 276-303.

Pattison, William D. *Beginnings of the American Rectangular Survey, 1784-1800*. Department of Geography Research Paper No. 60. Chicago: University of Chicago, Department of Geography, 1957.

Pedersen, Harald A. "Cultural Differences in the Acceptance of Recommended Practices." *Rural Sociology* 16 (1951): 37-49.

Perret, Maurice E. *Les Colonies Tessionoises en Californie*. Lausanne: F. Rouge, 1950.

Perrigo, Lynn I. *Our Spanish Southwest*. Dallas: Banks, Upshaw, & Company, 1960.

Perrin, Richard W.E. "German Timber Farmhouses in Wisconsin: Terminal Examples of a Thousand-Year Building Tradition." *Wisconsin Magazine of History* 44 (1961): 199-202.

—. "Log Sauna and the Finnish Farmstead: Transplanted Architectural Idioms in Northern Wisconsin." *Wisconsin Magazine of History* 44 (1961): 284-6.

Perrin, Richard W.E. *Historic Wisconsin Buildings: A Survey of Pioneer Architecture 1835-70*. Milwaukee: Milwaukee Public Museum Press, 1962.

—. "Log Houses in Wisconsin." *Antiques* 89 (1966): 867-71.

—. *The Architecture of Wisconsin*. Madison: University of Wisconsin Press, 1967.

Peters, Victor. *All things Common: The Hutterian Way of Life*. Minneapolis: University of Minnesota Press, 1965.

Pillsbury, Dorothy. *Roots in Adobe*. Albuquerque: University of New Mexico, 1959.

Pillsbury, R. "The Urban Street Pattern as a Culture Indicator: Pennsylvania, 1682-1815." *Annals, Association American Geographers* 60 (1970): 428-46.

Pitt, Leonard. *The Decline of the Californias: A Social History of the Spanish-Speaking Californians, 1846-1890*. Los Angeles: University of California Press, 1966.

Post, Lauren C. *Cajun Sketches from the Prairies of Southwest Louisiana*. Baton Rouge: Louisiana State University Press, 1962.

Pounds, Jr., W.B. and H. Raup. "Northernmost Spanish Frontier in California as Shown by the Distribution of Geographic Names." *California Historical Society Quarterly* 32 (1953): 43-48.

Powell, Sumner C. *Puritan Village: The Formation of a New England Town.* Middletown, Conn.: Wesleyan University Press, 1963.

Proudfoot, A.B. "Irish Settlers in Alberta." *Ulster Folklife* 15/16 (1970): 216-23.

Qualey, Carlton C. "Pioneer Norwegian Settlement in Minnesota." *Minnesota History* 12 (1931): 247-80.

—. *Norwegian Settlement in the United States.* Northfield, Minn.: Norwegian-American Historical Association, 1938.

Raaen, Aagot. *Grass of the Earth: Immigrant Life in the Dakota Country.* Northfield, Minn.: Norwegian-American Historical Association, 1950.

—. *Measure of My Days.* Fargo: North Dakota Institute for Regional Studies, 1953.

Ragatz, Lowell J. *A Swiss Family in the New World: Letters of Jakob and Ulrich Buhler.* Menasha, Wis.: Edward Bros. Inc., 1963.

Raine, James Watt. *Saddlebag Folk: The Way of Life in the Kentucky Mountains.* Evanston: Row, Peterson, 1942.

Rasmussen, Wayne D. (ed.). *Readings in the History of American Agriculture* Urbana: University of Illinois Press, 1960.

Raup, Hallock F. *The German Colonization of Anaheim, California.* Berkely: University of California Press, 1932.

—. "The Italian-Swiss Dairymen of San Luis Obispo County, California." *Yearbook, Association Pacific Coast Geographers* 1 (1935): 3-8.

Rolle, Andrew F. *The Immigrant Upraised: Italian Adventurers and Colonists in an Expanding America.* Norman: University of Oklahoma Press, 1968.

Rowe, W.J. "Old World Legacies in America." *Folklife* 6 (1968): 68-82.

Rowse, Alfred L. *The Cornish in America.* London: Macmillan & Co., 1969.

Rutman, Darrett B. *Husbandmen of Plymouth: Farms and Villages in the Old Colony 1620-92.* Boston: Beacon Press, 1967.

Saarinen, Oiva W. "The Pattern and Impact of Finnish Settlement in Canada." *Terra* 79 (1968): 113-20.

Sabbe, Philemon D. and Leon Buyse. *Belgians in America.* Tielt: Richard Roose, 1960.

Sanchez, George I. *Forgotten People: A Study of New Mexicans.* Albuquerque: Calvin Horn, 1967.

Sas, A. "Dutch Concentrations in Rural Southwestern Ontario." *Annals, Association American Geographers* 48 (1958): 185-94.

Sauer, Carl. "Historical Geography and the Western Frontier." In Willard, James F. and J. Goodykoontz (eds.). *The Trans-Mississippi West.* Boulder: University of Colorado Press, 1930.

Schermerhorn, R.A. *These Our People.* Boston: Heath, 1949.

Schmidt, L.B. "The History of American Agriculture as a Field for Research." *Agricultural History* 14 (1940): 117-26.

Schock, Adolph. *In Quest of Free Land.* Assen: Royal Vanqorcum, 1964.

Schreiber, William I. *Our Amish Neighbors.* Chicago: University of Chicago Press, 1962.

—. "The Pennsylvania Dutch Bank Barn in Ohio." *Journal Ohio Folklore Society* 2 (1967): 15-28.

Schultze, G. "Evolution of the Areal Patterns of German and Polish Settlement in Milwaukee." *Erdkunde* 10 (1956): 136-41.

Scofield, Edna. "The Origin of Settlement Patterns in Rural New England." *Geographical Review* 28 (1938): 652-63.

Scott, Franklin D. *Wertmuller: Artist and Immigrant Farmer.* Chicago: Swedish Pioneer Historical Society, 1963.

Séguin, Robert-Lionel. *Les granges du Quebec du XVIIe au XIXe siècle.* No. 2 de la Série des Bulletins d'Histoire. Ottawa: Musée National du Canada Bulletin 192, 1963.

—. *Les Civilizations traditionnels de l' "habitant" aux 17 et 18 siècles.* Montreal: Fides, 1967.

—. *La Maison en Nouvelle-France.* No. 5 de la Série des bulletins de Folklore. Ottawa: Musée National du Canada Bulletin 266, 1968.

Shannon, James P. *Catholic Colonization on the Western Frontier.* Cambridge: Yale University Press, 1957.

—. "Bishop Ireland's Connemara Experiment." *Minnesota History* 25 (1957): 205-213.

Shoemaker, Alfred L. "Barracks." *Pennsylvania Folklife* 9 (1958): 3-11.

—. (ed.). *The Pennsylvania Barn.* 2nd ed. Kutztown: Pennsylvania Folklife Society. 1959.

Shurtleff, Harold. *The Log Cabin Myth.* Cambridge: Harvard University Press, 1939.

Shyrock, Richard H. "The Pennsylvania Germans in American History." *Pennsylvania Magazine of History and Biography* 63 (1939): 333-46.

—. "Cultural Factors in the History of the South." *Journal Southern History* 5 (1930): 333-46.

—. "British versus German Traditions in Colonial Agriculture." *Mississippi Valley Historical Review* 26 (1939-40): 39-54.

Skrabanek, R.K. and Vernon J. Parenton. "Social Life in a Czech-American Rural Community." *Rural Sociology* 15 (1950): 221-31.

—. "Forms of Cooperation and Mutual Aid in a Czech-American Rural Community." *Southwest Social Science Quarterly* 30 (1949): 183-7.

Sloane, Eric. *A Museum of Early American Tools.* New York: Wilfred Funk, 1964.

—. *A Reverence for Wood.* New York: Funk and Wagnalls, 1965.

Smith, Charles H. *The Coming of the Russian Mennonites: An Episode in the Settling of the Last Frontier, 1874-1884.* Berne, Ind.: Mennonite Book Concern, 1927.

Smith, Elmer L. *The Amish.* Witmer, Pa.: Applied Arts, 1966.

Steinmetz, Rollin C. and Charles S. Rice. *Vanishing Crafts and Their Craftsmen.* New Brunswick, N.J.: Rutgers University Press, 1959.

Stephenson, George M. *American Immigration 1820-1924.* Boston: Russell & Russell, 1926.

Tarver, James D. "Intra-Family Farm Succession Practises." *Rural Sociology* 17 (1952): 266-71.

Thomas, William J. and Florian Znaniecki. *The Polish Peasant in Europe and America.* 5 vols. Boston: Dover Publications, 1918-20.

Tower, J. and W. Wolf. "Ethnic Groups in Cullman County, Alabama." *Geographical Review* 33 (1943): 276-85.

Traquair, R. *The Old Architecture of Quebec.* Toronto: University of Toronto Press, 1947.

Trewartha, Glen T. "French Settlement in the Driftless Hill Land." *Annals, Association American Geographers* 28 (1938): 179-200.

—. "Types of Rural Settlement in Colonial America." *Geographical Review* 36 (1946): 569-96.

Trindel, Roger T. "Building in Brick in Early America." *Geographical Review* 58 (1968): 484-87.

Valetta, Clement. "Italian Immigrant Life in Northampton County, Pennsylvania, 1890-1915." *Pennsylvania Folklife* 14:3 (1965): 36-45; *Ibid.,* 15:1 (1965): 39-48.

Van Cleef, Eugene. "The Finn in America." *Geographical Review* 6 (1918): 185-214.

—. "Finnish Settlement in Canada." *Geographical Review* 42 (1952): 253-60.

—. "The Finns of the Pacific Coast of the United States, and Consideration of the Problem of Scientific Land Settlement." *Annals, Association American Geographers* 30 (1940): 25-38.

Vanderhill, Burke G. and Davie E. Christensen "The Settlement of New Iceland." *Annals, Association American Geographers* 53 (1963): 350-63.

Vaughan, Alder T. *New England Frontier: Puritans and Indians 1620-75.* Boston: Little & Brown, 1963.

Vedder, R.K. and L.E. Gallaway. "The Settlement Preferences of Scandinavian Emigrants to the United States, 1850-1960." *Scandinavian Economic History Review* 18 (1970): 159-76.

Vicero, Ralph D. "French-Canadian Settlement in Vermont Prior to the Civil War." *Professional Geographer* 13 (1971): 290-94.

Vogt, Evan Z. and Ethel M. Albert. *People of Rimrock: A Study of Values in Five Cultures.* New York: Atheneum, 1970.

Von Wasielewski, H.T. "Das Obere Conestogatal: Ein Stuck Deutschpennsylvanischer Kulturlandschaft." *Mitt Geographische Gesellschaft in Munchen* 32 (1939): 165-237.

Wacker, Peter O. *The Musconetcong: A Study in Historical Geography*. New Brunswick, N.J.: Rutgers University Press, 1968.

—. "Cultural and Commercial Associations of Traditional Smokehouses in New Jersey." *Pioneer America* 3 (1971): 25-34.

—, and R.T. Trindell. "The Log House in New Jersey: Origins and Diffusion." *Keystone Folklore Quarterly* 13 (1969): 248-68.

Warkentin, John. "Mennonite Agricultural Settlements of Southern Manitoba." *Geographical Review* 49 (1959): 342-68.

Webb, Walter Prescott. *The Great Plains*. Boston: Ginn & Company, 1931.

Welsh, Peter C. "Woodworking Tools, 1600-1900." *Contributions from the Museum of History and Technology*. US National Museum Bulletin 241, Paper 51. Washington: Smithsonian Institute, 1966.

Wertenbaker, Thomas J. *The First Americans 1607-90*. New York: Macmillan, 1927.

—. *The Founding of American Civilization: The Middle Colonies*. New York: Cooper Square Publishers, 1938.

—. *The Old South: The Founding of American Civilization*. New York: Cooper Square Publishers, 1942.

—. *The Puritan Oligarchy: The Founding of American Civilization*. New York: Cooper Square Publishers, 1947.

Weslager, C.A. "Log Structures in New Sweden during the Seventeenth Century." *Delaware History* 5 (1952-53): 77-95.

—. *The Log Cabin in America: From Pioneer Days to the Present*. New Brunswick, N.J.: Rutgers University Press, 1969.

West, Robert C. "The Term 'Bayou' in the United States: A Study in the Geography of Place Names." *Annals, Association American Geographers* 44 (1954): 63-74.

Whitaker, A.P. "The Spanish Contribution to American Agriculture." *Agricultural History* 3 (1929): 1-14.

Wilhelm, E.J., Jr. "Folk Settlement Types in the Blue Ridge Mountains." *Keystone Folklore Quarterly* 12 (1967): 151-74.

Wilhelm, Hubert G.J. "German Settlement and Folk Building Practises in the Hill Country of Texas." *Pioneer America* 3 (1971): 15-24.

Wilson, Eugene M. "Some Similarities Between American and European Folk Houses." *Pioneer America* 3 (1971): 8-14.

Wittke, Carl. *The Germans in America: A Student's Guide to Localized History*. New York: Teachers College Press, 1967.

Wood, David. "Scandinavian Settlers in Canada Revisited." *Geografiska Annaler* 49 (1967): 1-9.

Wood, Ralph (ed.). *The Pennsylvania Germans*. Princeton, N.J.: Prentice-Hall, 1942.

Wright, Martin. "The Antecedents of the Double-Pen House Type." *Annals, Association American Geographers* 48 (1958): 107-117.
Wust, Klaus (ed.). *The Virginia Germans.* Charlottesville: University Press of Virginia, 1969.
Wytrawl, Joseph A. *America's Polish Heritage.* Detroit: Endurance Press, 1961.
Yuzyk, P. *The Ukranians in Manitoba: A Social History.* Toronto: University of Toronto Press, 1953.
Zelinsky, Wilbur. "The Log House in Georgia." *Geographical Review* 43 (1953): 173-93.
—. "Generic Terms in the Place Names of the Northeastern United States." *Annals, Association American Geographers* 45 (1955): 319-49.
—. "The New England Connecting Barn." *Geographical Review* 48 (1958): 540-53.
—. "Walls and Fences." *Landscape* 8 (1959): 14-20.

II

REFERENCES: GOVERNMENT PUBLICATIONS,
PRINTED SOURCES, AND MANUSCRIPTS

Canada. *Census of Canada, 1851.* RG 31. MSS in National Archives, Ottawa.
Canada. *Census of Canada, 1861.* RG 31. MSS in National Archives, Ottawa.
Canada. Peter Robinson Papers, 1822-44. MSS in Provincial Archives of Ontario, Toronto.
Great Britain. Colonial Office Corresponsence, Newfoundland. Series 1, vols. 1-6, 9-10, 12-30, 32-47, 49-68, 1574-1697. MSS in Provincial Archives, St John's.
Great Britain. Colonial Office Correspondence, Newfoundland. Series 194, vols. 1-279, 1696-1922. MSS in Provincial Archives, St John's.
Great Britain. Colonial Office Correspondence, Lower & Upper Canada. MG11, Series Q, vols. 1-431, 1760-1841. MSS in National Archives, Ottawa.
Great Britain. Parliament. *Appendix Colonel Cockburn's Instructions & Reports on Emigration.* London, 1828. In National Archives, Ottawa.
Great Britain. Parliament. *Papers Relative to Emigration to Canada.* London, 1847. In National Archives, Ottawa.
Great Britain. Parliament. *Report of the Select Committee of the House of Lords on Colonization from Ireland.* VI, London, 1847. In National Archives, Ottawa.
Great Britain. Parliament. *Select Committee on Emigration from the United Kingdom. Minutes of Evidence.* London, 1827. In National Archives, Ottawa.
Ireland. *Report of the Commissioners Appointed to Take the Census of Ireland for the Year 1841.* Dublin: Queen's Printer, 1843.

New Brunswick. Board of Agriculture. *Annual Reports of the Board of Agriculture, New Brunswick.* Nos. 1-10. Fredericton, 1861-70. In University of New Brunswick Library, Fredericton.

New Brunswick. Department of Crown Lands. *Crown Land Records,* Northumberland County. Vols. 1-9, 1787-1833. MSS in Confederation Building, Fredericton.

New Brunswick. Department of Crown Lands. Land Petitions, Northumberland County. Vols. 1-9, 1763-1860. MSS in Newcastle Courthouse, New Brunswick.

New Brunswick. Department of Public Works. "Highways Recorded in the County of Northumberland." 1819-69. MSS in Newcastle Courthouse, New Brunswick.

New Brunswick. Parish Records. Bartibogue, Northumberland, 1790-1826. Nelson, Northumberland, 1826-60. MSS in Roman Catholic Church, Nelson Parish.

Newfoundland. Governor's Office. "An Account of Inhabitants Residing in the Harbour and District of St John's, 1794-95." MSS in Memorial University Library, St John's.

Newfoundland. Department of Colonial Secretary. *Census of Newfoundland, 1836.* In Memorial University Library, St John's.

Newfoundland. Department of Colonial Secretary. *Census of Newfoundland and Labrador, 1857.* In Memorial University Library, St John's.

Newfoundland. Department of Colonial Secretary. *Abstract Census and Return of Population, etc. of Newfoundland, 1869.* In Memorial University Library, St John's.

Newfoundland. Department of Colonial Secretary. *Census of Newfoundland and Labrador, 1891.* In Memorial University Library, St John's.

Newfoundland. Department of Colonial Secretary. Correspondence, Series 1, vols. 1-215, 1794-1932. MSS in Provincial Archives, St John's.

Newfoundland. Department of Colonial Secretary. *Registry of Grants,* 1810-1930. MSS in Department of Mines, Agriculture and Resources, Confederation Building, St John's.

Newfoundland. House of Assembly, *Journals* 1833-41; 1843-65. In Memorial University Library, St John's.

Newfoundland. Letter Book of Saunders and Sweetman. Placentia, 1788-1804. MSS in Arts & Culture Library, St. John's.

Newfoundland. Supreme Court, Registrar's Office. *Registry of Wills* 1 (1810-40), 2(1840-64). MSS in Courthouse, St John's.

Newfoundland. Surrogate Court Records, Placentia, 1757-1803. MSS in Arts & Culture Library, St John's.

Ontario. Assessment Rolls. RG 21. Ennismore Township, 1827, 1828, 1830, 1839-41. Emily, 1820-40. MSS in Provincial Archives, Toronto.

Ontario. Douro Township Council Reports, 1850-80. MSS in Township Hall, Douro, Peterborough County.

Ontario. Will of George O'Connell, 1848. MSS in Emily Township, Victoria County.

Ontario. William Moher Diaries, 1855-85. MSS in Douro Township, Peterborough County.

The Gleaner and Northumberland Schediasma, Chatham. 1829-30. University of New Brunswick Library, Fredericton.

The Mercantile Journal, St John's. 1816-24. Provincial Archives, St John's.

The Mercury, Newcastle. 1826-30. University of New Brunswick Library, Fredericton.

The Morning Courier, St John's. 1844-55. Arts and Culture Library, St John's; 1853-75. Provincial Archives, St John's.

The Newfoundlander, St John's. 1827-82. Provincial Archives, St John's.

The Patriot, St John's. 1834-37, 1840-61. Arts and Culture Library, St John's.

Peterborough Daily Examiner, Peterborough. May 15, 1925. Peterborough Public Library, Peterborough.

The Pilot, St John's. 1825-53. Provincial Archives, St John's.

Public Ledger, St John's. 1827-82. Provincial Archives, St John's.

The Royal Gazette and New Brunswick Advertiser, Fredericton. 1787-1837. University of New Brunswick Library, Fredericton.

Royal Gazette and Newfoundland Advertiser, St John's. 1810-1816, 1836-47, 1850-89. Arts and Culture Library, St John's.

III

REFERENCES: MAPS

Newfoundland. Department of Colonial Secretary. *Registry of Grants.* In Confederation Building, St John's.

Patterson, James A. *Map of the County of Victoria, 1877.* C.VI. 420. In National Archives, Ottawa.

Roe and Colby. *Map of Northumberland County, New Brunswick.* R.220. Northumberland, 1876. In National Archives, Ottawa.

IV

REFERENCES: BOOKS AND ARTICLES

Aalen, F.H.A. "Transhumance in the Wicklow Mountains." *Ulster Folklife* 10 (1964): 65-72.

—. "Enclosures in Eastern Ireland: A General Introduction." *Irish Geography* 5 (1965): 29-33.

—. "The Evolution of the Western Irish House." *Journal Royal Society Antiquaries Ireland* 96 (1966): 47-58.

—. "Furnishings of Traditional Houses in the Wicklow Hills." *Ulster Folklife* 13 (1967): 61-67.

Adams, William F. *Ireland and Irish Emigration to the New World.* New Haven: Yale University Press, 1932.

Alcock, N.W. "Devonshire Linhays: A Vernacular Tradition." *Devonshire Association, Report and Transactions* 95 (1963): 117-30.

—. "Devon Farmhouses, Part I." *Devonshire Association, Report and Transactions* 100 (1968): 13-28.

—. "A Devon Farm: Bury Barton, Lapford." *Devonshire Association, Report and Transactions* 98 (1966): 105-31.

Andrews, J.H. "Some Sources for the Study of Enclosure in Ireland Between the 16th and 19th Centuries." *Irish Geography* 5 (1965): 36-37.

—. "Changes in the Rural Landscape of the Late Eighteenth and Early Nineteenth Century Ireland: an Example from County Waterford." *Area: Institute British Geographers* 1 (1970): 55-56.

Anspach, Lewis A. *A History of the Island of Newfoundland.* London: Published for Author, 1819.

Arensberg, Conrad M. and Solon T. Kimball. *Family and Community in Ireland.* Cambridge: Harvard University Press, 1940.

Barbeau, Marius. "The Field of European Folk-Lore in America." *Journal American Folklore* 32 (1919): 185-97.

Barley, M.W. *The English Farm House and Cottage.* London: Routledge and Kegan Paul, 1961.

Benedict, Ruth. *Patterns of Culture.* Cambridge, Mass.: Riverside Press, 1934.

Bishko, Charles J. "The Peninsular Background of Latin American Cattle Ranching." *Hispanic American Historical Review* 32 (1952): 491-515.

—. "The Iberian Background of Latin American History: Recent Progress and Continuing Problems." *Ibid.*, 36 (1956): 50-80.

Blegen, Theodore C. *Grass Roots History.* New York: Kennikat Press, 1947.

—. (ed.). *Land of Their Choice: The Immigrants Write Home.* Minneapolis: University of Minnesota Press, 1955.

Bonnycastle, R.H. *Newfoundland in 1842: A Sequel to the "Canadas in 1841."* 2 vols. London: H. Colburn, 1842.

Bourke, P.M. Austin. "The Agricultural Statistics of the 1841 Census of Ireland. A Critical Review." *Economic History Review* 18 (1965): 376-91.

Briggs, Martin Shaw. *The Homes of the Pilgrim Fathers in England and America 1620-1685.* London: Oxford University Press, 1932.

Buchanan, R.H. "Rural Settlement in Ireland." In Stephens, Nicholas and Robin E. Glasscock (eds.). *Irish Geographical Studies in Honour of E. Estyn Evans.* Belfast: Queen's University Press, 1970: 146-61.

Campbell, Åke. "Notes on the Irish House," *Folkliv* 1 (1937): 207-34.

Collins, E.J.T. "Harvest Technology and Labour Supply in Britain, 1790-1850." *Economic History Review* 22 (1969): 453-73.

—. "Labour Supply and Demand in European Agriculture, 1800-1880." In Jones, E.L. and S.J. Woolf (eds.). *Agrarian Change in Economic Development: The Historical Problems.* London: Methuen, 1969.

Commager, Henry Steele (ed.). *Immigration and American History: Essays in Honour of Theodore C. Blegen.* Minneapolis: University of Minnesota Press, 1961.

Cousens, S.H. "The Regional Variations in Emigration from Ireland between 1821 and 1841." *Institute British Geographers, Transactions and Papers* 37 (1965): 15-29.

Crawford, W.H. "The Woodlands of Brownlow's Derry." *Ulster Folklife* 10 (1964): 57-64.

Danaher, K. *In Ireland Long Ago.* Cork: Mercier Press, 1962.

De Fréine, Seán. *The Great Silence.* Dublin: Mercier Press, 1965.

Dinneen, Patrick S. *An English-Irish Dictionary.* Dublin: Educational Company of Ireland, 1927.

Dorson, Richard M. "The Shaping of Folklore Traditions in the United States." *Folklore* 78 (1967): 161-83.

Dundes, Alan. "The American Concept of Folklore." *Journal Folklore Institute* 3 (1966): 226-49.

Erixon, Sigurd. "West European Connections and Culture Relations." *Folkliv* 2 (1938): 137-72.

—. "The Age of Enclosures and Its Older Traditions." *Folklife* 4 (1966): 56-63.

Evans, E. Estyn. "Some Survivals in the Irish Open Field System." *Geography* 24 (1939): 24-63.

—. *Irish Folk Ways.* London: Routledge and Kegan Paul, 1957.

—. "Cultural Relics of the Ulster Scots in the Old West of North America." *Ulster Folklife* 11 (1965): 33-38.

Evans, Francis E. *The Emigrants' Directory and Guide.* Dublin: W. Curry, 1833.

Flatrès, P. *Géographie rurale de quatre countrées celtiques: Irlande, Galles, Cornwall, Man.* Rennes: Plihon, 1957.

Flynn, Monsignor. "The Parish of Placentia." *Newfoundland Quarterly* 36 (1936): 29-32.

Foster, George M. "What is Folk Culture." *American Anthropologist* 55 (1953): 159-73.

—. *Culture and Conquest: America's Spanish Heritage.* Viking Fund Publications in Anthropology No. 27. Chicago: Quadrangle Books, 1960.

Fox, J.R. "Kinship and Land Tenure on Tory Island." *Ulster Folklife* 12 (1966): 1-17.

Freeman, T.W. *Pre-Famine Ireland.* Manchester: Manchester University Press, 1957.

203

—. "The Typology of the Irish Spade." In Gailey, Alan and Alexander Fenton (eds.). *The Spade in Northern and Atlantic Europe.* Belfast: Queen's University Press, 1970.

Glassie, Henry. "The Types of Southern Mountain Cabin." In Jan H. Brunvand (ed.). *The Study of American Folklore.* New York: W.W. Norton, 1968.

—. "A Central Chimney Continental Log House from Cumberland County." *Pennsylvania Folklife* 18 (1968-69): 33-39.

—. "The Pennsylvania Barn in the South." *Pennsylvania Folklife* 15:2 (1965-66); 8-19; 15:4 (1966): 12-25.

—. *Pattern in the Material Folk Culture of the Eastern United States.* University of Pennsylvania Monographs in Folklore and Folklife No. 1. Philadelphia: University of Pennsylvania Press, 1969.

—, and MacEdward Leach. *A Guide for Collectors of Oral Traditions and Folk Cultural Material in Pennsylvania.* Philadelphia: University of Pennsylvania Press, 1968.

Graham, J.M. "Transhumance in Ireland." *Advancement of Science* 10 (1953): 74-79.

—. "Rural Society in Connacht 1600-40." In Stephens, Nicholas and Robin E. Glasscock (eds.). *Irish Geographical Studies in Honour of E. Estyn Evans.* Belfast: Queen's University Press, 1970, pp. 192-206.

—. "Southwest Donegal in the Seventeenth Century." *Irish Geography* 6 (1970): 136-53.

Hall, Basil. *Travels in North America.* 2 vols. Edinburgh: Carey, Lea and Carey, 1829.

Hansen, Marcus L. "The History of American Immigration as a Field for Research." *American Historical Review* 22 (1927): 500-18.

Hart, John Fraser. Review of Robert-Lionel Séguin, *Les granges du Quebec du XVIIe au XIXe siècle.* Ottawa: Musée Nationale du Canada Bulletin No. 192, 1963. In *Geographical Review* 55 (1965): 424-26.

Harvey, Nigel. *A History of Farm Buildings in England and Wales.* Newtown Abbott: David and Charles, 1970.

Hickey, William. *Hints on Emigration to Upper Canada.* Dublin: W. Curry, 1831.

Hill, George W. "The Use of the Culture-Area Concept in Social Research." *American Journal of Sociology* 47 (1941): 39-45.

Hill, Lord George. *Gweedore: Facts from Gweedore.* Dublin: Hatchard, 1845. 5th ed., 1887.

Hultkrantz, Ake. "Historical Approaches in American Ethnology." *Ethnologia Europaea* 1 (1967): 96-116.

Ianni, Francis. "Time and Place as Variables in Acculturation Research." *American Anthropologist* 60 (1958): 39-46.

Johnson, J.H. "The Two Irelands at the Beginning of the Nineteenth Century." In Stephens, Nicholas and Robin E. Glasscock (eds.). *Irish Geographical Studies in Honour of E. Estyn Evans.* Belfast: Queen's University Press, 1970.

—. "Partnership and Clachans in Mid-Nineteenth Century Londonderry." *Ulster Folklife* 9 (1963): 20-29.

Jones Hughes, T. "Land Holding and Settlement in the Cooley Peninsula of Louth." *Irish Geography* 4 (1961): 149-73.

—. "Landlordism in the Mullet of Mayo." *Irish Geography* 4 (1959): 16-34.

—. "Town and Baile in Irish Placenames." In Stephens, Nicholas and Robin E. Glasscock (eds.). *Irish Geographical Studies in Honour of E. Estyn Evans.* Belfast: Queen's University Press, 1970, pp. 244-58.

—. "Society and Settlement in Nineteenth Century Ireland." *Irish Geography* 5 (1965): 79-96.

Joyce, P.W. *English as We Speak it in Ireland.* London: Longmans, 1910.

Jukes, J.B. *Excursions in and About Newfoundland in the Years 1839-40.* London: John Murray, 1842.

Kane, Eileen. "Man and Kin in Donegal: A Study of Kinship Functions in a Rural Irish and Irish-American Community." *Ethnology* 7 (1968): 245-58.

Kelly, Kenneth. "Wheat Farming in Simcoe County in the Mid-Nineteenth Century." *Canadian Geographer* 15 (1971): 95-112.

Kilfoil, William P. *Johnville: The Centennial Story of an Irish Settlement.* Fredericton: Unipress, 1962.

Kirwin, William. "Lines, Coves and Squares in Newfoundland Names." *American Speech* 40 (1965): 163-70.

Kniffen, Fred. "Folk Housing: Key to Diffusion." *Annals, Association American Geographers* 55 (1965): 549-77.

—, and Henry Glassie. "Building in Wood in the Eastern United States: A Time-Place Perspective." *Geographical Review* 56 (1966): 40-66.

Kongas, Elli Kaija. "Immigrant Folklore: Survival or Living Tradition." *Midwest Folklore* 10 (1960): 117-23.

Langton, H.H. (ed.). *A Gentlewoman in Upper Canada: The Journals of Anne Langton.* Toronto: Clarke, Irwin & Company, Ltd., 1964.

Lacy, B. *Miscellaneous Poems Compos'd at Newfoundland on Board H.M. Ship "The Kinsale."* London: The Author, 1729.

Lucas, A.T. "Wattle and Straw Mat Doors in Ireland." *Studia Ethnographica Upsaliensia* 11 (1956): 29-32.

—. "An Fhóir: A Straw-Rope Granary." *Gwerin* 1 (1956-57): 68-77.

—. "An Fhóir: Further Notes." *Gwerin* 2 (1958-59): 2-20.

—. "Sea Sand and Shells as Manure." In Geraint Jenkins (ed.). *Studies in Folk Life.* London: Routledge and Kegan Paul, 1969.

—. "Paring and Burning in Ireland." In Stephens, Nicholas and Robin E. Glasscock (eds.). *Irish Geographical Studies in Honour of E. Estyn Evans.* Belfast: Queen's University Press, 1970, pp. 99-147.

MacAodha, B.J. " 'Souming' in the Sperrins." *Ulster Folklife* 2 (1956): 19-21.

McCourt, D. "Infield and Outfield in Ireland." *Economic History Review* 7 (1954-55): 369-76.

—. "Traditions of Rundale in and Around the Sperrin Mountains." *Ulster Journal Archaeology* 16 (1953): 69-84.

—. "The Rundale System in Donegal: its Distribution and Decline." *Donegal Annual* 3 (1955): 47-60.

—. "Surviving Openfield in County Londonderry." *Ulster Folklife* 4 (1958): 19-28.

McCracken, Eileen, "The Woodlands of Ireland circa 1600." *Irish Historical Studies* 11 (1959): 271-90.

MacDonagh, Oliver. "Irish Emigration to the United States and British Colonies During the Famine." In Edwards, R.D. and T.D. Williams (eds.). *The Great Famine.* Dublin: Browne and Nolan, 1956.

Mason, L. "The Characterization of American Culture in Studies of Acculturation." *American Anthropologist* 57 (1955): 1264-79.

Matley, Ian M. "The Origin of Infield-Outfield Agriculture in Scotland: The Linguistic Evidence." *The Professional Geographer* 18 (1966): 275-79.

Meredith, Mamie. "The Nomenclature of American Pioneer Fences." *Southern Folklore Quarterly* 15 (1951): 109-51.

Messenger, John C. *Inis Beag: Isle of Ireland,* New York: Holt, Rinehart, and Winston, 1969.

Moodie, Susanna. *Roughing it in the Bush.* Toronto: McClelland and Stewart, 1964. First published London, 1852.

Murray, Jean M. (ed.). *The Newfoundland Journal of Aaron Thomas.* Toronto: Longmans, 1968.

Ó Danachair, Caoimhín. "Traces of the Buaile in the Galtees." *Journal Royal Society Antiquaries Ireland* 75 (1945): 248-52.

—. "Hearth and Chimney in the Irish House." *Béaloideas* 16 (1946): 91-104.

—. "The Flail and Other Threshing Methods." *Journal of the Cork Archaeological Society* 60 (1955): 6-14.

—. "Irish Farmyard Types." *Studia Ethnographica Upsaliensia* 11 (1956): 6-15.

—. "Some Distribution Patterns in Irish Folklife." *Béaloideas* 25 (1957): 108-123.

—. "Materials and Methods in Irish Traditional Building." *Journal Royal Society Antiquaries Ireland* 87 (1957): 61-74.

—. "The Spade in Ireland." *Béaloideas* 31 (1963): 98-114.

—. "The Combined Byre-and-Dwelling in Ireland." *Folklife* 2 (1964): 58-75.

—. "The Use of the Spade in Ireland." In Gailey, Alan and Alexander Fenton (eds.). *The Spade in Northern and Atlantic Europe.* Belfast: Queen's University Press, 1970: 49-56.

O'Growney, Eugene. *Simple Lessons in Irish.* 3 vols. Dublin: M.H. Gill, 1936.

Oliver, Bruce W., "The Devonshire Cottage." *Devonshire Association, Report and Transactions* 81 (1949): 27-45.

Onions, C.T. (ed.). *The Shorter Oxford English Dictionary.* 2 vols. Oxford: Claredon Press, 1959.

Ó Ríordáin, S.P. and C.Ó. Danachair. "Lough Gur Excavations: Site J. Knockadoon." *Journal Royal Society Antiquaries Ireland* 77 (1947): 39-52.

Pickering, Joseph. *Inquiries of an Emigrant.* London: E. Wilson, 1832.

Poole, Thomas W. *The Early Settlement of Peterborough County.* Peterborough: Peterborough Printing Co., 1867. Reprinted 1967.

Price, C.A. "Immigration and Group Settlement." In Borrie, W.D. (ed.). *The Cultural Integration of Immigrants.* Paris: UNESCO, 1959.

Raup, H.F. "The Fence in the Cultural Landscape." *Western Folklore* 6 (1947): 1-7.

Riedl, Norbert F. "Folklore vs. 'Volkskunde.'" *Tennessee Folklore Society Bulletin* 121 (1965): 47-53.

—. "Folklore and the Study of Material Aspects of Folk Culture." *Journal of American Folklore* 79 (1966): 557-63.

—. "A Survey of Tennessee Folk Culture." Unpublished questionnaire. Department of Anthropology, University of Tennessee, 1967.

Rowe, John H. "Time Perspective in Ethnography." *Kroeber Anthropological Society Papers* 12 (1955): 55-61.

Schlesinger, Arthur M. "The Significance of Immigration in American History." *American Journal of Sociology* 27 (1921): 71-85.

Sheppard, June A. "Vernacular Buildings in England and Wales: A Survey of Recent Work by Architects, Archaeologists and Historians." *Institute British Geographers, Transactions* 40 (1966): 21-37.

Shoemaker, Alfred L. "Barracks." *Pennsylvania Folklife* 9 (1958): 3-11.

Spier, Robert F.G. "Tool Acculturation Among 19th Century California Chinese." *Ethno-history* 5 (1958): 97-117.

Spiro, Melford. "The Acculturation of American Ethnic Groups." *American Anthropologist* 57 (1955): 1240-52.

Stephenson, George M. "When America was the land of Canaan." *Minnesota History* 10 (1929): 237-59.

Stewart, Frances. *Our Forest Home.* Montreal: Gazette Printing and Publishing Company, 1902.

Strickland, Samuel. *Twenty-Seven Years in Canada West.* London: R. Bentley, 1853.

Thompson, Stith. "Advances in Folklore Studies." In Kroeber, A.L. (ed.). *Anthropology Today: An Encyclopoedic Inventory.* Chicago: University of Chicago Press, 1955.

Towns, P.G. "Early Life in Douro." *Peterborough Daily Examiner,* May 15, 1925.

Traill, Catherine Parr. *The Backwoods of Canada.* Toronto: McClelland and Stewart, reprint, 1968.

Whitaker, Ian. "The Harrow in Scotland." *Scottish Studies* 2 (1958): 149-65.

Williams, Glyn. "Incidence and Nature of Acculturation within the Welsh Colony of Chubut: A Historical Perspective." *Kroeber Anthropological Society Papers* 39 (1968): 72-87.

—. "Welsh Contributions to Explorations in Patagonia." *Geographical Journal* 135 (1969): 213-27.

Wix, Edward. *Six Months of a Newfoundland Missionary's Journal.* London: Smith, Elder and Co. 1836.

Wright, J. *English Dialect Dictionary.* London: Frowde, 1905.

Yoder, Don. "The Folklife Studies Movement." *Pennsylvania Folklife* 13 (1963): 43-65.

—. "Folklife." In Coffin, Tristan P. (ed.). *Our Living Traditions.* New York: Basic Books, 1968, pp. 47-57.

Young, Arthur. *A Tour In Ireland, 1776-1779.* 2 vols. Shannon: Irish University Press, 1970.

Zelinsky, Wilbur. "Walls and Fences." *Landscape* 8 (1959): 14-20.

Index

Acreage: Avalon farms, 52, 61, 63, 66; initial settlement, 24-27, 36, 40, 41, 42; Miramichi farms, 72-73; Peterborough farms, 74-76

Adopted traits, 3, 4, 6, 78, 171-72: farm outbuildings, 130-31, 133-35; farm tools, 109-10; fences, 106-7; field systems, 78-79; furniture, 164; grain harvesting, 113-14; house types, 159, 162-63; land clearing methods, 104-6; ploughing, 108; threshing, 97-98

Agglomerated settlements. *See* Farm clusters

Agricultural revolution: and Irish farming patterns, 35-36, 57-60; and technology, 4

Agricultural systems: compared in three study areas, 24-30. *See also* Arable farming; Cattle farming; Dairy farming; Pastoral farming

Animal husbandry. *See* Cattle farming; Livestock

Arable farming: on Avalon, 61-72; compared with pastoral, 5; in Ireland, 59-60; Miramichi area, 72-74; Peterborough area, 74-77; subsistence and Irish influence, 170-71; technology for, 86-92, 108-15; tillage boom in Ireland, 15, 36, 58. *See also* Pastoral farming; Wheat cultivation

Architecture: *See* Houses; Farm outbuildings

Artisans: Irish immigrants, 17-18

Atlantic trade, 30

Avalon Peninsula, Newfoundland: climate, 31-32; farm outbuildings, 119-25, 129, 131-32, 134, 136; field systems, 60-72, 79, 80; grain harvest, 96, 100-1; grain planting, 92, 93; haulage methods, 101-4; haymaking, 93-5; house types, early, 143-44, 157-58; house types, later, 147-55; Irish culture transferred, 170-72; land clearance, 24-25, 84-85; livestock, 73; origins of farm technology, 106-7, 109-14;

origins of house types, 159-64; origins of Irish immigrants, 16-17; period of migration, 18-20; root cellars, 128; potato harvest, 101; root crops, 90; settlement patterns, early, 14, 36-39, 42-43; settlement patterns, later, 44-49; tools, 89; topography, 30-31, 78-79; traditional folk festivals, 116-17; types of farming, 27; village types, 50-54

Bacon: sale in Peterborough, 30
'Baiting and burning': fertilization method in Ireland, 59; on Avalon, 62, 66, 80
Barley crop: climate for, 31; in Ireland, 55; Miramichi, 72
Barnaby, New Brunswick: boundaries, 86; description of a farm, 73-75; ethnic diversity, 24; farm outbuildings, 136; grain harvest, 97-98; grain planting, 92; haymaking, 94; house types, early, 144; settlement patterns, initial, 14, 21, 39-40, 42; settlement patterns, evolving, 48-49; village development, 51-52
Barnaby river: as trading link, 29
Barns, 122-27; Irish influence, 167; origins of types, 131-33, 137
Beans: in Ireland, 55; Miramichi area, 73
Boats: storage, 122
Boundaries, 79, 85-86: on Avalon, 60-61, 66-67; Miramichi area, 72; origins of types, 106-8; Peterborough area 74, 76-78
Branch, Avalon: acreage in cultivation, 66; ethnic homogeneity, 23; fishery, 30; grain harvest, 97; house types, 151; roads and marketing, 28; settlement patterns, early, 39; settlement patterns, evolving, 46;

village development, 50-51
Butter: production and sale on Avalon, 28, 67; in Ireland, 57; Miramichi area, 29, 74; Peterborough area, 30

Cabbages: on Avalon, 32, 63-64, 66; cultivation in New World, 27; in Ireland, 55, 60; Miramichi area, 73; planting methods, 93; storage, 128
Cape Shore, Avalon: acreages, 27; ethnic homogeneity, 23; farm outbuildings, 123-24, 136-37; field systems, 64, 66-72, 80-83; furniture, 153; grain planting, 92; handtools, 89; haulage, 102-4; haymaking, 93; house types, 143-44, 147-49, 151, 161-62; Irish culture transferred, 165-66, 170, 172; fencing, 85-86; landholding, 41; livestock, 73, 134; market links with St John's, 28-29; origins of farm technology, 106, 108, 110-11, 114-15; ploughing, 86, 88; population, 30; potato growing, 90; root cellars, 128; root crops, 90; settlement patterns, early, 14, 18-20, 39, 43; settlement patterns, evolving, 44-46, 48-49; threshing, 97, 115; topography, 30; types of farming, 27; vegetable planting, 93; village types, 50-53
Carters, in St John's, 52
Carts, 103-5: Irish influence, 167; origins of types, 116; storage in barns, 122
Cattle farming: on Avalon, 28, 67-68; beef production, 27, 30; in Ireland, 56; Miramichi area, 29, 74; Peterborough area, 30, 76-78. *See also* Livestock; Pastoral farming
'Changedale.' *See* 'Rundale'
Chatham, New Brunswick, 20, 29

Chimneys: Avalon, 148-51, 153, 155, 157; Ireland, 140-41; Miramichi and Peterborough areas, 157; origins of types, 161-64, 167

Churches 50-51, 54

Clachan': on Avalon, 51; and field systems, 56-58; Irish village pattern, 34, 43; survival in New World, 170

Climate: and farm buildings, 130-31, 133; and field systems, 79-80; and house types, 160-62; and Irish influence, 170, 173; in study areas, 31-32; and vegetable farming, 86-88

Cod fishery: on Cape Shore, 28-29; and communal labour, 106; and farming, 72; and field systems, 80-83; and Irish cultural survivals, 170; and Irish immigration to Newfoundland, 18; marketing, 27; population engaged in, 30; and settlement patterns, 51-52

Cod liver oil, 28

Coffey, John (Avalon), 44-45

Commercial farming, 27, 84, 170-72: Avalon, 52, 67, 80, 82-83; and development of technology, 113; in Ireland, 15, 56, 168; Miramichi area, 29, 74, 82; Peterborough area, 30, 53, 78-79, 82, 115, 132-33. See also Economic factors

Communal labour: on Avalon, 71-72; building, 126, 160; grain harvest, 96; haymaking, 93; in Ireland, 36, 56, 58; land clearing, 85; origins, 106. See also Partnership farming

Community halls, 51, 54

Cooking: utensils and food: on Avalon, 149, 151; in Ireland, 141; Miramichi and Peterborough areas, 158; origins, 161-62

Cork, Ireland: at time of migrations, 15; Gaelic speaking, 16; immigrants from, 13, 17, 21; suppliers to St John's, 27

Courtyard. See Farmyard

Cows, 130, 142. See also Cattle farming; Livestock

Crop rotation: on Avalon, 63-67; in Ireland, 55, 57-60; Irish influence, 166, 173; Miramichi area, 73-74; Peterborough area, 74-77

Crops: on Avalon, 61, 63-64, 66; comparisons of differing, 27, 31-32; in Ireland, 55, 57; Miramichi area, 72-74; other studies on, 5; Peterborough area, 76; storage, 118-119. See also individual crops

Cunards (Chatham), 29

Cuslett, Avalon, 97

Dairy farming: on Avalon, 27, 67-68; Miramichi area, 74. See also Cattle farming; Pastoral farming; names of individual products

Dispersed settlement patterns: Cape Shore, 81; in Ireland, 33-36; in New World, 36-44, 46, 48-49, 172-73; and village development, 50-54

Douro, Ontario: cattle farming, 77-78; grain harvest, 98; houses, 144, 146, 159; settlement, 14, 21; topography and field systems, 78

Downeyville, Ontario: acreages, 25; farm outbuildings, 137; field systems, 76-78; grain harvest, 101; house types, 146; occupations, 30; settlement patterns, 21, 41, 50; topography, 31, 78; village development, 51-54

Drainage: on Avalon, 62-63; in Ireland, 59

Economic factors: and agricultural systems, 24, 27, 29-30; and cooking,

163; and crop rotation, 63; and cultural adaptation, 169-171, 174; and enclosure in Ireland, 58; and farm outbuildings, 130-33, 137; and farm technology, 112-13; and field systems, 67, 75, 78-80, 83; and land clearing, 106-7; and migration to New World, 15-16, 169; and settlement patterns, 51-53

Emily Township, Ontario: ethnic diversity, 24; house types, 146, 159; settlement, 14

Enclosures: in Ireland, 35-36, 57-58, 60

English language in Ireland, 16

Ennismore, Ontario: acreages, 25; cattle farming, 77; crops and yields, 76; houses, 146, 158-59; land clearing, 104; settlement, 14, 21, 49; types of farming, 27

Ethnic homogeneity and diversity, 23-24

Extended family: in Ireland, 16, 56; in New World, 43. *See also* Kinship; Nuclear family

Farm clusters: on Avalon, 66-72, 81-82; in Ireland, 33-36; in New World, 43-44, 46-48, 52, 166

Farm outbuildings, 4, 5, 118-37; changes in New World, 165, 167, 171, 173; compared with houses, 147

Farmers: proportion of immigrants, 17-18, 30

Farming. *See* Agricultural systems; Arable farming; Cattle farming; Dairy farming; Market gardening

Farmsteads: acreage in New World, 27; on Avalon, 19, 20, 52; changes in New World, 165, 173; dispersed pattern, 42-44; initial types on Avalon, 36-39; initial types in Miramichi, 39-41; initial types in Peterborough area, 40-41; later patterns, 44-50; types in Ireland, 33-36. *See also* Houses

Farmyard, 118-19, 126, 130, 134-35

Fences, 85-87; on Avalon, 60-61, 66-67; Irish influence, 166; origins of types, 106-7; Peterborough area, 74, 77-78

Fermoy, Ireland, 17, 21

Fertilization: on Avalon, 61-63, 66; changes in New World, 166; and field systems, 80; in Ireland, 55, 57, 59; Miramichi area, 73; Peterborough area, 74; root crops, 62

Field forms and names: on Avalon, 64-67, 69; Irish influence, 166; Miramichi area, 73-75; Peterborough area, 76-77

Field systems, 4-5, 11, 55-83; changes in New World, 165-66, 170-71

Flatrock, Avalon, 143-44

Flax, 55

Floors: on Avalon, 153, 155; mud, 159; Peterborough and Miramichi areas, 158

Flour mills, 60, 98

Folk festivals 116-17, 173

Folklife: dialect and houses, 159; family traditions, 19-20; folk memory, houses, 143, 146; folk memory, linhays, 119, 122; and haymaking, 113; and ploughing, 88; studies on in New World, 6-8, 11; superstitions and houses, 155; traditions and hauling, 101; traditions on kinship, 16; traditions on marketing (Cape Shore), 28; traditions on markets (St John's), 27

Fredericton, New Brunswick, 97

Freshwater, Avalon: crop rotation and

land use, 63-66, 79-80, 83; dairy
farming, 67; ethnic homogeneity,
24; farm outbuildings, 123, 133;
farmyards, 134; fertilization, 62;
grain harvest, 97; handtools, 89;
hay farming, 95, 131; hearths, 149;
houses, 151, 153; Irish traits, 81;
origins of technology, 108, 111;
ploughing, 88; potato harvest, 101;
root cellars, 128; root crops, 73,
90; settlement, 14, 20; settlement
patterns, 36-38, 46-48; types of
farming, 27; village development,
52; yields per acre, 61
Fruit cultivation, 63
Furniture: on Avalon, 151, 153, 155,
158; in Ireland, 142-43; Irish influence, 167; origins of, 164; Peterborough and Miramichi areas, 158

Gaelic language, 16
Garden: on Avalon, 44, 46, 64, 66;
front garden, 63; kitchen garden,
63, 73, 85, 90, 92; sowing
time, 117
Gavelkind, 33
Gilmour & Rankin (Newcastle,
N.B.), 29
Goats: on Avalon, 67-68
Government aid: British and Irish
immigration, 21; New Brunswick
and settlement, 41-42, 48; Newfoundland and agricultural settlement, 19-20; Newfoundland and
land grants, 41; Ontario and gifts of
tools, 104, 109; Ontario housing
assistance, 146; Ontario and
settlement, 41-42
Grain cultivation: harvesting, 95-101,
111-15; in Ireland, 58-60; Irish,
influence, 166, 170; planting,
92-93; storage, 125-26, 132-33. *See*

also Arable farming
Grand Banks fishery, 18
Guirys (Downeyville), 50, 53

Halloween, 117
Handtools: and field forms, 79; grain
harvesting, 95-101; haymaking,
93-95, 112-15; Irish influence,
166-67; land clearing, 84-85, 104-6;
planting, 88-92, 108-11; potato
harvesting, 101; storage, 118, 122.
See also Machine technology;
Technology
Harrow, 92, 111
Harvesting: folk-festivals and, 116-17;
methods and tools for, 93-101;
origins of above, 111-16
Haulage: in agriculture, 101-5; Irish
influence, 167; origins of methods,
115-16; storage of equipment, 123
Hay: on Avalon, 63-64; harvesting,
93-95, 111-15; hauling, 102; hay
'barracks,' 127, 129-31; Irish influence, 167; Miramichi area, 73-74;
Peterborough area, 76; planting, 93;
storage in barns, 122, 125-26,
132-34; storage in linhays, 123,
131; yields on Avalon, 61, 66, 74
Hearths: on Avalon, 149-51, 155; in
Ireland, 140-42; Irish influence,
167; Miramichi area, 144, 157; origins of types, 159, 161-63; Peterborough area, 146, 157
Hogs: on Avalon, 67; housing of, 129,
132; Miramichi area, 29, 74; Peterborough area, 77
Horses: on Avalon, 67-68; and harvesting, 98; for hauling, 101; housing
of, 123; Miramichi area, 74; Peterborough area, 77; and ploughing,
88, 108
Houses, 4, 138-64: changes in New

World, 165, 167, 171-73; indoor
threshing and design, 115; other
studies on, 11. *See also* Farm outbuildings

Infield/Outfield system, 55-59
Inheritance, of land: on Avalon,
68-72; changes in New World, 170;
and field systems, 81-82; in Ireland,
33, 56, 58; in Miramichi area, 74;
and settlement patterns, 44-50 52
Invention, of material culture traits,
3-4, 171-72; threshing on Cape
Shore, 97, 115
Ireland: culture changes within,
165-69, 173; extent of culture
transfer from, 160-65, 170-74;
farm outbuildings, 118-19, 130-36;
field systems, 55-60; furniture,
154; grain harvest methods
transferred, 112; haulage, 116;
house types, 138-143, 145, 150,
152, 156; migration from, 13,
15-32; potato planting, 109-10;
settlement patterns, 33-36, 42-44;
threshing, 97; topography, 31-32;
village patterns transferred, 51-54.
See also Transferred traits
Irish famine, 1840, 21

Kilkenny, Ireland: infield cultivation,
59; migrants from, 13, 19, 20
Kinship: and communal labour, 106;
and farmsteads, 33; and field systems, 68-72, 80-81; in Ireland and
migrations, 16-17; and settlement
patterns, 43-44, 46, 49; and village
types, 51-53. *See also* Extended
family; Nuclear family
'Kish,' 102, 105, 115, 149, 167

Labour supply: and culture trans-

ferred, 170-71; and farm technology, 84, 108; and field systems,
79-80
Labourers, in Irish migration, 17-18
Land clearing: on Avalon, 61, 66-67,
69-70, 72, 82; and field systems,
78; initial, 24, 27, 41-42; Irish influence, 166, 170; later patterns,
44, 52; methods of, 84-86, 89; in
Miramichi, 72, 82; origins of
methods, 104-6; Peterborough area,
74-76, 80, 82
Landholding: on Avalon, 68, 71-72;
on Cape Shore, 68-72; change in
New World, 170; compared with
Irish, 41; and field systems, 78, 81;
in Ireland, 35, 56, 57, 59, 60; land
grants on Avalon, 19-20, 60-61;
Miramichi area, 42; Peterborough
area, 40, 42, 50; sales of land, 46,
48, 49, 53, 82; and settlement patterns, 41-43. *See also* Inheritance
Ley farming. *See* Pastoral farming
Linhay: on barns, 122; Cape Shore,
124; evolution of, 153; Freshwater,
123; origins of, 130-31, 133; roofs,
148; St John's area, 119-22
Livestock: on Avalon, 63, 66-68, 73;
culture transferred, 170; and field
system, 79; food for, 141; housing
of, 118, 120, 122-26, 131-33; Miramichi area, 73-74; ownership in
Ireland, 56; Peterborough area,
77-78; proprietory marks, 67-68,
74; tethering, 124, 133-34. *See also*
Cattle farming; Pastoral farming
Logy Bay, Avalon: fertilization, 62;
field forms, 64; and fishery, 83;
grain harvest, 96-97; house types,
143-44; marketing in St John's, 28;
settlement in, 14, 20
Longhouse: in Ireland, 119, 132, 134

.umbering: and communal labour, 106; and early immigration, 20-21; and farm outbuildings, 136-37; and field systems, 80; and land clearing methods, 104; Miramichi area, 29-30; Peterborough area, 30; and settlement patterns, 53

McGrath family (Patrick's Cove, Cape Shore), 68-72

Machine technology: grain harvest, 96-98, 101; haymaking, 113; introduction of, 85, 108, 171. *See also* Plough; Technology

Malt houses, 60

Market gardening: on Avalon, 27-29, 67; Miramichi area, 29

Markets: in Ireland, 53; Miramichi area, 29; in St John's, 27; and settlement near St John's, 52. *See also* Trade

Marriage patterns: and field systems on Avalon, 70; and settlement patterns, 46, 48-49

Mattock: in Ireland, 55-56; in New World, 88-89, 91, 166

May-day celebrations, 116

Meat production. *See* Cattle farming

Middle Cove, Avalon. *See* Outer & Middle Cove

Migrations, 4, 10, 15-32; causes of, 169-70; culture shock, 168-69; and cultural survivals, 172-73

Milk: sale in Avalon, 67. *See also* Dairy farming

Miramichi area: acreages, 25; climate, 31-32; ethnic homogeneity, 24; farm outbuildings, 124-26, 129, 131-34, 136; field systems, 72-74, 76, 79, 80, 82; folk festivals, 116-17; furniture, 154; grain, 92-93, 96-98, 100-1; haulage, 101, 103-4; haymaking, 93-95; house types, 144-45, 150, 155-59; Irish influence, 165-66, 170-72; land clearing, 24, 85-86, 104; migration to, 18; occupations, 30; origins of farm technology, 106-16; origins of house types, 159-64; origins of immigrants, 16-17; potatoes, 101; root cellars, 128; root crops, 90, 92; settlement patterns, 14, 20-21, 39-40, 41-42, 48-49; tools, 89; topography, 31, 78; trade, 27, 29; types of farming, 27; village types, 51-54

Mixed farming: and field systems, 80; and Irish influence, 172; Miramichi area, 27, 72; Peterborough area, 75-76. *See also* Arable farming; Cattle farming; Dairy farming; Pastoral farming

Munster, Ireland: chimneys, 140-41; conditions at time of migrations, 15-16; farmyards, 118; tools, 109-11

Nelson, New Brunswick, 158

New England: farm outbuildings, 131; fence antecedents, 106-7; Newfoundland emigration to, 52

New Englanders, near Irish settlers, 24

Newcastle, New Brunswick, 20, 29

Nowlanville, New Brunswick: boundaries, 86; house types, 158; settlement patterns, 14, 21, 42

Nuclear family: on Avalon, 68; and Irish influence, 172-73; and land holding, 35; in migrations, 16-17; and settlement patterns, 19-20, 43-44. *See also* Kinship

Oats: on Avalon, 63-64, 66, 96-97; on Cape Shore, 115; in Ireland, 31, 55; Miramichi area, 27, 72-73

O'Brien, John (Avalon), 63
O'Neills (Downeyville), 50
Openfield system: on Avalon, 68-72, 81-82; in Ireland, 35-36, 56-57, 59-60; Peterborough area, 76-77; survival in New World, 80-81, 165-66
Origins of culture traits, 165-74; farm outbuildings, 130-37; field systems, 78-83; house types, 159-64; other studies on, 8-14; technology, 104-17; village patterns, 51-54. *See also* Adopted traits; Invention; Transferred traits
Otonabee, Ontario, 146, 159
Outer & Middle Cove, Avalon: caplin for fertilization, 62; dairy farming, 67; farm outbuildings, 123, 128; field forms, 64; grain harvest, 97, 100; house types, 143, 151; settlement patterns, 14, 20, 38; trade, 28; village development, 51
Oxen, 77, 88, 108

Parish: as focus of community life, 51, 53-54
Partnership farming: on Avalon, 71-72, 82; in Ireland, 33, 56. *See also* 'Clachan'; Communal labour
Pastoral farming: on Avalon, 27, 32, 63-64, 66-67, 71-72, 82-83, 110, 115; and barns, 131, 133; and field systems, 79, 80, 82-83; in Ireland, 15, 56-57, 60; and Irish cultural survivals, 170; Miramichi area, 73-74; other studies on, 5; Peterborough area, 30, 76-78. *See also* Arable farming; Cattle farming; Dairy farming; Market gardening
Patrick's Cove, Avalon: grain harvest, 97; house types, 151; land holding, 68-72, 81-82

Peas: in Ireland, 55; Miramichi area, 73; Peterborough area, 76; planting, 93
Peterborough area: climate, 31-32; ethnic homogeneity, 24; farm outbuildings, 124-26, 129, 131-34, 136-37; field systems, 74-78, 80, 82; folk festivals, 116; furniture, 154; grain cultivation, 92-93, 96, 98, 100-1; haulage, 102-4; haymaking, 93-95; house types, 144-46, 150, 155-59; Irish culture transferred, 165-66, 170-71; land clearing, 24, 85-86; migration to, 15-18, 21; origins of farm technology, 106-16; origins of house types, 159-60, 162-64; potato harvest, 101; root cellars, 128; root crops 90, 92; settlement patterns, 40-43, 49-50; tools, 88-89; topography, 31, 78; trade, 27, 29-30; village development, 51, 53-54; wheat farming, 27, 79
Placentia, Avalon: early houses, 148, 153, 161; ethnic diversity, 23; roads and marketing, 28-29; seasonal Irish fishery, 18; settlement, 19
Ploughs, 86-88, 90, 108; and field system, 79; in Ireland, 55, 57; and Irish influence, 166; in potato harvest, 101
Population: Cape Shore, 19, 51, 66; Freshwater, 20; history in three areas, 44-50; settlement and occupations in three areas, 30; Miramichi area, 21; Peterborough area, 21; St John's area, 19-20
Port Hope, Ontario, 29-30
Potatoes: on Avalon, 27, 61, 63-64, 66; climate for, 31-32; cooking, 141; harvesting, 101; in Ireland, 55-59; Miramichi area, 73-74; Peterborough

area, 76; planting, 90, 93, 109-10. *See also* Root crops

Poultry: housing of, 118-19, 129, 134; marketing, 29

Quebec: exporter of shingles to Newfoundland, 148; origins for fence types, 107

Raspberries, cultivation on Avalon, 63

River access and transport: importance in Barnaby area, 29, 39-40, 42, 49, 52, 173; in Peterborough area, 29. *See also* Roads; Sea access

Roads: on Avalon, 28, 62; building and settlement duties, 42; in Ireland, 116; Miramichi area, 29; Peterborough area, 29-30. *See also* River access and transport; Sea access

Roofs: on Avalon, 143, 145, 147-48, 155; in Ireland, 139-40, 145; Irish influence, 167; Miramichi area, 144, 155; origins of, 160-61; Peterborough area, 146, 155; shingled, 148. *See also* Thatching

Root cellars, 121, 126-29; adoption of, 133; roofs, 148

Root crops: on Avalon, 32; fertilization, 62; harvesting, 101; Irish influence, 166; Miramichi area, 73; Peterborough area, 76; seedtime methods and tools, 89-92. *See also* names of individual crops

Rundale, landholding system in Ireland, 56, 59, 60. *See also* Landholding

St Brides, Avalon: grain harvest, 97; house types, 148-49; roads and marketing, 28-29; settlement patterns, 39, 46; village development, 50-51

St John's and area: acreages, 27; crop rotation, 63-64; ethnic diversity, 23-24; cod fishery, 72; farm outbuildings, 122-24; farmyards, 134; fencing, 85-86; fertilization, 62; field systems, 81-82; grain harvest, 95-98; haulage, 102-4; hay barracks, 127, 129-30; haymaking, 93; house types, 143, 145, 147-49, 151, 153; Irish influence, 165-66, 172; Irish population, 19-20; land clearance, 61; land titles, 41; linhay, 119-22, 130-31; livestock, 67, 134; market gardening, 27-28; occupations, 30; origins of house types, 160; origins of technology, 108, 110-11, 113, 115-16; ploughing, 86, 88; potatoes, 90, 101; root cellars, 126; settlement, 39, 42, 46-48; street patterns, 51-52; topography, 30-31; types of farming, 27; village development, 51-52

Sawmills, 51, 136, 137

Schools, 50-51

Scotland: immigrants from, 24; influences from, 109, 111

Sea access: on Avalon, 28-29, 42, 52; and settlement patterns, 173. *See also* Cod fishery; River access and transport; Roads

Semiwagan, New Brunswick: boundaries, 86; settlement patterns, 14, 21, 42, 48, 50

Settlement patterns, 4, 11, 33-54; extent changed in New World, 165-66, 172-73

Sheep: on Avalon, 67-68; housing of, 132; marketing, 29-30; Miramichi area, 74; Peterborough area, 77

Ship Cove, Avalon: field systems, 72; settlement, 19

Skerry, John (Cape Shore), 18-19

Sleds: for farm haulage, 103, 105, 115; Irish influence, 167
Social class, of immigrants, 17-18
Soils: on Avalon, 61, 66, 82; and field systems, 78, 82; Irish influence, 170; Peterborough area, 77; and settlement, 42
Spade: in Ireland, 55-56; Irish influence, 166; in New World, 88-91, 108-11; for potato harvest, 101. *See also* Handtools
'Square': use of term in Newfoundland, 46, 51-52
Squatting: on Avalon, 41
Stonewalls: as boundary lines, 86-87; chimneys, 149, 161; around farmyard, 133; origins of types, 107-8
Studding: barns, 123-24, 132-33; in houses on Avalon, 147, 155, 162; on linhays, 119-22; origins of, 134, 136
Subsistence farming: on Avalon, 24; and cod fishery, 51-52; and grain growing, 114-15; and Irish cultural survivals, 170-72; of root crops, 27
Sweetmans (Placentia): merchant, 18-19, 28

Technology, 4, 5, 11, 84-117: agricultural revolution, 4; changes in New World, 165-67, 170-71; and field system, 79-80; in Irish farming, 55-56, 59; storage of equipment, 118, 122-23, 126. *See also* Handtools; Machine technology
Thatching: on farm outbuildings, 121, 124, 128, 134; on houses on Avalon, 144, 148-49, 160; in Peterborough area, 159. *See also* Roofs
Threshing machine, 4, 97-98
Tillage farming. *See* Arable farming

Tilt: early house type on Avalon, 143-45, 147
Timothy: cultivated on Avalon, 66, 115; in Ireland, 111
Tipperary: immigrants to Miramichi, 21; origin of settlers, 13, 19, 20
Topography: effects on Irish survivals, 173-74; and field systems, 78-79, 81; other studies on, 5; of study area, 30-31
Townland, in Ireland, 53-54
Trade: on Avalon, 27-29, 52, 67; development of local stores, 51, 110; diffusion of material culture traits, 3; early settlers and surplus for, 24; international linkages, 27; in Ireland, 27, 53, 56, 60, 168; Miramichi area, 29, 42, 73, 74; Peterborough area, 27, 29-30; timber and migration, 20. *See also* Cod fishery; Commercial farming; Markets; Market gardening
Transferred traits, 3-4, 21-23; on Avalon, 171; farm outbuildings, 130, 133-34; farm technology, 106-11, 113-15; field systems, 78-83; folk festivals, 116-17; house types, 159-64; from Ireland to New World, 165, 170, 172-74; land clearing and fencing, 107-8; service centres, 53-54; settlement patterns, 42-43, 52-53
Transport. *See* River access and transport; Roads; Sea access
Turnips: on Avalon, 27, 61, 63-64; climate for, 31-32; in Ireland, 55, 57, 60; Miramichi area, 73; planting, 93

Ulster: farmyard, 118; spade, 109, 111
Ulster/Scottish immigrants, 24
Urbanization, 171

Vegetable cultivation: seedtime,
86-92; storage, 119, 126-29
Villages: development, 49-54; in Ireland, 34-35; Irish influence, 170.
See also Clachan

Walling, of houses: on Avalon, 143,
147-48, 155; in Ireland, 138-39;
Irish influence, 167; Miramichi
area, 144, 155, 157; Peterborough
area, 146, 155, 157; origins,
159, 160
Waterford, Ireland: acreages, 27; and
cod fishery off Newfoundland, 18;
Gaelic speaking, 16; origin of
settlers, 13, 19, 20; trade with St
John's, 27
Westcountry, England: connections

with Ireland and Newfoundland,
18; immigrants to Avalon, 23-24;
influence on Avalon, 172; influence
on farm outbuildings, 130, 131;
influence on farm technology, 114;
influence on houses, 161, 163-64;
trade with St John's, 27
Wexford, Ireland: bread ovens, 163;
infield cultivation, 59; origin of
settlers, 13, 19-20
Wheat cultivation: climate for, 31-32;
comparisons of, 27; in Ireland, 55;
Miramichi area, 72-73; Peterborough area, 29-30, 53, 75-76, 79;
and village styles, 53

Yields: on Avalon, 61, 66; Miramichi
area, 72-73